Computers which can use
TIM HARTNELL'S
GIANT BOOK
OF COMPUTER GAMES

VIC 20

Apple II and IIe (and clones)

Commodore 64

Atari

IBM PC (and all clones)

TRS-80 Models 1, 2, and 3

TRS-80 Model 100

TRS-80 Color Computer

Texas Instruments TI99/4a
(with extended BASIC)

Timex Sinclair 2000 series
(string-handling needs modification)

Plus any computer furnished with Microsoft BASIC

(BASIC Conversion Chart included)

TIM HARTNELL'S

Giant Book of Computer Games

Tim Hartnell

Ballantine Books · New York

Library of Congress Catalog Card Number: 83-91157

ISBN 0-345-31609-6

Manufactured in the United States of America

First American Edition: April 1984

Designed by Gene Siegel

10 9 8 7 6 5 4 3 2 1

CONTENTS

INTRODUCTION

Once upon a time it was not easy to write and play games with computers. Back in the dim, dark past, it could cost you $80 to $100 *an hour* just to rent access to a time-shared mainframe via a terminal. And the only output you had was on the printout of a noisy, hard-to-read teleprinter. Think what those restrictions would have done to your current pattern of spending hours lovingly debugging, and improving, your latest masterpiece.

We, fortunately, do not have to suffer such medieval conditions. The luxury of having a computer of your own, driving a TV screen, with unrestricted access to the machine, allows you to work for as long as you like creating games and other programs.

In this book, you'll find a collection of my favorite computer games. I hope some of them will soon be up and running on your computer, and are stored with your own favorite programs. They're sure to provide you with a lot of fun in the weeks ahead.

I've tried to produce a set of games which will provide varied entertainment, to cater to your game interests, whatever they may be. As you'll see by glancing through this book, the games range from "classic" board games like CHESS and REVERSI/OTHELLO, through just-for-fun simulations like the wacky MISTRESS OF XENOPHOBIA, to the demanding ADVENTURE programs STRONGHOLD OF THE DWARVEN LORDS and THE BANNOCHBURN LEGACY. There are more than 40 games in this book, which I wrote to ensure your computer never gets the chance to voice the complaint, "I've got nothing to do," again.

I've deliberately written the book so that it is "open-ended." That is, in contrast to many other collections of games programs on the market, I've assumed you'll want to adapt and improve the programs once you get them up and running. Therefore, with many of them I've included program breakdowns, some line by line, so you know what each section of code is doing. As well, the introduction to each section discusses a bit about the philosophy of writing games of that type, has a word or two to say about the basic algorithms which you can use to create games of that sort yourself, and generally aims to give you a solid background against which you can expand and develop your own game-writing skills.

1

Near the back of the book you'll even find a section devoted entirely to game ideas which you can convert into computer games.

Getting the programs running

I deliberately wrote the programs in this book in the most general version of BASIC I could. Therefore, you'll find no PEEKs and POKEs, no use of graphic character sets, and no use of such commands as SOUND or PLAY. I've assumed you have access to READ and DATA, and that your screen is around 32 to 40 characters wide (and you'll find, if you have a computer like the VIC-20 with a screen which is not that wide, it is very easy to adapt the program output to fit, as many of the games only use the width of a playing board, say 12 characters). Standard string-handling commands (such as LEFT$, RIGHT$, and MID$) are used, and these will need to be converted to the Timex-Sinclair "string-slicing" mechanism if you have a computer such as the T/S 1500 or the T/S 2068. This is not difficult to do, and I've kept even string-handling to a minimum in these programs so that the majority of programs should run on your system just by being typed in directly.

Of course, you'll probably have to play with the display a little, in order to make it as effective as possible. I expect, by the way, that you'll modify and adapt the programs to make the most of your system, adding sound and color, plus your own system's graphics, wherever you can.

Many of the programs reprint the board, or playing field, after each turn. For simplicity, I've preceded these "reprints" with a CLS command to clear the screen. Some systems demand a command of the PRINT "CLR" type, so I'll expect you to make that replacement whenever you come to it. More importantly, you'll find that after the screen has been cleared at the start of the game, the output of the program can be made much more effective by replacing the CLS with a "home" command, so that the program reprints "on top of itself" each time round. This gives the impression in a program like ROBOT MINEFIELD for example, that the robots are moving. The same can be seen in the board games. Actually having the pieces *move* on the board is highly effective, and adds much to your enjoyment when running the programs.

Therefore, if your system has a means of resetting the cursor to the top of the screen without clearing it first (such as PRINT AT 0,0 or PRINT @ 0 or LOCATE 1,1 or the like) make sure you put this in the place of the CLS at the start of the reprint section.

These programs were written on an IBM PC®. On this computer, if I want to generate random integers in the range, say, 1 to 10, I use

2

a command of the type A = INT(RND * 10) + 1. You'll find this format is used throughout the book. If your system does not accept this, you may have to substitute either A = RND(10) or A = INT(RND(0) * 10) + 1 or A = INT(RND(1) * 10) + 1 (and you may well need to precede this with LET). You probably know exactly how to do it right now, but if you're not sure, look up RND or "random numbers" in your system's manual.

The computer on which I developed the programs always gives the same sequence of random numbers each time the program is run. As numbers which are more or less genuinely randomly distributed are needed in many programs, I've seeded the random number generator in each case by one of two methods.

I've either used INKEY$ to hold the program in a loop, incrementing a variable as I do so, until a key is pressed, and then use that variable to seed the random number generator (as in RANDOMIZE N) or have taken the seconds part of the built-in clock on my computer as the seed (which gives rise to that rather terrifying-looking line RANDOMIZE VAL (RIGHT$(TIME$,2)) in many of the programs).

If your computer does not produce the same numbers in the same sequence every time you run the program, drop these lines altogether. Alternatively, just use RANDOMIZE (or RAND) without a following number, if your system accepts that. Again, your manual will tell you what to do. If you're not sure what to do, and your computer will not accept the long line including TIME$, then just leave it out altogether. The program will function perfectly well without it.

Although much of the output within quote marks in PRINT statements is in lower-case, all programs (with the exception of the CHESS one, which needs lower-case letters to signify the human's pieces) expect input in upper case letters. If your system does not have lower-case letters, simply put the material in PRINT statements in upper-case. It has been put in lower-case just because I think it looks better, but it has nothing to do with the actual running of the program.

You'll probably find, in fact, that when you get to entering the programs you'll automatically make the small changes needed to accommodate the special features of your system. I've included the above notes in the book just to make sure you can get the programs up and running as quickly as possible. However, you may well find you don't need them at all. So don't be intimidated by the length of this initial section of the book.

The majority of the programs in this book will fit well within 8K. THE BANNOCHBURN LEGACY is the exception, which demands nearly 17K on my system. CHESS occupies 8K, with the shorter programs generally under 4K. If you have trouble getting a program into your system because of shortage of memory, cut out the REM statements (the majority of GOSUB and GOTO calls do not reference the leading REM, but go to the actual routine itself which follows the identifying REM), and shorten the PRINT statements. It is impossible to predict exactly how much memory the programs will take on your system, because of the different ways memory is organized, and the working space the program requires differs from system to system.

To maximize the length of program you can get into your machine (and to keep program entry time down to a minimum) few of the programs include instructions. These are in the text. However, if you have the memory (and the inclination) you can easily add a "Do you want instructions" line as part of the initialization subroutine, and then include a shortened form of the instructions from the text in your program.

I've followed structured programming techniques in all programs which lent themselves to that approach. This is explained in the material supporting the CHESS program. You may well find, as I did when I actually decided to put all the advice I'd read in books and articles into action, that working in a "top down" manner made writing and modifying programs a much simpler, and more precise, activity than it had been before. As a bonus, it is much easier to get a program up and running when it's written this way. Most importantly, you can get to the fun parts—actually running the thing—much more quickly.

Many programs include a delay loop. As the actual delay produced will depend on your system, you should adjust these dummy loops (which are generally held in subroutines at the very end of the program) so that the screen display is as effective as possible.

Finally, a word about variables. In several cases complete words (such as SCORE) have been used as variable names. However, only the first two letters of the name are significant. If your system only accepts two-letter variable names, enter just the first two letters (such as SC in our example). Even if your system only recognizes the first two letters of a variable name, you should include the name in full if your system will accept it. You will find that it will be easier to understand what is happening within a program if you do this.

I think we should get to the fun parts immediately.

Good game-playing!

Tim Hartnell
London,
May 1983

Board Games

Some games could not have existed without computers.

Think of the whole range of Space Intruder types of games and the Pacperson ones. These could have not come into being before the computer—using a TV-like screen for output—was developed. Many other games, of course, predate the computer by thousands of years. However, more and more of these traditional games have now been computerized, with board games being as popular with computer games players as they were with players in precomputer days.

In this section of the book, we have a generous crop of board games:

- CHESS

- GOMOKU

- FOUR IN A ROW

- CHECKERS

- SHOGUN (HASAMI SHOGI)

- AWARI

- KNIGHTSBRIDGE

- REVERSI (OTHELLO)

We'll start this section of the book with a discussion on how board games can be easily modified to make it possible for a computer to handle them. Apart from AWARI, the ideas we'll discuss in the next few pages have been applied to every board game in this section of the book.

There is a common thread which holds together all the programs in this section of the book, a thread which you can also use to help you develop programs to play your favorite board games. Look first at this diagram. It shows a checkerboard numbered to make it easy for the computer to handle.

You can indicate any square on the board by referring to the number along the left-hand side, (such as 3), then the number along the top (such as 4). In this case, the line numbered 3 (along the left-hand side) and the line numbered 4 (along the top) meet at the square numbered 34. If you wish to move a piece, you can do so by entering the number of the square you're moving from (such as 55), then the number you're moving to (such as 66) and the computer can understand exactly what you're doing. There is no need to change the numbers entered by the human player into another set in order to allow the computer to interpret them.

That is the first "secret" of writing board games so your computer can play them. The second is that a board numbered in this way has another great advantage over one which is simply numbered from one to 64 in order. When you move a piece in any direction on this board—no matter where you start—the difference between the squares is the same.

I'll try to expand on that somewhat cryptic statement. If you move one square up and to the right—like the move of a piece in checkers—you will move from, say, 24 to 35; or from 53 to 64; or from 71 to 82. But notice that no matter where you are on the board, the difference between your starting and ending squares is always 11. If you move diagonally up to the left, you'll move from, say, 26 to 35 (plus 9), or 66 to 75 (also plus 9) or from 22 to 31 (plus 9 again).

This predictability makes it relatively simple to create a board which the computer can handle.

How the computer plays

Imagine the computer has a checkers piece on the square numbered 24. It could be programmed to check each square on the board, and every time it found one of its own pieces, could check if there was a human piece on the square numbered the same as its piece (that is, 24 in this example), plus 11 (that is, on 35); and it could check to see whether the square which was 11 past that, 46, was blank. If it found that all these conditions were true, the computer could jump over square 35 into square 46, and capture the piece currently occupying 35.

This, in essence, is how many computer board games—from checkers, through Reversi, to chess—work, based on a simple 8 by 8 grid numbered in this way.

If you were writing chess on this board (as the CHESS game we'll look at shortly was, in fact, written), you could specify the moves of, for example, the knight, by knowing it can always move to squares which are the following "numerical distances" from the square on which the piece now sits:

```
21   12   -8   -19   -21   -12   19   8
```

Try it now, by placing a coin on square number 55, and move it as if it were a knight, working out the mathematical relationship between the starting square, and the square you're moving to. You should find the differences are the same as the numbers listed above.

The programs in this section, and in many other parts of this book, were written in a "top down" manner, in an attempt to produce a structured program which is relatively easy to follow and modify. Many of the programs were written by entering the following "bare code" at the start:

```
10   REM NAME OF GAME
20   GOSUB 9000:REM INITIALISE
30   GOSUB 8000:REM PRINT BOARD
```

```
40     GOSUB 1000:REM COMPUTER MOVES
50     GOSUB 8000:REM PRINT BOARD
60     GOSUB 7000:REM HUMAN MOVES
70     Check if human has won or computer has
       won and if so branch to end of
       game message...
80     GOTO 30
```

This structure was written, in nearly all cases, before I had the slightest idea how I was to accomplish the goals I had set myself for each of the subroutines.

All programs were written out completely on paper before the computer was even turned on, so that a version of the game could be "hand run" before starting to actually grapple with the game on the computer. This enabled the worst bugs to be caught right at the beginning.

I strongly advise you to follow a similar process when you write programs. I had read this advice myself, in several articles and books, and—predictably enough—had ignored it, until I found myself on a two-week holiday in Wales, miles from the nearest computer store, with a burning desire to write a chess program. The program in this book is based on that original program, written on paper in a rented cottage on the Welsh coast, and dreamed up as my dog and I wandered for miles along the seafront.

Among the many great advantages I discovered regarding programming on paper in this way was the willingness with which I completely discarded whole blocks of code if they were found to be unworkable. It is much more difficult to decide to erase a whole section of code from a program once you actually have it in the computer than it is to just tear up a piece of paper. The temptation—when lines of program are actually in the computer—is to fiddle with them, in an attempt to make them work, at least after a fashion.

Working on paper, then, tends to prevent having code which really should not be in a program from somehow being patched together to make it work. Working with a structured outline, such as that I've described, makes it simple to know which parts of the program carry out which task. I know, for example, in the outline above, that the board is printed by the subroutine starting at line 8000. Therefore, if the board comes out looking a bit odd, I know immediately which section of the code I should concentrate on.

As well as helping in the early "get it working" stage, a structured program tends to invite improvements. Once you have, for example, your own CHECKERS program up and running, you can go back to it some time in the future to try and make it play a little better by going just to that part of the code which covers the computer's game. You will not have to wade through vast acres of code, trying to work out just what each line does, and which particular lines control the computer's play.

The methods I've just outlined are used throughout this and most other sections of the book. It may prove instructive to look through some of the programs to follow through the listing, and work out which section does what. In many programs, you'll see that I've included lines of asterisks as a REM statement. These break the program into separate modules which should help you follow the program through.

□CHESS

CHESS is one of the greatest challenges which can face a computer programmer. To analyze how a human plays chess, and then to try and break that analysis into a number of ideas which can be expressed clearly enough to be written into a program, is a formidable task.

It cannot be claimed that this CHESS program is a particularly successful attempt to surmount the challenge I've described. While it plays chess on a reasonably coherent basis, it does not play well, and should prove no real challenge to defeat. Why then include it in the book, alongside other games which are practically unbeatable?

I've put the CHESS program in this book precisely because chess has proved such an attraction to computer programmers. Very few chess programs have ever been published (I know of one which appeared in *Creative Computing* magazine in December 1981, under the title Chess C.4, by Michael Rakaska; two others which appear in books; and the machine level listing of Sargon II), which suggests how difficult a task it is to produce a program of this type. I felt that the very rarity of published chess programs gave weight to any argument in favor of including this one.

The possibility of a machine playing chess against man has occupied men's minds for hundreds of years. A chess-playing automaton built by Baron von Kempelen, which played its first exhibition match before royalty in Vienna in 1770, captured the imagination of much of Europe. Unfortunately, the machine was little more than an elaborate conjuring trick, with a man in a hidden compartment operating the playing mechanism. It was a highly successful fraud, nevertheless, and an examination of its moves shows the man stuffed inside the device certainly knew his chess. While doing some research into the history of game-playing at the British Museum, I found in the British Library a book from the last century, *50 Games Played by the Chess Automaton,* which some earnest reader had annotated in the last 100 years. The human players came in for more scathing comments—such as "This move brands the player as a beginner!"—than the machine ever received.

But despite its reputation, the machine could not really play chess. The first real approach to a device which would play a complete game of chess (as opposed to machines, a few of which were built early this century, to play particular endgames) was in 1949, when on March 9 Claude Shannon, then a research worker at Bell Telephone Laboratories, Murray Hill, New Jersey, presented a paper called *Programming a Computer for Playing Chess* at a New York convention.

As David Levy points out in his fascinating book *Chess and Computers* (Computer Science Press, Inc., Potomac, Maryland, 1976) the real significance of Shannon's paper lies not only in the fact that it was first, but that "many of Shannon's original ideas can still be seen in today's programs" (p. 40).

Shannon said in that paper that the number of possible moves in a 40-move game approached 10 raised to the 120th power, a number which is of the same order as the atoms in the universe. Clearly any program which attempted to evaluate all those moves would be around a long time (say 10 to the 90th power years) before the first king's pawn made its foray out towards the center.

To make the program in this book play, and to get it to play reasonably quickly, demanded—as I'm sure you can appreciate—a number of compromises. I traded in-depth evaluation against some rough and ready playing ideas (such as programming the computer to move pieces to help hold the center as much as possible; to develop knights as soon as possible in a game; to capture by a pawn, regardless of the fact that the pawn faced immediate capture, whenever possible; to hold the king as immobile as possible, at least in the early stages of the game, when a cowardly approach would seem to make good sense; and to allow pieces with vast mobility—such as the queen—a randomly weighted decision-making mechanism which would ensure it did not sail off to the other side of the board just because a clear channel was open for it to do so).

I followed a clear structure in laying out the program, which has ensured that it plays as quickly as possible. The structure, in fact, is not as transparent as I hoped it would be when I first wrote the program. The complexity and number of demands put upon the computer by the game when I finally got the program up and running meant that my best-laid plans of producing a clearly structured program went somewhat astray. Nevertheless, the program does play extremely quickly, and if it does not play well, at least it is an opponent with quirks which can never fail to exasperate and amuse.

At the end of the listing there is a section which will tell you how to modify the program to get it to play against itself. This is a fascinating demonstration program, and one which never fails to arouse interest when it is up and running, especially from those who consider themselves experts at the game. I ran one game of "auto-chess," with a printer connected, and before the program listing I'll show you that, so you can judge for yourself what sort of an opponent the computer will make.

The "auto-chess" variation makes use of the exchange sides option within the game, swapping sides after each move. When you swap sides, as you can do if you feel the computer could do with some help, and you give it the side you were playing on, the pieces are exchanged as if they were reflected across a mirror placed at the center of the board. That is, a queen swapping sides ends up on the correct-colored square, and so on. Try the exchange a few times when you're playing and the operation of this mechanism will be quite clear.

A final word, before we get down to our demonstration program. The computer must be watched to make sure it does not cheat. It will only do so extremely rarely, but (unless you're feeling particularly generous) if it—for example—moves into check you should take this as a sign that the program wishes to resign. Again, the machine sometimes has problems getting out of check. Here you may wish to be a bit more tolerant, as it will usually manage to do so within the next move or so. Alternatively, you can regard any such failure by the computer as an acknowledgment of your superior play.

Before the listing of the program, I'll show you a few stages in a game played by the computer against itself. The computer changed sides after each move, and printed the board after every second move.

```
   A B C D E F G H              A B C D E F G H

8  R N B Q K B N R  8        8  R N B Q K B N R  8
7  P P P P P P P P  7        7  P P P . P P P P  7
6  . . . . . . . .  6        6  . . . . . . . .  6
5  . . . . . . . .  5        5  . . . P . . . .  5
4  . . . p . . . .  4        4  . . . p . . . .  4
3  . . . . . . . .  3        3  . . . . . . . .  3
2  p p p . p p p p  2        2  p p p . p p p p  2
1  r n b q k b n r  1        1  r n b q k b n r  1

   A B C D E F G H              A B C D E F G H
```

********************************* *************************************

14

```
   A B C D E F G H              A B C D E F G H

8  R N B Q K B N R  8        8  R N B Q K B N R  8
7  P P P . P P P P  7        7  P P . . P P P P  7
6  . . . . . . . .  6        6  . . P . . . . .  6
5  . . . P . . . .  5        5  . . . P . . . .  5
4  . . . p . . . .  4        4  . . . p . . . .  4
3  . . . . p . . .  3        3  . . . . p . . .  3
2  p p p . . p p p  2        2  p p p . . p p p  2
1  r n b q k b n r  1        1  r n b q k b n r  1

   A B C D E F G H              A B C D E F G H
```

****

```
   A B C D E F G H              A B C D E F G H

8  R N B Q K B N R  8        8  R N B Q K B N R  8
7  P P . . P P P P  7        7  P P . . P . P P  7
6  . . P . . . . .  6        6  . . P . . . . .  6
5  . . . P . . . .  5        5  . . . P . P . .  5
4  . . . p . . . .  4        4  . . . p . . . .  4
3  n . . p . . . .  3        3  n . . p . . . .  3
2  p p p . . p p p  2        2  p p p . . p p p  2
1  r . b q k b n r  1        1  r . b q k b n r  1

   A B C D E F G H              A B C D E F G H
```

****

```
   A B C D E F G H              A B C D E F G H

8  R N B Q K B N R  8        8  R . B Q K B N R  8
7  P P . . P . P P  7        7  P P . . P . P P  7
6  . . P . . . . .  6        6  N . P . . . . .  6
5  . . . P . P . .  5        5  . . . P . P . .  5
4  . . . p . . . .  4        4  . . . p . . . .  4
3  n . p . p . . .  3        3  n . p . p . . .  3
2  p p . . . p p p  2        2  p p . . . p p p  2
1  r . b q k b n r  1        1  r . b q k b n r  1

   A B C D E F G H              A B C D E F G H
```

******************************* **************************

```
    A B C D E F G H              A B C D E F G H

8   R . B Q K B N R  8       8   R . B Q K B . R  8
7   P P . . . . P P  7       7   P P . . . . P P  7
6   N . P . P . . .  6       6   N . P . P N . .  6
5   . . . P . P . .  5       5   . . . P . P . .  5
4   . . . p . p . .  4       4   . p . p . p . .  4
3   n . p . p . . .  3       3   n . p . p n . .  3
2   p p . . . . p p  2       2   p . . . . . p p  2
1   r . b q k b n r  1       1   r . b q k b . r  1

    A B C D E F G H              A B C D E F G H
```

****

```
    A B C D E F G H              A B C D E F G H

8   R . B Q K B . R  8       8   R . B Q K B . R  8
7   P P . . . . P P  7       7   P P . . . . P P  7
6   . . P . P N . .  6       6   . . P . . N . .  6
5   . . . P . P . .  5       5   . . . P P P . .  5
4   . p . p . p . .  4       4   . p . p . p . .  4
3   n . . p n . . .  3       3   n . . p n . . .  3
2   p . . . . . p p  2       2   p . . . . . p p  2
1   r . b q k b . r  1       1   r . b q k b . r  1

    A B C D E F G H              A B C D E F G H
```

****

```
    A B C D E F G H              A B C D E F G H

8   R . B Q K B . R  8       8   R . B Q K B . R  8
7   P P . . . . P P  7       7   P P . . . . P P  7
6   . . P . . . . .  6       6   . . P . . . . .  6
5   . . . P p P . N  5       5   . . . P p P . N  5
4   . p . . p . . .  4       4   . p . . p . n .  4
3   n . . p n . . .  3       3   n . . p . . . .  3
2   p . . . . p p    2       2   p . . . . p p    2
1   r . b q k b . r  1       1   r . b q k b . r  1

    A B C D E F G H              A B C D E F G H
```

****

```
        A B C D E F G H              A B C D E F G H

    8   R . B Q K B . R   8      8   R . B Q K B . R   8
    7   P . . . . P P     7      7   P . . . . . P     7
    6   . . P . . . .     6      6   . . P . . . P .   6
    5   . P . P p P . N   5      5   . P . P p P . N   5
    4   . p . . . p . n   4      4   . p . . . p . n   4
    3   n . . . p . p .   3      3   n . . . p . p .   3
    2   p . . . . . p     2      2   p . . . . . p     2
    1   r . b q k b . r   1      1   r . b q k b . r   1

        A B C D E F G H              A B C D E F G H
```

****

Now here is the listing of the chess game:

```
10 REM Chess
20 GOSUB 2970
30 GOTO 60
40 GOSUB 2580
50 GOSUB 2820
60 GOSUB 2580
70 REM ********************************
80 IF A$ = "S" THEN END
90 IF A$ = "X" THEN PRINT "EXCHANGING SIDE
S":GOSUB 3540:A$ = ""
100 IF A$ = "P" THEN GOSUB 3730
110 REM ********************************
120 FOR Z = 1 TO 16:T(Z) = 0:NEXT Z
130 U = 0
140 PRINT "Please stand by"
150 FOR Q = 1 TO 64:IF A(S(Q))>=BB AND A(S
(Q)) <=RB THEN U = U +1:T(U) = S(Q):IF A(S
(Q))=KB THEN KM=S(Q)
160 NEXT Q:IF U<3 THEN GOTO 2230
170 GOTO 650
180 FOR Q = 1 TO U:IF A(T(Q))=KB THEN T(Q)
=T(U):T(U) = KM
190 NEXT Q
200 Q = INT(RND*3)
210 IF A$ = "C" THEN Q = 0
220 IF Q<U THEN Q = Q + 1
230 Z = T(Q):GOSUB 280
```

```
240 IF MM = 1 THEN GOSUB 2500:GOTO 40
250 IF Q<U THEN 220
260 GOTO 2360
270 REM *********************************
280 IF A(Z) = QB THEN GOSUB 910
290 IF A(Z) = RB THEN GOSUB 1170
300 IF A(Z) = BB THEN GOSUB 1420
310 IF A(Z) = NB THEN GOSUB 1690
320 IF A(Z) = PB THEN GOSUB 2240
330 RETURN
340 REM *********************************
350 IF A(X) = 107 THEN MM = 0: Q = Q + 1:R
ETURN
360 IF X + 9 > 88 THEN 380
370 IF A(X + 9)<83 AND A(X + 9)>65 AND RND
<.96 THEN RETURN
380 IF X - 11<11 THEN 400
390 IF A(X-11)<83 AND A(X-11)>65 AND RND<.
96 THEN RETURN
400 AD = 0
410 AY = 0
420 AX = X + Q(AY + AD)
430 IF AX<11 OR AX>88 THEN 460
440 AP = A(AX)
450 IF AP = Q OR AP = R AND RND>.8  OR AP
= B AND RND >.5 THEN RETURN
460 AY = AY + 1
470 IF AY < 8 THEN 420
480 AD = AD + 7
490 IF AD<56 THEN 410
500 AY = 1
510 AX = X + N(AY)
520 IF AX<11 OR AX>88 THEN 540
530 IF A(AX) = N THEN RETURN
540 AY = AY + 1
550 IF AY<9 THEN 510
560 AY = 1
570 AX = X + K(AY)
580 IF AX<11 OR AX>88 THEN 600
590 IF (A(AX)=K OR A(AX)=P) AND RND>.1 THE
N RETURN
600 AY = AY + 1
610 IF AY<9 THEN 570
620 MM = 1
```

```
630 RETURN
640 REM *********************************
650 Z = KM
660 Y = 0
670 Y = Y + 1
680 X = Z + N(Y)
690 IF X<11 OR X>88 THEN 600
700 IF A(X) = N THEN 1870
710 IF Y<8 THEN 670
720 REM *********************************
730 D = 0
740 Y = 1
750 X = Z + Q(Y + D)
760 IF X<11 OR X>88 THEN 810
770 IF A(X) = B OR A(X) = Q OR A(X) = R TH
EN 1870
780 IF A(X)<>E THEN 810
790 Y = Y + 1
800 IF Y<8 THEN 750
810 D = D + 7
820 IF D<49 THEN 750
830 X = Z + 11
840 IF X>88 THEN 860
850 IF A(X)=P THEN 1870
860 X = Z - 11
870 IF X<11 THEN 180
880 IF A(X)=P THEN 1870
890 GOTO 180
900 REM *********************************
910 D = 0
920 Y = 1
930 X = Z + Q(Y + D)
940 IF X<11 OR X>88 THEN 1000
950 IF A(X)=42 OR A(X)>=BB AND A(X)<=RB TH
EN 1000
960 IF A(X)>=B AND A(X)<=R THEN GOSUB 350:
IF MM <> 1 THEN 1000
970 IF MM = 1 THEN RETURN
980 Y = Y + 1
990 IF Y<7 THEN 930
1000 D = D + 7
1010 IF D < 42 THEN 920
1020 RETURN
1030 REM *********************************
```

```
1040 D = 0
1050 Y = 1
1060 X = Z + Q(Y + D)
1070 IF X<11 OR X>88 THEN 1130
1080 IF A(X)<>E THEN 1130
1090 IF RND>.5 THEN GOSUB 350:IF MM = 0 TH
EN GOTO 1130
1100 IF MM = 1 THEN RETURN
1110 Y = Y + 1
1120 IF Y<8 THEN GOTO 1060
1130 D = D + 7
1140 IF D<49 THEN 1050
1150 RETURN
1160 REM ********************************
1170 D = 0
1180 Y = 1
1190 X = Z + R(Y + D)
1200 IF X<11 OR X>88 THEN 1260
1210 IF A(X)=-99 OR A(X)>=BB AND A(X)<=RB
THEN 1690
1220 IF A(X)>=B AND A(X)<=R THEN GOSUB 350
:IF MM = 0 THEN GOTO 1260
1230 IF MM = 1 THEN RETURN
1240 Y = Y + 1
1250 IF Y<7 THEN 1190
1260 D = D + 7
1270 IF D<21 THEN 1180
1280 RETURN
1290 REM ********************************
1300 D = 0
1310 Y = 1
1320 X = Z + R(Y + D)
1330   IF X<11 OR X>88 THEN 1390
1340 IF A(X)<>E THEN 1390
1350 IF RND<.1 THEN GOSUB 350
1360 IF MM = 1 THEN RETURN
1370 Y = Y + 1
1380 IF Y < 7 THEN 1320
1390 D = D + 7
1400 IF D<21 THEN 1310
1410 RETURN
1420 IF A(Z) <> BB THEN RETURN
```

```
1430 D = 0
1440 Y = 1
1450 X = Z + B(Y + D)
1460 IF X<11 OR X>88 THEN 1520
1470 IF A(X)=-99 OR A(X)>=BB AND A(X)<=RB
THEN 1520
1480 IF A(X)>=B AND A(X)<=R THEN GOSUB 350
:IF MM <> 1 THEN 1520
1490 IF MM = 1 THEN RETURN
1500 Y = Y + 1
1510 IF Y<7 THEN 1450
1520 D = D + 7
1530 IF D<21 THEN 1440
1540 RETURN
1550 REM ********************************

1560 D = 0
1570 Y = 1
1580 X = Z + B(Y + D)
1590 IF X<11 OR X>88 THEN 1650
1600 IF A(X) <> E THEN 1650
1610 IF RND>.05 THEN GOSUB 350:IF MM <> 1
THEN 1650
1620 IF MM = 1 THEN RETURN
1630 Y = Y + 1
1640 IF Y<7 THEN 1580
1650 D = D + 7
1660 IF D<21 THEN 1570
1670 RETURN
1680 REM ********************************

1690 Y = 1
1700 X = Z + N(Y)
1710 IF X<11 OR X>88 THEN 1750
1720 IF A(X) =-99 THEN 1750
1730 IF A(X)>=B AND A(X)<=R THEN GOSUB 350

1740 IF MM = 1 THEN RETURN
1750 Y = Y + 1
1760 IF Y<9 THEN 1700
1770 RETURN
1780 REM ********************************

1790 Y = 0
```

```
1800 X = Z + N(INT(RND*8 + 1))
1810 IF X<11 OR X>88 THEN 1800
1820 IF A(X) =-99 THEN 1800
1830 Y = Y + 1
1840 IF A(X) = E THEN GOSUB 350
1850 IF MM = 1 OR Y > 20 THEN RETURN
1860 GOTO 1800
1870 YK = 1
1880 Z = KM
1890 X = Z + K(YK):X1 = X
1900 IF X<11 OR X>88 THEN 2200
1910 IF A(X)=-99 OR A(X)>65 AND A(X)<83 TH
EN 2200
1920 IF A(X)>97 AND A(X)<115 THEN 2200
1930 Z = X
1940 Y = 0
1950 Y = Y + 1
1960 X = Z + N(Y)
1970 IF X<11 OR X>88 THEN 1990
1980 IF A(X)=N THEN 2200
1990 IF Y<8 THEN 1950
2000 REM *********************************

2010 D = 0
2020 Y = 1
2030 X = Z +Q(Y + D)
2040 IF X<11 OR X>88 THEN 2090
2050 IF A(X)=B OR A(X)=Q OR A(X)=R THEN 22
00
2060 IF A(X)<>E THEN 2090
2070 Y = Y + 1
2080 IF Y<8 THEN 2030
2090 D = D + 7
2100 IF D<49 THEN 2030
2110 X = Z + 11
2120 IF X>88 THEN 2140
2130 IF A(X)=P THEN 2200
2140 X = Z - 11
2150 IF X<11 THEN 2170
2160 IF A(X) = P THEN 2200
2170 X = X1:Z = KM
2180 MM = 1
2190 GOSUB 2500:GOTO 40
2200 YK = YK + 1
```

```
2210 Z = KM
2220 IF YK<9 THEN 1880
2230 PRINT "I concede, champ!":END
2240 X = Z + 9
2250 IF A(X)>=B AND A(X)<=R THEN MM = 1:IF
 A(X)=P AND RND<.2 THEN MM = 0
2260 IF MM = 1 THEN RETURN
2270 IF Z = 12 THEN RETURN
2280 X = Z - 11
2290 IF A(X)>=B AND A(X)<=R THEN MM = 1:IF
 A(X)=P AND RND<.2 THEN MM = 0
2300 RETURN
2310 REM ********************************

2320 IF Z - 10*(INT(Z/10))=7 AND A(Z-1)=E
AND A(Z-2)=E AND (A(Z-13)=E OR A(Z-13)=42)
 AND (A(Z+7)=E OR A(Z+7)=-99) THEN X = Z -
 2:MM = 1:RETURN
2330 IF A(Z-1)=E AND A(Z-12)<98 AND A(Z+8)
<98 THEN X=Z-1:MM = 1:RETURN
2340 IF RND<.05 AND A(Z-1)=E THEN X=Z-1:MM
=1
2350 RETURN
2360 Q = INT(RND*RND*5):IF Q>U THEN 2360
2370 IF Q<U THEN Q = Q + 1
2380 Z = T(Q)
2390 IF A(Z)=PB THEN GOSUB 2320
2400 IF A(Z)=NB THEN GOSUB 1790
2410 IF A(Z)=BB THEN GOSUB 1560
2420 IF A(Z)=RB THEN GOSUB 1300
2430 IF A(Z)=QB THEN GOSUB 1040
2440 IF A(Z)=KB AND A$<>"C" AND RND<.07 TH
EN GOSUB 1870
2450 IF MM=0 AND Q<U THEN GOTO 2370
2460 IF MM=1 THEN GOSUB 2500:GOTO 40
2470 UK = UK + 1:IF UK>8 THEN 2230
2480 GOTO 2360
2490 REM ********************************

2500 IF A(Z)=KB AND A$<>"C" AND RND>.1 THE
N MM=0:GOTO 2360
2510 IF A(Z)=PB AND ((X-10*INT(X/10) > Z-1
0*INT(Z/10) OR ABS(X-Z)>11)) THEN MM=0:U =
 U + 1:GOTO 230
```

```
2520 IF A(X) = K   THEN PRINT "CHECK": MM=0
:U = U + 1:GOTO 230
2530 A(X) = A(Z):A(Z) = E
2540 PRINT "I will move from ";
2550 FZ=INT(Z/10):PRINT CHR$(FZ+64);Z-10*F
Z;" to ";:FX=INT(X/10):PRINT CHR$(FX+64);X
-10*FX:FOR O = 1 TO 1000:NEXT O
2560 RETURN
2570 REM *********************************

2580 CLS
2590 GOSUB 2670
2600 FOR X=8 TO 1 STEP -1
2610 PRINT TAB(10);X;" ";
2620 FOR Y = 10 TO 80 STEP 10
2630 IF A(Y+1)=PB THEN A(Y+1)=QB
2640 IF A(Y+8)=B THEN A(Y+8)=Q
2650 PRINT CHR$(A(X+Y));" ";
2660 NEXT Y:PRINT X:NEXT X:MM = 0
2670 PRINT:PRINT TAB(14);"A B C D E F G H"
:PRINT
2680 REM *********************************

2690 RETURN
2700 Z = KM
2710 QK = 0
2720 M = Z + K(QK)
2730 IF M<11 OR M>88 THEN 2780
2740 IF A(M)=-99 OR A(M)>65 AND A(M)<83 OR
 MM=0 THEN 2780
2750 X = M
2760 KM=Z
2770 RETURN
2780 IF QK<8 THEN 2720
2790 IF A$<>"C" THEN RETURN
2800 GOTO 2230
2810 REM *********************************

2820 PRINT
2830 INPUT "FROM (LETTER,NUMBER)";A$
2840 IF LEN(A$)<>2 THEN 2820
2850 INPUT "TO";B$
2860 IF LEN(B$)<>2 THEN 2850
2870 X = 10*(ASC(A$)-64)+VAL(RIGHT$(A$,1))
```

```
2880 Y = 10*(ASC(B$)-64)+VAL(RIGHT$(B$,1))

2890 PRINT "Enter C - check"
2900 PRINT "      P - to print board"
2910 PRINT "      X - to exchange sides"
2920 PRINT "      S - to stop game"
2930 INPUT "Or press RETURN to continue";A
$
2940 IF A(Y)>=75 AND A(Y)<=82 THEN GOSUB 3
660
2950 A(Y) = A(X):A(X) = 46:RETURN
2960 REM ********************************

2970 CLS:PRINT "PLEASE ENGAGE CAPS LOCK":P
RINT"THEN PRESS RETURN"
2980 N = N + 1:IF INKEY$ = "" THEN 2980
2990 RANDOMIZE N:CLS:PRINT "Please stand b
y"
3000 DEFINT A - Z
3010 MM=0:A$=""
3020 DIM A(99),R(28),B(28),N(8),Q(56),K(8)
,Z(88),S(64),T(16)
3030 P=112: R=114: N=110: B=98: Q=113: K=1
07: E=46
3040 PB=80: RB=82: NB=78: BB=66: QB=81: KB
=75
3050 FOR Z = 1 TO 99:A(Z) = - 99:NEXT Z
3060 REM ********************************

3070 FOR Z = 1 TO 64:READ X:READ Y:A(X)=Y:
NEXT Z
3080 DATA 18,82,28,78,38,66,48,81
3090 DATA 58,75,68,66,78,78,88,82
3100 DATA 17,80,27,80,37,80,47,80
3110 DATA 57,80,67,80,77,80,87,80
3120 DATA 16,46,26,46,36,46,46,46
3130 DATA 56,46,66,46,76,46,86,46
3140 DATA 15,46,25,46,35,46,45,46
3150 DATA 55,46,65,46,75,46,85,46
3160 DATA 14,46,24,46,34,46,44,46
3170 DATA 54,46,64,46,74,46,84,46
3180 DATA 13,46,23,46,33,46,43,46
3190 DATA 53,46,63,46,73,46,83,46
3200 DATA 12,112,22,112,32,112,42,112
```

```
3210 DATA 52,112,62,112,72,112,82,112
3220 DATA 11,114,21,110,31,98,41,113
3230 DATA 51,107,61,98,71,110,81,114
3240 REM ********************************

3250 RESTORE 3270
3260 FOR Z = 1 TO 8:READ N(Z):NEXT Z
3270 DATA 19,-19,21,-21,-8,8,12,-12
3280 FOR Z = 1 TO 28:READ R(Z):NEXT Z
3290 DATA 10,20,30,40,50,50,50
3300 DATA -1,-2,-3,-4,-5,-5,-5
3310 DATA -10,-20,-30,-40,-50,-50,-50
3320 DATA 1,2,3,4,5,5,5
3330 RESTORE 3350
3340 FOR Z = 1 TO 28:READ B(Z):NEXT Z
3350 DATA -11,-22,-33,-44,-55,-55,-55
3360 DATA 11,22,33,44,55,55,55
3370 DATA 9,18,27,36,45,45,45
3380 DATA -9,-18,-27,-36,-45,-45,-45
3390 RESTORE 3290
3400 FOR Z = 1 TO 56:READ Q(Z):NEXT Z
3410 FOR Z = 1 TO 8:READ K(Z):NEXT Z
3420 DATA 1,11,9,10,-10,-9,-11,-1
3430 FOR Z = 1 TO 64:READ S(Z):NEXT Z
3440 DATA 46,56,36,66,47,57,45,55
3450 DATA 37,67,35,65,28,78,27,77
3460 DATA 44,54,26,76,38,68,17,87
3470 DATA 18,88,34,64,25,75,16,86
3480 DATA 48,24,74,15,85,14,84,43
3490 DATA 53,33,62,23,73,52,42,62
3500 DATA 32,83,13,72,22,12,82,41
3510 DATA 51,31,61,21,71,11,81,58
3520 CLS:RETURN
3530 REM ********************************

3540 FOR Z = 11 TO 88:Z(Z) = A(Z): NEXT Z
3550 FOR Z = 11 TO 88:X = Z - 10*INT(Z/10)

3560 IF X = 0 OR X = 9 THEN 3580
3570 A(Z) = Z(Z + 9 - X*2)
3580 NEXT Z
3590 FOR Z = 11 TO 88:M = A(Z)
3600 IF M>=B THEN A(Z) = A(Z) + PB - P
3610 IF M<=RB AND M>=BB THEN A(Z) = A(Z) -
```

```
 PB + P
3620 NEXT Z
3630 GOSUB 2580
3640 RETURN
3650 REM *********************************

3660 CM=INT(RND*4) + 1
3670 ON CM GOSUB 3690,3700,3710,3720
3680 FOR J = 1 TO 1000:NEXT J:RETURN
3690 PRINT "Well done!":RETURN
3700 PRINT "Good move":RETURN
3710 PRINT "Great move, champ!":RETURN
3720 PRINT "Got me...":RETURN
3730 LPRINT "*****************************
***"
3740 GOSUB 3800
3750 FOR X=8 TO 1 STEP -1
3760 LPRINT TAB(5);X;" ";
3770 FOR Y = 10 TO 80 STEP 10
3780 LPRINT CHR$(A(X+Y));" ";
3790 NEXT Y:LPRINT X:NEXT X
3800 LPRINT:LPRINT TAB(9);"A B C D E F G H
":LPRINT
3810 RETURN
```

If you wish to get the computer to play against itself, change line 2580 to the following:

```
2580 CLS:PRINT "Player"PR"at top of screen"
```

and change the first 10 lines of the program so that they read as follows:

```
15 PR = 1
20 GOSUB 2970
30 GOTO 60
40 GOSUB 2580
50 A$ = "X"
60 IF PR = 2 THEN PR = 1: GOTO 80
70 PR = 2
80 IF A$ = "S" THEN END
90 IF A$ = "X" THEN PRINT "EXCHANGING SIDE
S":GOSUB 3540:A$ = ""
100 IF PR = 2  THEN GOSUB 3730
```

27

If you want the computer to trigger your printer from time to time during a game, to give you "snapshots" of the program in action, add the following:

```
3730 IF RND >.08 THEN RETURN
3735 LPRINT "********************************
"
3740 GOSUB 3800
```

How the program works

We'll have a look at a few parts of the chess program now, so that if you decide to modify it to improve its play, you'll know which bits to attack first.

As explained in the introduction to this section of the book, the program starts with a series of subroutine calls which are cycled through as the game progresses. After the first REM statement identifying the program, the computer goes to the subroutine from line 2970 which initializes the variables. Next, line 30 jumps to line 60, which calls up the board printing subroutine at line 2580. This routine, like the other board-printing routines in this section, starts off with a clear screen (CLS) command. If you have a HOME key, or similar (such as PRINT @ 0, PRINT AT 0,0 or LOCATE 1,1) you should put this in the place of the CLS. Then the board will simply be reprinted over its old image, which gives a very effective impression of the pieces moving. It is far more satisfactory than clearing the screen each time the board must be reprinted.

After the board is printed, the program continues past line 60 into the computer move section. First it checks the status of A$, which is a string set by the player after each move. If A$ equals S then the human player has signaled a desire to quit the game, so the program ends. If A$ has been set to X (for exchange) the program goes to the subroutine from line 3540 to swap sides. If A$ is equal to P, the computer moves to the subroutine from line 3730 which dumps the current board to the printer.

Now the computer play begins in earnest. First, the T array (which will hold the location of the computer pieces) is filled with zeroes, and the piece counter variable (U) is set to zero. The loop in lines 150 and 160 goes through each square on the board, counting the pieces (U is incremented each time a piece is found, and storing the location of each piece in the elements of the T array. When the king (variable KB, for "king black") is found, the variable KM (for "king marker") is set equal to that, so the computer knows where its king is at all times. If U is less than three (line 160) then the computer

28

goes to line 2230 to concede the game. It has no endgame strategy, and tends to flounder if it has too few pieces.

Line 170 jumps the action to 650, where a long routine checks whether the king is in check. Each section of the code in this part of the program checks for danger from a particular piece. The first part, from 650 to 710, checks for danger from human knights, while the next (730 to 890) looks for lurking queens, bishops, rooks, and pawns. If no danger has been found, so the program flow is not redirected by the numerous GOTOs in this section, line 890 sends the program back to 180 where it starts looking for a move.

Lines 180 and 190 reshuffle the contents of the T array, so that the king is the very last piece in the array. In general, the computer will try to move its pieces in terms of their position within this array, so if the king is at the end, it will only move if the computer judges no other move is worthwhile. As I said before the listing, this is one of my rough and ready chess-playing ideas and is based on the principle that if the king moves as little as possible, it is unlikely to get into danger. This, of course, is not always true. However, for the kind of chess the program plays it is a reasonable assumption, and certainly less dangerous than the alternative, which would see the king belting around exposing himself to danger at every turn.

Now Q is set to either 0, 1, or 2 by line 210 and reset to 0 in line 210 if the human has signaled C for check. Q determines where in the T array the computer will start looking for its move. The random element is introduced here so that the computer does not always do the same thing when confronted with similar board positions. One is added to Q if Q is less than U (that is, less than the total number of pieces the computer has on the board) and then Z is set equal to that element of the T array, which is the location of the computer piece on the board.

The subroutine at line 280 is now called. If you look at that subroutine, you'll see that lines 280 to 320 determine which piece it is dealing with. The computer plays black, and to make it easy to follow what is happening in the listing, QB is used to indicate the queen ("queen black"), RB is the rook, BB the bishop, NB the knight, and PB the pawn. So the computer—in this little subroutine—just finds out what piece it has in hand, and then directs the computer to the relevant subroutine to check for a capture by that piece.

Now you should be getting an idea of how the program works. Essentially, it finds its pieces; if it is not in check it puts the pieces in an order dictated by the layout of the board (that will be explained when we get to the end of the program listing) with the king at the end of this list; then it looks for a capture with each of the pieces in turn.

29

The most important variable (after KM, the king marker) is MM (which stands for "machine move"). You'll see MM in line 240. MM is set initially to zero, and only gets reset to one when a move is found. Line 240 checks the value of MM and if it finds it is a one, knows that a move has been found, so goes to the subroutine from line 2500. Here it checks to see that (a) it is not trying to move its king without due cause; (b) that it is not moving a pawn unintelligently; and (c) that it is not just about to capture the human's king. Any of these three cases will cause the MM flag to be reset to zero, and the action reverts to line 230 to find another move. (If the computer finds case "c" is true, it prints CHECK on the screen, then continues looking for its move.)

If it finds that the three conditions are not true, then it actually makes the move (line 2530 makes the needed changes to the elements of the A array, the array that actually holds the board), then tells you—using lines 2540 and 2550—the move it is to make, then returns to the start of the program where the board is reprinted.

If, however, MM was not equal to one when the computer came to line 240, it then moves on to 250 where the machine checks that it has not used up all its pieces (which will be the case if Q equals U), and if it finds it has not, goes back to line 220, where Q is incremented by one, and the process begins again. If, however, Q is equal to U, the computer decides it cannot make a legal move, and goes to 2360 to look for a non-capture move. The next section, as we've already discussed, sends the action to various parts of the program which control individual pieces.

If we look at the section from line 2360, we see that it starts by setting Q to a random number between zero and four. The use of the double RND ensures that it will tend to choose lower numbers in that range more often than higher ones. Z is set equal to the Qth element of the T array (as before when we were looking for captures) and then the lines from 2390 to 2440 send the program to the sections of code which control their moves.

We won't look at each of these sections for individual piece moves because each of them works in a similar way. Understand the basic principle of one, and you can easily deduce how the others work.

We'll look at the section which moves a knight, as we have already had some discussion (in the introduction to this section of the book) of how knights move. Look at the section of code from line 1790. As you'll discover when we look at the initialization section of the program, an array is set up for each piece which holds the possible moves (in terms of a numerical displacement from the starting square) for that piece. The Q array holds the possible queen moves, the B array, the moves the bishop can make, and so on. Therefore, we know the N array, which is referred to in line 1800, holds the legal moves of the knight.

In this line, the variable X is set equal to Z (the square the piece occupies) plus an element (chosen at random) of the N array. Line 1810 checks to see that this possible "destination" square is not off the board (which it would be if its value was less than 11 or greater than 88) or equal to -99 (which would also mean it was off the board). Y is the variable which counts the number of potential moves tried. It is incremented by one in line 1830, and then the computer checks the value now held by A(X), which is the destination square. If it finds it holds the value E (for "empty") then it knows it can move into that square. But it does not necessarily just leap into A(X) just because this is an empty square.

First it goes to the subroutine from line 350 which checks to see if the intended destination square is under attack. On returning from that destination it checks (line 1850) to see if MM is equal to one. If it is, the computer knows the move it is considering has been approved, and so moves to the section of code which actually makes the move. If Y is greater than 20, which means 20 moves have been tried without success, then this also triggers a return, so a new piece can be tried. If both these conditions are found to be false, the computer goes back to line 1800 to get a new knight move at random.

In essence, this is how every possible move is generated, and tested. The knight is a little simpler than the other pieces because it can leap over intervening pieces. The other pieces have to check that a clear path exists for them to carry out their intended move, but this is not very difficult to achieve.

If you move now to the section of the program from line 2970, you'll see that the initialization takes place here. First the computer asks the player to "ENGAGE CAPS LOCK . . . THEN PRESS RE-TURN." The computer counts how long this takes (using N as a counter) and uses this value to seed the random number generator. As in all programs in this book, if your RANDOMIZE function works differently from this, change the line to suit your particular dialect of BASIC. Line 3000 ensures that all variables will be treated as integer variables. This is included to maximize the running speed, but can be left out without harm if you do not have a DEFINT on your computer. MM (machine move, remember) is set to zero in line 3010 and A\$ (which holds messages from the player such as the desire to exchange sides) is set to the null string.

A number of arrays are now dimensioned. A holds the board itself, R the rook moves, B the bishop moves, N the knight moves, Q the queen moves, K the king moves, Z the exchange sides mechanism, S the priority sequence which determines the order in which squares are checked for pieces, and T the location of the pieces on the board before each move is made.

The next two lines initialize the variables which are the human and computer pieces as follows:

```
P  - human pawn
R  - human rook
N  - human knight
Q  - human queen
K  - human king
E  - an empty square
PB - computer pawn
RB - computer rook
NB - computer knight
BB - computer bishop
QB - computer queen
KB - computer king
```

The next line (3050) fills the A array (which will hold the board) with a dummy value (-99). This ensures that any square which is not subsequently given a value will be ignored when the program is running. This program, by the way, uses a numbered board similar to the one shown at the start of this section of the book, but it is "on its side and back to front," with a layout as follows:

```
18 28 38 48 58 68 78 88 *8
17 27 37 47 57 67 77 87 *7
16 26 36 46 56 66 76 86 *6
15 25 35 45 55 65 75 85 *5
14 24 34 44 54 64 74 84 *4
13 23 33 43 53 63 73 83 *3
12 22 32 42 52 62 72 82 *2
11 21 31 41 51 61 71 81 *1
**************************
A  B  C  D  E  F  G  H
```

The next section of the program fills the arrays, with the Z loop (in line 3070) putting all the pieces in their place for the start of the game. The next section is fairly obvious when you examine it, with 3260 putting the values for knight moves into the N array, 3280 doing the same for the rook and 3340 for the bishop. The DATA pointer is then restored to line 3290, the start of the rook information, so that the Q array (for the queen) can be filled with the locations for both the rook and the bishop because, of course, the queen is able to make the moves of both pieces.

Line 3430 fills the S array with the numbers in DATA statements line 3430 to 3510. These are probably the key reason why the program runs so quickly when it is underway. This series of numbers is the order in which the squares on the board are checked. If you compare this sequence with the "numbered board" given on the previous page, you'll be able to work out the sequence. It starts with the squares in front of the starting position of the two key pawns followed by the squares either side of those, before moving back to look at the squares where the key pawns begin the game. Once you've worked through this list, you may well want to modify this sequence. This array, more than any other, determines the kind of game the computer will play. If you don't agree with the sequence I've set up, by all means change it and see what effect this has on the game the computer plays.

The "exchange sides" routine is from 3540 to 3640. A series of comments when the computer loses a piece ("Great move, champ!" and so on) is generated by the routine from 3660 to 3720. The final section of code dumps the current board to the printer.

☐ GOMOKU

You'll find GOMOKU an easy game to learn, but one which is almost impossible to win. The computer plays extremely well in this program, which is based on one written by Graham Charlton.

You have to try to get five of your pieces (the H's) in a row in any direction, while the computer is trying to do the same.

Have a look at these board positions from the start of one game I played against the program. Studying the printouts will show you how the game unfolds, and will show you how to play it:

```
   1 2 3 4 5 6 7 8              1 2 3 4 5 6 7 8
1  . . . . . . . .  1        1  . . . . . . . .  1
2  . . . . . . . .  2        2  . . . . . . . .  2
3  . . . C . . . .  3        3  . . . C . . . .  3
4  . . . . . . . .  4        4  . . . . . . . .  4
5  . . . . H . . .  5        5  . . . . H . . .  5
6  . . . . . . . .  6        6  . . . C . . . .  6
7  . . H . . . . .  7        7  . . H . . . . .  7
8  . . . . . C . .  8        8  . . . . . C . .  8
   1 2 3 4 5 6 7 8              1 2 3 4 5 6 7 8


   1 2 3 4 5 6 7 8              1 2 3 4 5 6 7 8
1  . . . . . . . .  1        1  . . . . . . . .  1
2  . . . . . . . .  2        2  . . . . . . . .  2
3  . . . C . . . .  3        3  . . . C . . . .  3
4  . . . . . . . .  4        4  . . . . . . . .  4
5  . . . . H . . .  5        5  . . . . H C H .  5
6  . . . C C . . .  6        6  . . . C C . . .  6
7  . . H . H . . .  7        7  . . H . H . . .  7
8  . . . . . C . .  8        8  . . . . . C . .  8
   1 2 3 4 5 6 7 8              1 2 3 4 5 6 7 8
```

```
  1 2 3 4 5 6 7 8                1 2 3 4 5 6 7 8
1 . . . . . . . .  1           1 . . . . . . . .  1
2 . . . . . . . .  2           2 . . . . . . . .  2
3 . . . C . . . .  3           3 . . . C . . . .  3
4 . . . . . . . C  4           4 . . . C . . . C  4
5 . . . . H C H .  5           5 . . . . H C H .  5
6 . . . C C H . .  6           6 . . . C C H . .  6
7 . . H . H . H .  7           7 . . H . H . H .  7
8 . . . . . C . .  8           8 . . . . . C . .  8
  1 2 3 4 5 6 7 8                1 2 3 4 5 6 7 8


  1 2 3 4 5 6 7 8                1 2 3 4 5 6 7 8
1 . . . . . . . .  1           1 . . . . . . . .  1
2 . . . . . . . .  2           2 . . . . . . . .  2
3 . . . C . . . .  3           3 . . . C . . . .  3
4 . . . C . . . C  4           4 . . . C . . C C  4
5 . . . . H C H .  5           5 . . . H H C H .  5
6 . . . C C H . .  6           6 . . . C C H H .  6
7 . . H C H H . .  7           7 . . H C H H H C  7
8 . . . . . C . .  8           8 . . . . . C . .  8
  1 2 3 4 5 6 7 8                1 2 3 4 5 6 7 8
```

Here's the listing for your very own game of GOMOKU:

```
10 REM GOMOKU
20 GOSUB 750
30 GOSUB 130
40 GOSUB 240
50 GOSUB 130
60 GOSUB 320
70 GOSUB 130
80 IF L>3 THEN PRINT:PRINT "I WIN!!":END
90 GOTO 40
100 E = A
110 E = E + N: IF A(E)<>Z THEN RETURN
120 K = K + 1:GOTO 110
130 CLS
140 PRINT:PRINT:PRINT
150 PRINT TAB(12);"1 2 3 4 5 6 7 8"
160 FOR A = 1 TO 8:PRINT TAB(8);A;" ";
170 FOR B = 2 TO 9
```

```
180 PRINT CHR$(A(A*10 + B));" ";
190 NEXT B
200 PRINT A
210 NEXT A
220 PRINT TAB(12);"1 2 3 4 5 6 7 8"
230 RETURN
240 PRINT:PRINT
250 PRINT "Please enter your move..."
260 INPUT G
270 G = G + 1
280 IF G<12 OR G>89 OR A(G)<>46 THEN 260
290 Z = H
300 A(G) = Z
310 RETURN
320 A = G
330 L = 0
340 FOR X = 1 TO 4:K = 0:N = X(X)
350 GOSUB 100
360 N = - N:GOSUB 100
370 IF K>L THEN L = K
380 NEXT X
390 IF L>3 THEN PRINT:PRINT "You win!!":END

400 T = 1
410 IF T<>2 THEN Z = C
420 IF T = 2 THEN Z = H
430 G = 0:H1 = 0:L = 0
440 FOR A = 12 TO 89
450 M = 0
460 IF A(A)<>46 THEN 570
470 FOR X = 1 TO 4:K = 0:N = X(X)
480 GOSUB 100
490 N = - N:GOSUB 100
500 IF K>L THEN H1 = 0:L = K
510 IF L<>K THEN 540
520 IF T=1 AND L<4 OR (T=2 OR T=3) AND L<2
THEN 540
530 M = M + 1
540 NEXT X
550 IF M<=H1 THEN 570
560 H1 = M:G = A
570 NEXT A
580 IF H1<>0 THEN 650
590 T = T + 1: IF T<>4 THEN 410
```

```
600 A = 1
610 G = INT(RND*77) + 13
620 IF A(G) = 46 THEN 650
630 A = A + 1:IF A<100 THEN 610
640 PRINT:PRINT "I concede the game":PRINT"
to a master!!":END
650 A(G) = C
660 Z = C:A = G:L = 0
670 FOR X = 1 TO 4
680 K = 0
690 N = X(X)
700 GOSUB 100
710 N = -N:GOSUB 100
720 IF K>L THEN L=K
730 NEXT X
740 RETURN
750 CLS
760 DIM A(100),X(4)
770 FOR C = 1 TO 8
780 FOR B = 2 TO 9
790 A(C*10 + B) = 46
800 NEXT B
810 NEXT C
820 FOR Q = 1 TO 4
830 READ Z: X(Q) = Z
840 NEXT Q
850 DATA 1,9,10,11
860 H = ASC("H"):C = ASC("C")
870 PRINT:PRINT "Enter Y if you want the"
880 PRINT "first move, N if you don't"
890 N = 0
900 N = N + 1
910 A$ = INKEY$
920 IF A$ <> "y" AND A$ <> "Y" AND A$ <> "n
" AND A$ <> "N" THEN 900
930 RANDOMIZE N
940 CLS
950 IF A$ = "y" OR A$ = "Y" THEN RETURN
960 FOR J = 1 TO INT(RND*12) + 1
970 READ Z
980 NEXT J
990 A(Z) = C
1000 RETURN
1010 DATA 34,35,44,46,47,54,55,56,57,66
```

☐ FOUR IN A ROW

In this game, FOUR IN A ROW, as its name suggests, the aim is to get four of your pieces (the H's) in a line in any direction, before the computer (using the C's) manages to do so.

You indicate your choice of move by specifying the column in which you want to move your piece. The piece then drops to the lowest available position within that column.

The computer plays this game fairly well, and surprisingly quickly, considering the number of times it can go through those loops within the program.

I was not particularly pleased when I finished the first hand-written version of this program, because it seemed to me that I had taken a "brute force" approach to solving the problem. I was sure there would be a more clever way to do it. However, I continued with the program, and then entered it into the computer. It won the first game, even though it played a little oddly, so I knew I was onto a winner, despite the programming approach. Then, when thinking about it later I realized that if the program was correctly structured (as it was), had no redundant code (and it hasn't, as far as I can see), ran quickly and well, it did not need "fiddling" to make the programming more tricky. Transparent code is always better than overly clever convoluted code which, although it may occupy less space, and may run a few microseconds faster, is almost impossible to modify.

So the program you have here is my "brute force" version. It is generously supplied with REM statements so you have little trouble in working out what each section of code does. It should also prove fairly simple to modify, once you have played a few games with it in its present form.

In this version of FOUR IN A ROW, the computer always allows the human to have the first move, and bases its initial move on that made by the human. You may wish to modify the program so that there is an option for the computer to have the opening move.

Before we get to the listing of FOUR IN A ROW, here's one game played against the program:

```
. . . . . . .          . . . . . . .
. . . . . . .          . . . . . . .
. . . . . . .          . . . . . . .
. . . . . . .          . . . . . . .
. . . . . . .          . . . . . . .
. . . . . . .          . . . C . . .
. . . H . . .          . . . H . . .
1 2 3 4 5 6 7          1 2 3 4 5 6 7
```

Stand by for my move...

Your move...

Which column do you
wish to move into? 3

```
. . . . . . .          . . . . . . .
. . . . . . .          . . . . . . .
. . . . . . .          . . . . . . .
. . . . . . .          . . . . . . .
. . . C . . .          . . . C . . .
. . H H C . .          H C H H C . .
1 2 3 4 5 6 7          1 2 3 4 5 6 7
```

```
. . . . . . .          . . . . . . .
. . . . . . .          . . . . . . .
. . . C . . .          C . . C . . .
. . H H . . .          C C H H H . .
. H C C C . .          H H C C C . .
H C H H C . .          H C H H C . H
1 2 3 4 5 6 7          1 2 3 4 5 6 7
```

Your move...   Your move...

Which column do you   Which column do you
wish to move into? 5   wish to move into? 7

39

```
. . . . . .
H . . . . .
C . C . . . .
C . H C . . .
C C H H H . C
H H C C C . H
H C H H C . H
1 2 3 4 5 6 7
```

```
. . . . . .
H . . . . .
C . C H . . .
C . H C . . .
C C H H H . C
H H C C C . H
H C H H C C H
1 2 3 4 5 6 7
```

Your move...

Which column do you
wish to move into? 4

Your move...

Which column do you
wish to move into? 6

```
. . . . . .
H . C . . . .
C . C H . . .
C . H C H . .
C C H H H C C
H H C C C H H
H C H H C C H
1 2 3 4 5 6 7
```

```
. . C . . . .
H . C H . . .
C . C H . . .
C . H C H . .
C C H H H C C
H H C C C H H
H C H H C C H
1 2 3 4 5 6 7
```

```
. . C C . . .
H . C H . . .
C . C H . . .
C . H C H . H
C C H H H C C
H H C C C H H
H C H H C C H
1 2 3 4 5 6 7
```

```
. . C C . . .
H . C H . . .
C C C H . . .
C H H C H . H
C C H H H C C
H H C C C H H
H C H H C C H
1 2 3 4 5 6 7
```

Your move...

Which column do you
wish to move into? 2

I've defeated you,
human!

This is the listing for FOUR IN A ROW:

```
10 REM Four-in-a-row
20 GOSUB 1090:REM INITIALISE
30 GOSUB 860:REM PRINT BOARD
40 GOSUB 680:REM WIN CHECK
50 GOSUB 980:REM HUMAN MOVE
60 GOSUB 860:REM PRINT BOARD
70 GOSUB 680:REM WIN CHECK
80 GOSUB 110:REM COMPUTER MOVE
90 GOTO 30
100 REM **************
110 REM COMPUTER MOVE
120 PRINT:PRINT "Stand by for my move..."
130 B = 10
140 B = B + 1
150 IF A(B) = - 9 THEN 180
160 IF A(B) = C THEN X = C:GOTO 210
170 IF A(B) = H THEN X = H:GOTO 210
180 IF B < 77 THEN 140
190 GOTO 480
200 REM ****************************
210 REM FOUR IN ROW DANGER/CHANCE?
220 REM ACROSS
230 IF A(B+1) = X AND A(B+2) = X AND A(B+3
) = E AND A(B + 13) <> E THEN MOVE = B + 3
:GOTO 650
240 IF A(B-1) = X AND A(B-2) = X AND A(B-3
) = E AND A(B + 7) <> E THEN MOVE = B - 3:
GOTO 650
250 IF A(B+1) = X AND A(B+2) = X AND A(B-1
) = E AND A(B + 9) <> E THEN MOVE = B - 1:
GOTO 650
260 IF A(B-1) = X AND A(B+2) = X AND A(B+1
) = E AND A(B+11) <> E THEN MOVE = B + 1:G
OTO 650
270 IF A(B+1) = X AND A(B-1) = X AND A(B+2
) = E AND A(B+12) <> E THEN MOVE = B + 2:G
OTO 650
280 IF A(B+1) = X AND A(B-1) = X AND A(B-2
) = E AND A(B+8) <> E THEN MOVE = B - 2:GO
TO 650
290 IF A(B-1) = X AND A(B-2) = X AND A(B+1
```

```
) = E AND A(B+11) <> E THEN MOVE = B + 1:G
OTO 650
300 REM DOWN
310 IF B > 20 THEN IF A(B-10) = X AND A(B-
20) = X AND A(B+10) = E AND A(B+20) <> E T
HEN MOVE = B + 10:GOTO 650
320 REM DIAGONALS
330 IF A(B+11) = X AND A(B+22) = X AND A(B
-11) = E AND A(B-1) <> E THEN MOVE = B - 1
1:GOTO 650
340 IF A(B+9) = X AND A(B+18) = X AND A(B-
9) = E AND A(B+1) <> E THEN MOVE = B - 9:G
OTO 650
350 REM ****************
360 REM MAKE/BLOCK THREE?
370 REM ACROSS
380 IF A(B+1) = X AND A(B+2) = E AND A(B+1
2) <> E THEN MOVE = B + 2:GOTO 650
390 IF A(B+1) = X AND A(B-1) = E AND A(B+9
) <> E THEN MOVE = B - 1:GOTO 650
400 IF A(B-1) = X AND A(B-2) = E AND A(B+8
) <> E THEN MOVE = B - 2:GOTO 650
410 REM VERTICAL
420 IF A(B+10) = X AND A(B-10) = E AND A(B
) <> E THEN MOVE = B - 10:GOTO 650
430 REM DIAGONAL
440 IF A(B+9) = X AND A(B-9) = E AND A(B+1
) <> E THEN MOVE = B - 9:GOTO 650
450 IF B > 11 THEN IF A(B+11) = X AND A(B-
11) = E AND A(B-1) <> E THEN MOVE = B - 11
:GOTO 650
460 GOTO 180
470 REM ************
480 REM SINGLE MOVES
490 FOR N = 1 TO 3
500 M(N) = 0
510 NEXT N
520 COUNT = 0
530 FOR B = 11 TO 77
540 IF A(B) <> C AND A(B) <> H THEN 600
550 IF  A(B+1) = E AND A(B+11) <> E THEN C
OUNT = COUNT + 1:M(COUNT) = B + 1
560 IF  A(B-1) = E AND A(B+9) <> E THEN CO
UNT = COUNT + 1:M(COUNT) = B - 1
```

```
570 IF  A(B-10) = E AND A(B) <> E THEN COU
NT = COUNT + 1:M(COUNT) = B - 10
580 IF  A(B-11) = E AND A(B-1) <> E THEN C
OUNT = COUNT + 1:M(COUNT) = B - 11
590 IF  A(B-9) = E AND A(B+1) <> E THEN CO
UNT = COUNT + 1:M(COUNT) = B - 9
600 NEXT B
610 IF COUNT <> 0 THEN 640
620 PRINT:PRINT "I think we should call it
 a draw"
630 PRINT:PRINT:PRINT:END
640 MOVE = M(INT(RND*COUNT) + 1)
650 A(MOVE) = C
660 RETURN
670 REM *********
680 REM WIN CHECK
690 X = H
700 B = 10
710 B = B + 1
720 IF A(B) <> X THEN 770
730 IF A(B+1) = X AND A(B+2) = X AND A(B+3
) = X THEN 800
740 IF B > 30 THEN IF A(B-10) = X AND A(B-
20) = X AND A(B-30) = X THEN 800
750 IF B > 33 THEN IF A(B-11) = X AND A(B-
22) = X AND A(B-33) = X THEN 800
760 IF B > 27 THEN IF A(B-9) = X AND A(B-1
8) = X AND A(B - 27) = X THEN 800
770 IF B < 77 THEN 710
780 IF X = H THEN X = C:GOTO 700
790 RETURN
800 REM WIN FOUND
810 PRINT:PRINT
820 IF X = H THEN PRINT "You've beaten me,
 human!"
830 IF X = C THEN PRINT "I've defeated you
, human!"
840 PRINT:PRINT:PRINT:END
850 REM ***********
860 REM PRINT BOARD
870 CLS:PRINT:PRINT
880 FOR K = 10 TO 70 STEP 10
890 PRINT TAB(5);
900 FOR J = 1 TO 7
```

```
910 PRINT CHR$(A(K + J));" ";
920 NEXT J
930 NEXT K
940 PRINT TAB(5);"1 2 3 4 5 6 7"
950 PRINT:PRINT
960 RETURN
970 REM **********
980 REM HUMAN MOVE
990 PRINT "Your move...":PRINT
1000 PRINT "Which column do you wish to"
1010 INPUT "move into";J
1020 Z = J
1030 Z = Z + 10
1040 IF A(Z + 10) = E THEN 1030
1050 IF A(Z) = E THEN A(Z) = H:RETURN
1060 PRINT "You can't move there"
1070 GOTO 1000
1080 REM **********
1090 REM INITIALISE
1100 CLS
1110 DEFINT A - Z
1120 RANDOMIZE VAL(RIGHT$(TIME$,2))
1130 DIM A(109),M(30),P(6)
1140 E = ASC(".")
1150 H = ASC("H"):C = ASC("C")
1160 FOR B = 1 TO 109
1170 A(B) = E
1180 D = B - 10*INT(B/10)
1190 IF D = 0 OR D > 7 OR B < 11 OR B > 77
THEN A(B) = -9
1200 NEXT B
1210 RETURN
```

☐ CHECKERS

The game of CHECKERS has a long and honorable history. R. C. Bell (in his book *Discovering Old Board Games*, Shire Publications, Aylesbury, UK, 1980) says it was invented around 1100, "probably in the south of France, using Backgammon tablemen on a chequered chessboard with the Alquerque method of capture" (pp. 35-36). The *Encyclopedia of Sports, Games and Pastimes* (Fleetway House, London, c. 1935) puts it much further back in time: "Forms of it were known in ancient Egypt, Greece and Rome, while the game was played in the mid-seventeenth century much as it is today" (p. 237).*

Regardless of its age, it is a very popular game around the world, with many European countries having regional variations on the game of their own. Continental draughts (checkers is generally known as draughts outside the US), for example, is played on a board of 100 squares with each player starting the game with 20 pieces. It was developed in the early 1700s.

This CHECKERS program plays the game you are probably most familiar with. It plays swiftly, and reasonably well, although its lack of endgame strategy often leads to a dramatic collapse in the final moments of a game.

CHECKERS is played between you and the computer. Each of you is attempting to take (that is jump over to capture, then remove from the board) the other player's pieces, or to confine the opponent's pieces so no more moves are possible.

The game is generally played on a board with 64 squares, which are alternately light and dark. In this program, the board (as you can see from the sample game we have shortly) is a series of dots, with your pieces shown as H's (for human) and the machine's pieces as C's (for clever).

When the game begins, you're at the bottom of the screen, playing up, and the computer is at the top playing down. As the program is currently set up, the computer always has the first move. If you want the first move then delete line 50.

All moves must be made along diagonals. Individual pieces can

---

*Both these books are very fine resources for game ideas to turn into computer programs. R. C. Bell's book (and others by that author) is particularly recommended. The *Encyclopedia* has been out of print for many years, but you may find a copy of it in a secondhand shop. It was very widely distributed in the UK in the late 'thirties, and includes much fascinating information, including full details on how to build and fly your own airplane.

only move forward, that is, toward the opponent's starting side. Pieces are converted into "kings" when they reach the back rank across the board. Your kings are shown as K's, the computer's kings are dollar signs. Kings can move either forward or back. After capturing a piece, by jumping over it into the vacant square immediately behind the captured piece, you can move again if there is a further capture which can be made.

Here is a series of board positions from one game I played against the program:

```
COMPUTER: 0
   HUMAN: 0


   1 2 3 4 5 6 7 8
8  . C . C . C . C  8
7  C . C . C . C .  7
6  . C .   . C . C  6
5  .   . C .   .    5
4  .   .   .   .    4
3  H . H . H . H .  3
2  . H . H . H . H  2
1  H . H . H . H .  1
   1 2 3 4 5 6 7 8


   COMPUTER: 0
      HUMAN: 1


   1 2 3 4 5 6 7 8
8  .   .   . C . C  8
7  C . C . C . C .  7
6  . C . H . C . C  6
5  C .   . C .   .  5
4  .   .   .   . H  4
3  H . H . H . H .  3
2  . H . H . H . H  2
1  .   . H .   . H  1
   1 2 3 4 5 6 7 8


Can you jump again

(Y or N)?
```

```
COMPUTER: 0
   HUMAN: 0


   1 2 3 4 5 6 7 8
8  . C .   . C . C  8
7  C . C . C . C .  7
6  .   . C . C . C  6
5  C .   . C .   .  5
4  . H .   .   . H  4
3  . H . H . H .    3
2  . H . H .   . H  2
1  H . H . H . H .  1
   1 2 3 4 5 6 7 8


   COMPUTER: 0
      HUMAN: 2


   1 2 3 4 5 6 7 8
8  . K .   . C . C  8
7  C .   . C . C .  7
6  .   .   . C . C  6
5  C . C . C .   .  5
4  .   .   .   . H  4
3  H . H . H . H .  3
2  . H . H . H . H  2
1  . H .   . H .    1
   1 2 3 4 5 6 7 8
```

46

```
        COMPUTER: 2
         HUMAN: 2


  1 2 3 4 5 6 7 8
8 .   .   . C . C   8
7 C .   .   . C .   7
6 . K . C . C .     6
5 . C . C . C .     5
4 .   .   .   . H   4
3 H .   . H . H .   3
2 .   . H . H . H   2
1 $ . H .   . H .   1
  1 2 3 4 5 6 7 8
```

```
                        COMPUTER: 2
                         HUMAN: 3


                  1 2 3 4 5 6 7 8
                8 .   .   . C . C   8
                7 C .   .   . C .   7
                6 .   . C . C .     6
                5 .   . C . C .     5
                4 .   . K .   . H   4
                3 H .   . H . H .   3
                2 .   . H . H . H   2
                1 $ . H .   . H .   1
                  1 2 3 4 5 6 7 8
```

Can you jump again
(Y or N)?

```
        COMPUTER: 4
         HUMAN: 3


  1 2 3 4 5 6 7 8
8 .   .   . C . C   8
7 C .   .   . C .   7
6 .   . C . C .     6
5 .   .   . C .     5
4 .   .   .   . H   4
3 H .   . H . H .   3
2 .   .   . H . H   2
1 $ . H . C . H .   1
  1 2 3 4 5 6 7 8
```

```
                        COMPUTER: 4
                         HUMAN: 3


                  1 2 3 4 5 6 7 8
                8 .   .   .   . C   8
                7 .   . C .   . 7
                6 . C . C . C . C   6
                5 H .   .   . C .   5
                4 .   . H .   . H   4
                3 .   .   . H .     3
                2 .   .   . H . H   2
                1 $ . H . $ . H .   1
                  1 2 3 4 5 6 7 8
```

```
         COMPUTER: 4
         HUMAN:  4


      1 2 3 4 5 6 7 8
   8  .   .   .   .      8
   7    . H . C . C .    7
   6  .   . C . C . C    6
   5    .   .   . C .    5
   4  .   . H .   . H    4
   3    .   .   . H .    3
   2  .   .   . H . H    2
   1  $ . H . $ . H .    1
      1 2 3 4 5 6 7 8
```

```
                            COMPUTER: 6
                            HUMAN:  6


                         1 2 3 4 5 6 7 8
                      8  .   .   .   .      8
                      7    .   . C . C .    7
                      6  .   .   .   . C    6
                      5    . H .   . C .    5
                      4  . $ .   . H . H    4
                      3    .   .   . H .    3
                      2  .   .   . C . H    2
                      1    .   .   . H .    1
                         1 2 3 4 5 6 7 8
```

```
         COMPUTER: 7
         HUMAN:  8


      1 2 3 4 5 6 7 8
   8  .   .   .   . K    8
   7    .   .   .   .    7
   6  .   .   .   . C    6
   5    .   . .   .      5
   4  $   .   . . H      4
   3  $ .   . H . H .    3
   2  .   .   . $ . H    2
   1    . $ .   .   .    1
      1 2 3 4 5 6 7 8
```

```
                            COMPUTER: 8
                            HUMAN:  9


                         1 2 3 4 5 6 7 8
                      8  .   . K .   .      8
                      7    .   . K .   .    7
                      6  .   . H . K      6
                      5    .   .   .   .    5
                      4  .   .   . C .      4
                      3    . $ . $ .        3
                      2  .   .   .   .      2
                      1    .   .   .   .    1
                         1 2 3 4 5 6 7 8
```

48

```
COMPUTER: 9          COMPUTER: 11
   HUMAN: 10            HUMAN: 10


  1 2 3 4 5 6 7 8          1 2 3 4 5 6 7 8
8 .   . K .   .   8      8 .   .   .   .   8
7   . H .   .   . 7      7   .   .   .   . 7
6 .   .   .   .   6      6 . K . $ .   .   6
5   . $ .   .   . 5      5   .   .   .   . 5
4 .   .   .   .   4      4 .   .   .   .   4
3   .   .   . K   3      3   .   .   .   . 3
2 . $ .   .   .   2      2 . $ .   .   .   2
1   .   .   .   . 1      1   .   .   .   . 1
  1 2 3 4 5 6 7 8          1 2 3 4 5 6 7 8
```

This is the complete listing for **CHECKERS**:

```
10 REM CHECKERS
20 GOSUB 1010
30 REM DELETE LINE 50 FOR HUMAN
40 REM     TO HAVE FIRST MOVE
50 GOTO 90
60 REM ******************************
70 GOSUB 600
80 GOSUB 760
90 GOSUB 600
100 GOSUB 130
110 GOTO 70
120 REM ******************************
130 FOR X = 1 TO 10:S(X) = 0:NEXT X
140 SC = 0:A = 89
150 A = A - 1
160 IF Q(A) <> C AND Q(A) <> CK THEN 240
170 B = 0:IF A < 29 THEN B = 2
180 B = B + 1
190 M = A + N(B)
200 IF M > 88 OR M < 11 THEN 240
210 IF (Q(M)=H OR Q(M)=HK) AND Q(M+N(B))=E
 THEN 280
220 IF Q(M)=E THEN IF (Q(M-11)<>H AND Q(M-
11)<>HK) THEN IF (Q(M-9)<>H AND Q(M-9)<>HK
) AND Q(M+9)<>HK THEN IF ((Q(M+22)<>HK OR
Q(M+18)<>HK) AND (Q(M+9)<>C OR Q(M+9)<>CK
```

```
     OR Q(M+11)=C OR Q(M+11)=CK)) AND Q(M+11)<>
     HK THEN GOSUB 400
230  IF B < 2 OR (Q(A)=CK AND B < 4) THEN 1
     80
240  IF A > 11 THEN 150
250  FL = 0:IF Q(22) = C OR Q(24) = C OR Q(
     26) = C OR Q(28) = C THEN GOSUB 1270
260  IF FL = 1 THEN 570
270  GOTO 420
280  Q(M+N(B)) = Q(A):Q(M) = E:Q(A) = E
290  CO = CO + 1
300  GOSUB 600
310  A = M + N(B)
320  B = 0
330  B = B + 1
340  IF (A+2*N(B)<11 OR A+2*N(B)>88) AND B
     < 4 THEN 330
350  M = A + N(B)
360  IF Q(M) = C AND B > 3 THEN RETURN
370  IF (Q(M)=H OR Q(M)=HK) AND Q(M+N(B))=E
     THEN 280
380  IF B < 2 OR (Q(A) = CK AND B<4) THEN 3
     30
390  RETURN
400  IF SC < 10 THEN SC = SC + 1
410  S(SC)=100*A + B + 20:RETURN
420  IF SC = 0 THEN 470
430  XC = INT(RND*SC) + 1
440  A = INT(S(XC)/100)
450  M = A + N(S(XC) - 100*A - 20)
460  GOTO 570
470  SC = SC + 1: A = INT(RND*88) + 1
480  IF Q(A) <> C AND Q(A) <> CK THEN 550
490  B = 0
500  B = B + 1
510  M = A + N(B)
520  IF M > 88 OR M < 11 THEN 540
530  IF Q(M) = E THEN 570
540  IF B < 2 OR Q(A) = CK AND B < 4 THEN 5
     00
550  IF SC < 300 THEN 470
560  PRINT:PRINT "I concede the game":END
570  Q(M) = Q(A):Q(A) = E
580  RETURN
```

```
590 REM ******************************
600 CLS:PRINT:PRINT
610 PRINT "      COMPUTER:"CO
620 PRINT "        HUMAN:"HU:PRINT:PRINT
630 PRINT "   1 2 3 4 5 6 7 8"
640 FOR F = 80 TO 10 STEP - 10
650 PRINT F/10;" ";
660 FOR G = 1 TO 8:PRINT CHR$(Q(F + G));"
";:NEXT G
670 PRINT F/10:NEXT F
680 PRINT "   1 2 3 4 5 6 7 8"
690 IF CO = 12 OR HU = 12 THEN 710
700 RETURN
710 IF HU = 12 THEN PRINT "You have won"
720 IF CO = 12 THEN PRINT "I have won"
730 PRINT "Thanks for the game":END
740 REM ******************************
750 REM 99 TO CONCEDE
760 PRINT:PRINT
770 PRINT "Enter your move"
780 INPUT "From";A
790 IF A = 99 THEN GOTO 730
800 IF Q(A) <> H AND Q(A) <> HK THEN 780
810 INPUT "To";B
820 IF Q(B) <> E THEN 810
830 Q(B) = Q(A):Q(A) = E
840 REM ******************************
850 FOR T = 11 TO 17:IF Q(T) = C THEN Q(T)
 = CK
860 NEXT T
870 FOR T = 82 TO 88:IF Q(T) = H THEN Q(T)
 = HK
880 NEXT T
890 REM ******************************
900 IF ABS(A - B) < 12   THEN RETURN
910 TY = RND
920 IF TY < .3 THEN PRINT "Good move":GOSU
B 1340
930 IF TY > .7 THEN PRINT "Got me!":GOSUB
1340
940 HU = HU+1:Q((A + B)/2)=E:GOSUB 600
950 FOR T = 82 TO 88:IF Q(T) = H THEN Q(T)
 = HK
960 NEXT T
```

```
970 PRINT:INPUT "Can you jump again (Y or
N)";A$
980 IF A$ <>"y" AND A$ <> "Y" THEN RETURN
990 A = B:GOTO 800
1000 REM ******************************
1010 REM Initialise
1020 CLS:PRINT "Press any key":N = 1
1030 N = N + 1:IF INKEY$ = "" THEN 1030
1040 CLS
1050 PRINT "Please stand by"
1060 DIM Q(99),N(4),S(10)
1070 H = ASC("H"):HK = ASC("K")
1080 C = ASC("C"):CK = ASC("$")
1090 E = 32:OF = - 99
1100 FOR M = 1 TO 99:Q(M) = OF:NEXT M
1110 FOR M = 1 TO 64
1120 READ D:READ G
1130 Q(D) = G: NEXT M
1140 DATA 81,46,82,67,83,46,84,67,85,46,86
,67,87,46
1150 DATA 88,67,71,67,72,46,73,67,74,46,75
,67,76,46
1160 DATA 77,67,78,46,61,46,62,67,63,46,64
,67
1170 DATA 65,46,66,67,67,46,68,67,51,32,52
,46
1180 DATA 53,32,54,46,55,32,56,46,57,32,58
,46
1190 DATA 41,46,42,32,43,46,44,32,45,46,46
,32
1200 DATA 47,46,48,32,31,72,32,46,33,72,34
,46,35,72
1210 DATA 36,46,37,72,38,46,21,46,22,72,23
,46,24,72
1220 DATA 25,46,26,72,27,46,28,72,11,72,12
,46,13,72
1230 DATA 14,46,15,72,16,46,17,72,18,46
1240 FOR M = 1 TO 4:READ X:N(M) = X:NEXT M

1250 DATA -11, -9, 11, 9
1260 CO = 0:HU = 0:RETURN
1270 IF Q(22)=C AND Q(11)=E THEN A=22:M =
11:FL = 1:RETURN
1280 IF Q(22)=C AND Q(13)=E THEN A=22:M =
```

```
13:FL = 1:RETURN
1290 IF Q(24)=C AND Q(13)=E THEN A=24:M =
13:FL = 1:RETURN
1300 IF Q(24)=C AND Q(15)=E THEN A=24:M =
15:FL = 1:RETURN
1310 IF Q(26)=C AND Q(15)=E THEN A=26:M =
15:FL = 1:RETURN
1320 IF Q(26)=C AND Q(17)=E THEN A=26:M =
17:FL = 1:RETURN
1330 RETURN
1340 FOR O = 1 TO 1000:NEXT O:RETURN
```

☐ SHOGUN

SHOGUN is based on the Japanese board game HASAMI SHOGI. In this game, generally played on the corner of a GO board, you move in any direction (forward, backwards, or sideways) in a straight line. Diagonal moves are not allowed. As well, you can jump over a piece (again in a straight line). You can jump over your own pieces, or an enemy piece.

The jumped piece is not removed from the board. You capture a piece by *squeezing* it between two of yours. That is, you get one piece of yours on either side (except along a diagonal) of a computer's piece, and it is removed from the board. A piece is not captured if it moves between two of the opponent's pieces.

There are no double moves. You do not get an extra move following a capture. In the original game, the aim is to remove all your opponent's pieces from the board. However, this is a fairly slow game, and could take an eternity if played against the computer in this way. Therefore, I've written it so that the game is won by the first player to capture six of the opponent's pieces.

You'll find that the game will more or less teach you how to play it just by watching how it moves. Don't forget the fact that you can jump over your pieces, or the computer's pieces. This is a recommended tactic to get pieces well out into the board near the beginning of the game to get the game moving.

Here's the listing for SHOGUN:

```
10 REM Shogun
20 REM Make sure your computer is in
   upper case mode
30 GOSUB 790
40 GOSUB 90
50 GOSUB 460
60 GOSUB 630
70 GOSUB 460
80 GOTO 40
90 REM CAPTURE
100 A = 99
110 IF A(A) <> C THEN 190
120 IF A(A - 10) = E THEN IF A(A - 9) = H
  THEN IF A(A - 8) = C THEN B = A - 10:GOT
O 350
130 IF A(A - 10) = E THEN IF A(A - 11) =
H THEN IF A(A - 12) = C THEN B = A - 10:
```

```
GOTO 350
140 IF A(A - 10) = E THEN IF A(A + 11) =
H THEN IF A(A + 12) = C THEN B = A - 10:
GOTO 350
150 B = 1
160 IF A + 2*C(B) < 11 OR A + 2*C(B) > 99
 THEN GOTO 180
170 IF A(A + C(B)) = E AND A(A + 2*C(B))
= H AND A(A + 3*C(B)) = C THEN A(A + 2*C(
B)) = E:CS = CS + 1: GOTO 340
180 IF B<4 THEN B = B + 1: GOTO 160
190 IF A > 11 THEN A = A - 1: GOTO 110
200 REM Non-capture
210 COUNT = 0
220 COUNT = COUNT + 1
230 A = RND*89 + 11
240 IF A(A) = C THEN 270
250 IF COUNT < 200 THEN 220
260 PRINT "Shogun Master": PRINT "I give
you the victory!":END
270 B = 1
280 IF A + 2*C(B) < 11 THEN 300
290 IF (A(A + C(B)) = C OR A(A + C(B)) =H
) AND A(A + 2*C(B)) = E THEN B = A + 2* C
(B):GOTO 350
300 IF A(A + C(B)) = E THEN 330
310 IF B < 4 THEN B = B + 1: GOTO 280
320 GOTO 250
330 REM Computer moves
340 B = A + C(B)
350 B1 = B - 10*(INT(B/10))
360 A(B) = C: A(A) = E
370 IF B1 > 7 THEN 390
380 IF A(B + 1) = H AND A(B + 2) = C THEN
 A( B + 1) = E:CS = CS + 1
390 IF B1 < 3 THEN 410
400 IF A(B - 1) = H AND A(B - 2) = C THEN
 A(B - 1) = E: CS = CS + 1
410 IF A > 89 THEN 430
420 IF A( B + 10) = H AND A( B + 20 ) = C
 THEN A( B + 10 ) = E: CS = CS + 1
430 IF A < 29 THEN RETURN
440 IF A( B - 10) = H AND A( B - 20) = C
THEN A( B - 10) = E: CS = CS + 1
```

```
450 RETURN
460 REM Board printout
470 CLS:REM Put HOME here if your
    computer supports it
480 PRINT TAB(15);"1 2 3 4 5 6 7 8 9"
490 FOR M = 90 TO 10 STEP - 10
500 PRINT TAB(13)CHR$(M/10 + 64);" ";
510 FOR N = 1 TO 9
520 PRINT CHR$(A(M + N));" ";
530 NEXT
540 PRINT CHR$(M/10 + 64)
550 NEXT
560 PRINT TAB(15);"1 2 3 4 5 6 7 8 9"
570 PRINT:PRINT ,"Computer:"CS
580 PRINT ,"Human:"HS
590 IF CS > 6 OR HS > 6 THEN 610
600 RETURN
610 IF CS > HS THEN PRINT:PRINT "I win!":
END
620 PRINT:PRINT "You win!":END
630 REM player move
640 INPUT "From (letter,no)";A$
650 IF A$ = "S" THEN END
660 IF LEN (A$) <> 2 THEN 640
670 PRINT "From "A$" to ";:INPUT B$
680 IF LEN (B$) <> 2 THEN 670
690 A = 10 *(ASC (A$) - 64) + VAL (RIGHT$
(A$,1))
700 B = 10 *(ASC (B$) - 64) + VAL (RIGHT$
(B$,1))
710 Y = VAL (RIGHT$(B$,1))
720 A(B) = H: A(A) = E
730 IF A(B + 1) = C AND A(B + 2) = H AND
Y <= 7 THEN A(B + 1) = E: HS = HS + 1
740 IF A(B - 1) = C AND A(B - 2) = H AND
Y >=3  THEN A(B - 1) = E: HS = HS + 1
750 IF B > 79 THEN 770
760 IF A(B + 10) = C AND A(B + 20) = H TH
EN A(B + 10) = E:HS = HS + 1
770 IF B >= 31 THEN IF A(B - 10) = C AND
A(B - 20) = H THEN A(B - 10) = E:HS = HS
+ 1
780 RETURN
790 REM initialise
```

```
800 REM Seed random number generator
810 PRINT "Press any key"
820 N = 1
830 N = N + 1
840 IF INKEY$ = "" THEN 830
850 RANDOMIZE N
860 DEFINT A - Z
870 CLS
880 DIM A(129), C(4)
890 H = 72: C = 67: E = 42
900 FOR Z = 11 TO 29
910 IF Z = 20 THEN Z = 21
920 A(Z) = H
930 NEXT
940 FOR Z = 31 TO 79
950 IF 10*INT(Z/10) = Z THEN Z = Z + 1
960 A(Z) = E
970 NEXT
980 FOR Z = 81 TO 99
990 IF Z = 90 THEN Z = 91
1000 A(Z) = C
1010 NEXT
1020 HS = 0
1030 CS = 0
1040 FOR Z = 1 TO 4
1050 READ C(Z)
1060 NEXT
1070 DATA -10, -1, 1, 10
1080 GOSUB 460
1090 RETURN
```

☐ AWARI

AWARI is one of a series of pebble-in-pits games generally known under the name of "Mancala." The game is played from Africa to the Philippines, and will now move into your home, via a very clever computer opponent.

As you can see from the sample game, which starts below, the game begins with six "pits" (the letters A to F and L to G) facing each player. Your pits are those from L to G. Each pit contains three seeds at the beginning of the game. Choosing any pit on your side, you pick up all the seeds from it, and then proceed to move in a clockwise direction, sowing a seed in each pit as you go past it. You do not sow any seeds in the pits at either end of the board, the ones which start off as zeroes.

If your final seed lands opposite an empty pit, then all the seeds in the pit you've landed in become yours, and are transferred to your "home." Your home is the zero to the left of the board, the computer's home is the zero to the right.

The game continues until either side is completely empty, so the player cannot move. At this point, the player with the largest number of seeds in his or her pit is the winner. The computer plays well in this game, but with practice you'll learn to defeat it. Don't expect too many victories in the early games. Remove the INPUT Z$ in line 270 if you don't want to see the computer's move before it is made. Also, you can delete the loop in line 40 to get maximum speed (although the computer plays very swiftly even in its present form).

Here's a game I played against my own computer:

```
        A    B    C    D    E    F
        3    3    3    3    3    3
   0                                   0
        3    3    3    3    3    3
        L    K    J    I    H    G


I'll move from C

        A    B    C    D    E    F
        3    3    0    4    4    4
   0                                   0
        3    3    3    3    3    3
        L    K    J    I    H    G
```

Which pit to start with? H


```
     A   B   C   D   E   F
     3   3   0   4   4   4
 0                           0
     3   4   4   4   0   3
     L   K   J   I   H   G


     A   B   C   D   E   F
     3   3   0   0   0   5
 0                           5
     3   4   4   4   1   4
     L   K   J   I   H   G


     A   B   C   D   E   F
     0   1   1   2   1   5
 8                           7
     4   1   1   5   0   0
     L   K   J   I   H   G
```


Which pit to start with? I


```
     A   B   C   D   E   F
     1   2   1   2   1   5
 8                           7
     5   2   2   0   0   0
     L   K   J   I   H   G
```


I'll move from A


```
     A   B   C   D   E   F
     0   3   1   2   1   5
 8                           7
     5   2   2   0   0   0
     L   K   J   I   H   G
```

Which pit to start with? L

```
    A   B   C   D   E   F
    1   4   2   3   2   5
  8                       7
    0   2   2   0   0   0
    L   K   J   I   H   G
```

Which pit to start with? G

```
    A   B   C   D   E   F
    3   5   1   0   0   0
  9                      15
    0   0   0   1   2   0
    L   K   J   I   H   G
```

I'll move from B

```
    A   B   C   D   E   F
    3   0   2   1   1   0
  9                      16
    0   0   0   1   2   1
    L   K   J   I   H   G
```

Which pit to start with? I

```
    A   B   C   D   E   F
    3   0   0   1   1   0
 11                      16
    0   0   1   0   2   1
    L   K   J   I   H   G
```

I'll move from E

```
        A   B   C   D   E   F
        3   0   0   1   0   1
11                              16
        0   0   1   0   2   1
        L   K   J   I   H   G
```

Which pit to start with? H

```
        A   B   C   D   E   F
        0   1   0   0   0   0
14                              17
        0   0   3   1   0   0
        L   K   J   I   H   G
```

I'll move from B

```
        A   B   C   D   E   F
        0   0   1   0   0   0
14                              20
        0   0   0   1   0   0
        L   K   J   I   H   G
```

Which pit to start with? I

```
        A   B   C   D   E   F
        0   0   0   0   0   0
15                              20
        0   0   1   0   0   0
        L   K   J   I   H   G
```

That's the end of the game

And I'm the winner!

My score was 20
and yours was 15

This is the listing for AWARI:

```
10 REM Awari
20 GOSUB 930:REM Initialise
30 GOSUB 770:REM Print board
40 FOR P = 1 TO 500:NEXT P
50 GOSUB 160:REM Machine move
60 GOSUB 770:REM Print board
70 GOSUB 620:REM Human move
80 CW = 0:HW = 0
90 FOR C = 1 TO 12
100 IF C<7 THEN CW = CW + A(C)
110 IF C>6 THEN HW = HW + A(C)
120 NEXT C
130 IF CW = 0 OR HW = 0 THEN 510
140 GOTO 30
150 REM **************************
160 REM Machine move
170 GM = 0:C = 0
180 C = C + 1
190 IF A(C) = 0 THEN 180
200 Z = C + A(C)
210 IF Z > 12 THEN Z = Z - 12
220 IF Z > 6 THEN IF  A(Z - 6) <> 0 AND A(
Z) = 0 AND A(Z - 6) > GM THEN GM = C
230 IF Z < 7  THEN IF (Z + 6) <> 0 AND A(Z
) = 0 AND A(Z + 6) > GM THEN GM = C
240 IF C < 6 THEN 180
250 IF GM = 0 THEN 370
260 C = GM
270 PRINT "I'll move from "CHR$(64 + C):IN
PUT Z$
280 FOR Z = C TO C + A(C)
290 IF Z > 12 THEN A(Z - 12) = A(Z - 12) +
 1
300 IF Z < 13 THEN A(Z) = A(Z) + 1
310 NEXT Z
320 Z = C + A(C) - 1:IF Z > 12 THEN Z = Z
- 12
330 A(C) = 0
340 B(2) = B(2) + A(13 - Z):A(13 - Z) = 0
350 RETURN
360 REM *************************
```

```
370 REM Non-score move
380 W = 0
390 W = W + 1
400 C = INT(RND#6) + 1
410 IF A(C) <> 0 THEN 440
420 IF W < 20 THEN 390
430 GOTO 510
440 PRINT "I'll move from "CHR$(64 + C):IN
PUT Z$
450 FOR Z = C TO C + A(C)
460 IF Z < 13 THEN A(Z) = A(Z) + 1
470 IF Z > 12 THEN A(Z - 6) = A(Z - 6) + 1

480 NEXT Z
490 A(C) = 0:GOTO 350
500 REM ***************************
510 REM End of game
520 GOSUB 770
530 PRINT:PRINT "That's the end of the gam
e"
540 PRINT
550 IF B(1) > B(2) THEN PRINT "You're the
winner!"
560 IF B(1) < B(2) THEN PRINT "And I'm the
 winner!"
570 IF B(1) = B(2) THEN PRINT "It looks li
ke a draw!"
580 PRINT:PRINT "My score was"B(2)
590 PRINT  "and yours was"B(1)
600 END
610 REM ***************************
620 REM Human move
630 INPUT "Which pit to start with";A$
640 B = ASC(A$) - 64
650 IF B < 7 OR B > 12 THEN 630
660 CO = B:Z = B + A(B):IF Z > 12 THEN Z =
 Z - 12
670 M = A(Z)
680 FOR Z = B TO B + A(B)
690 IF Z > 12 THEN A(Z - 12) = A(Z - 12) +
 1
700 IF Z < 13 THEN A(Z) = A(Z) + 1
710 NEXT Z
```

```
720 Z = B + A(B) -1:IF Z > 12 THEN Z = Z -
   12
730 IF M = 0 THEN B(1) = B(1) + A(13 - Z):
A(13 - Z) = 0
740 A(CO) = 0
750 RETURN
760 REM **************************
770 REM Print board
780 CLS:PRINT:PRINT:PRINT
790 PRINT "    A  B  C  D  E  F":PRINT "
  ";
800 FOR C = 1 TO 6
810 PRINT A(C);
820 NEXT C
830 PRINT:PRINT B(1)"                    "B(2
):PRINT "    ";
840 FOR C = 12 TO 7 STEP - 1
850 PRINT A(C);
860 NEXT C
870 PRINT:PRINT "    L  K  J  I  H  G"
880 PRINT:PRINT
890 RETURN
900 PRINT "I move from "CHR$(64 + GM)
910 C = GM
920 REM **************************
930 REM Initialise
940 CLS
950 RANDOMIZE VAL(RIGHT$(TIME$,2))
960 DIM A(12),B(2)
970 FOR C = 1 TO 12
980 A(C) = 3
990 NEXT C
1000 RETURN
```

☐ KNIGHTSBRIDGE

KNIGHTSBRIDGE is one of the few games which I can claim I invented completely (although, of course, the idea of naming it after a London suburb came from the two inventors of KENSINGTON). I make habit of reading games books to get ideas, and often when I walked in the woods around London, I'd take a book with me to read when I felt like a rest. I was walking one Sunday afternoon near Ruislip Lido thinking about a passage I'd just read in a book which said that chess evolved from an Indian game in which the throw of a die dictated which piece was to move.

From that starting point, I thought of a game in which all the pieces were chess knights (hence the name of the game) and a die was used to say which piece had to move. KNIGHTSBRIDGE evolved from that idea.

It is played on a seven by seven board. The computer tells you which piece you must move (each piece is indicated by entering a two-digit number, the first being the coordinates of the square you're moving to down the side of the board, the second digit being the coordinates of the square across the top), and then leaves you to decide where you will move to. All pieces move like chess knights, and all moves are checked to see if they are legal before you are allowed to move.

You capture by landing on top of an enemy piece. The first player to capture five of the enemy's seven pieces is the winner. There are no multiple jumps.

You'll find the computer plays swiftly and well.

Here's the inventor of the game being thrashed by his own invention:

My score is 0
and yours is 0

```
  1 2 3 4 5 6 7
  --------------
7 C . C C C C C 7
6 . . . C . . . 6
5 . . . . . . . 5
4 . . . . . . . 4
3 . . . . . . . 3
2 . . . . . . . 2
1 H H H H H H H 1
  --------------
  1 2 3 4 5 6 7
```

You must move the
piece on 17 ? 36

My score is 0
and yours is 0

```
  1 2 3 4 5 6 7
  --------------
7 C . C . C C C 7
6 . . . C . C . 6
5 . . . . . . . 5
4 . . . . . . . 4
3 . . . . . H . 3
2 . . . . . . . 2
1 H H H H H H . 1
  --------------
  1 2 3 4 5 6 7
```

You must move the
piece on 15 ? 34

My score is 0
and yours is 0

```
  1 2 3 4 5 6 7
  --------------
7 C . C . C C C 7
6 . . . . . C . 6
5 . . . . . C . 5
4 . . . . . . . 4
3 . . . H . H . 3
2 . . . . . . . 2
1 H H H H . H . 1
  --------------
  1 2 3 4 5 6 7
```

You must move the
piece on 34 ? 53

My score is 0
and yours is 0

```
  1 2 3 4 5 6 7
  --------------
7 C . . . C C C 7
6 . . . . C C . 6
5 . . H . . C . 5
4 . . . . . . . 4
3 . . . . . H . 3
2 . . . . . . . 2
1 H H H H . H . 1
  --------------
  1 2 3 4 5 6 7
```

You must move the
piece on 12 ? 33

66

```
   My score is 3
   and yours is 2

   1 2 3 4 5 6 7
   --------------
7  . . . . C C C  7
6  . . C . . . .  6
5  . . . H . . .  5
4  . . . . . . .  4
3  . . . . . H .  3
2  . . H . . C .  2
1  . . . H . . .  1
   --------------
   1 2 3 4 5 6 7
```

You must move the
piece on 23 ? 44

```
   My score is 4
   and yours is 2

   1 2 3 4 5 6 7
   --------------
7  . . . . C C C  7
6  . . . . . . .  6
5  . . . H . . .  5
4  . . . C . . .  4
3  . . . . . H .  3
2  . . . . . C .  2
1  . . . H . . .  1
   --------------
   1 2 3 4 5 6 7
```

You must move the
piece on 14 ? 26

```
   My score is 4
   and yours is 3

   1 2 3 4 5 6 7
   --------------
7  . . . . C . C  7
6  . . . . . . .  6
5  . . . H C . .  5
4  . . . C . . .  4
3  . . . . . H .  3
2  . . . . . H .  2
1  . . . . . . .  1
   --------------
   1 2 3 4 5 6 7
```

You must move the
piece on 36 ? 55

```
   My score is 5
   and yours is 4

   1 2 3 4 5 6 7
   --------------
7  . . . . . . C  7
6  . . . . . . .  6
5  . . . C H . .  5
4  . . . C . . .  4
3  . . . . . . .  3
2  . . . . . H .  2
1  . . . . . . .  1
   --------------
   1 2 3 4 5 6 7
```

This victory is the first
step in our plan to take
over the entire earth!

This is the listing for **KNIGHTSBRIDGE**:

```
10 REM Knightsbridge
20 GOSUB 760:REM Initialise
30 GOSUB 490:REM Print board
40 IF HU = 5 OR CO = 5 THEN 680:REM End of
   game
50 GOSUB 300:REM Computer moves
60 GOSUB 490:REM Print board
70 IF HU = 5 OR CO = 5 THEN 680:REM End of
   game
80 GOSUB 110:REM Player moves
90 GOTO 30
100 REM ***********************
110 REM Player moves
120 Q = 0
130 M = INT(RND*66) + 11
140 Q = Q + 1
150 IF Q = 500 THEN 680
160 IF H(M) <> 72 THEN 130
170 PRINT "You must move the piece on"M
180 INPUT N
190 IF N = 99 THEN Q = 500:GOTO 680
200 REM *** Check if move legal ***
210 P = 0
220 CT = 1
230 IF M + Z(CT) = N THEN P = 1
240 IF CT < 8 THEN CT = CT + 1:GOTO 230
250 IF P = 0 THEN PRINT "Illegal move":GOT
O 180
260 IF H(N) = 67 THEN HU = HU + 1:PRINT "W
ell played!":FOR R = 1 TO 500:NEXT R
270 H(M) = 46: H(N) = 72
280 RETURN
290 REM ***********************
300 REM Computer moves
310 Q1 = 0
320 Q1 = Q1 + 1
330 K = INT(RND*66) + 11
340 IF Q1 = 500 THEN 680
350 IF H(K) <> 67 THEN 320
360 PRINT "I have to move the piece on"K
370 W = 1
```

```
380 IF K + Z(W) < 11 OR K + Z(W) > 77 THEN
    400
390 IF H(K + Z(W)) = 72 THEN PRINT "Gotcha
!!":CO = CO + 1:FOR P = 1 TO 200:NEXT P:GO
TO 450
400 IF W < 8 THEN W = W + 1:GOTO 380
410 W = 1
420 IF (K + Z(W) < 11 OR K + Z(W) > 77 ) A
ND W < 8 THEN W = W + 1:GOTO 420
430 IF H(K + Z(W)) <> 46 AND W < 8 THEN W
= W + 1:GOTO 430
440 IF W = 8 AND H(K + Z(W)) <> 46 THEN Q1
 = 500:GOTO 680
450 X = K:Y = K + Z(W)
460 H(X) = 46:H(Y) = 67
470 RETURN
480 REM *********************
490 REM Print board
500 CLS:PRINT:PRINT:PRINT
510 PRINT TAB(8);"My score is"CO
520 PRINT TAB(8);"and yours is"HU
530 PRINT
540 PRINT TAB(8);"1 2 3 4 5 6 7"
550 PRINT TAB(8);"--------------"
560 FOR M = 70 TO 10 STEP - 10
570 PRINT TAB(5);M/10;
580 FOR N = 1 TO 7
590 PRINT CHR$(H(M + N));" ";
600 NEXT N
610 PRINT M/10
620 NEXT M
630 PRINT TAB(8);"--------------"
640 PRINT TAB(8);"1 2 3 4 5 6 7"
650 PRINT
660 RETURN
670 REM *********************
680 REM End of game
690 GOSUB 490
700 IF HU = 5 THEN PRINT "You have beaten
me, human"
710 IF CO = 5 THEN PRINT "This victory is
the first":PRINT "step in our plan to take
":PRINT "over the entire earth!"
```

```
720 IF Q = 500 THEN PRINT "I accept your w
ish to concede"
730 IF Q1 = 500 THEN PRINT "I concede to a
 Master"
740 END
750 REM ***********************
760 REM Initialise
770 CLS:PRINT "Please stand by...human"
780 DIM H(99),Z(8)
790 X = 0:Q1 = 0:Q = 0
800 RANDOMIZE VAL(RIGHT$(TIME$,2))
810 HU = 0:CO = 0:REM Scores
820 FOR A = 1 TO 99
830 IF A>77 OR A=70 OR A=60 OR A=68 OR A=6
9 OR A=50 OR A=59 OR A=40 OR A=48 OR A=49
THEN 880
840 IF A=30 OR A=38 OR A=39 OR A=20 OR A=2
8 OR A=29 OR A=18 OR A=19 OR A<11 THEN 880

850 H(A) = 46
860 IF A>70 AND A<78 THEN H(A) = 67
870 IF A>10 AND A<18 THEN H(A) = 72
880 NEXT A
890 FOR A = 1 TO 8:READ Z(A):NEXT A
900 DATA -8, -21, -12, -19, 19, 12, 21, 8
910 RETURN
```

□ REVERSI/ OTHELLO

The final program in the board-games section of this book is RE-VERSI, which is often called OTHELLO.* Invented in the late eighteen hundreds, it is played on an ordinary eight by eight board. When it is played on a board, you use pieces which have different colors on each side. The game begins with four pieces placed on the center squares.

From this point on, you move by placing one of your pieces next to a computer piece or pieces, with another of your pieces further on. When that happens, all the computer pieces "reverse" to become your pieces.

Here's how it works. Suppose a line of pieces looked like this:

OXXXX

and you decided to put your piece (the 0) at the end of the line like this:

OXXXXO

The computer pieces would reverse, so the line looked like this after your move:

OOOOOO

The game continues until every square on the board is filled, or neither player can move. As you can see, fortunes can change swiftly in this game, as rows branching off your position (such as on the diagonals) can be changed with a single move.

If you cannot move at any time, you signal this to the computer by entering a zero.

REVERSI is a very enjoyable game to play. Writing in *Creative Computing* magazine (June 1981, p. 188), David Levy tenders the opinion that it is "one of the best games ever invented, simply because the rules can be learned in no more than a minute, yet the game can take years to master." He goes on to observe that although

---

*Othello is a registered trademark of Gabriel Industries, Inc., USA and Mine of Information, UK.

the game is much simpler than chess, it is more complex than checkers.

Although the modern game is called Othello, and was "invented" by Goro Hasegawa in Tokyo in 1971, the only difference between it and Reversi is the fact that the first four positions must be as in the sample game you'll see following this description.

Back in the 1880s, when the game was first invented in London, two gentlemen—Lewis Waterman and John W. Mollett—both claimed to be the originators of the game. Stephen Kimmel (writing in *Creative Computing* magazine, July 1981, p. 94) says he believes Waterman has the strongest case for being the inventor of Reversi, because he had the details published first in a series of articles in the magazine, *The Queen* (which concentrated on "affairs of interest to ladies").

Regardless of who should get the credit, Hasegawa, Waterman, or Mollett, it is a great game, and this program (based on one written by Graham Charlton) puts up a spirited defense. This sample run shows the early stages of one game:

```
    COMPUTER IS X              COMPUTER IS X
      HUMAN IS O                 HUMAN IS O

    1 2 3 4 5 6 7 8           1 2 3 4 5 6 7 8
1   . . . . . . . .  1     1  . . . . . . . .  1
2   . . . . . . . .  2     2  . . . . . . . .  2
3   . . . . . . . .  3     3  . . . . . . . .  3
4   . . . X O . . .  4     4  . . . X O . . .  4
5   . . . O X . . .  5     5  . . X X X . . .  5
6   . . . . . . . .  6     6  . . . . . . . .  6
7   . . . . . . . .  7     7  . . . . . . . .  7
8   . . . . . . . .  8     8  . . . . . . . .  8
    1 2 3 4 5 6 7 8           1 2 3 4 5 6 7 8
```

Computer: 2   Computer: 4

Human: 2   Human: 1

72

```
      COMPUTER IS X                    COMPUTER IS X
       HUMAN IS O                       HUMAN IS O

   1 2 3 4 5 6 7 8                   1 2 3 4 5 6 7 8
 1 . . . . . . . .  1             1 . . . . . . . .  1
 2 . . . . . . . .  2             2 . . . . . . . .  2
 3 . . . . . . . .  3             3 . . . . . . . .  3
 4 . . . X O . . .  4             4 . . . X O . . .  4
 5 . . X O X . . .  5             5 . . X O X . . .  5
 6 . . O . . . . .  6             6 . . X . . . . .  6
 7 . . . . . . . .  7             7 . . X . . . . .  7
 8 . . . . . . . .  8             8 . . . . . . . .  8
   1 2 3 4 5 6 7 8                   1 2 3 4 5 6 7 8
```

Computer: 3

Human: 3

Computer: 5

Human: 2

```
      COMPUTER IS X                    COMPUTER IS X
       HUMAN IS O                       HUMAN IS O

   1 2 3 4 5 6 7 8                   1 2 3 4 5 6 7 8
 1 . . . . . . . .  1             1 . . . . . . . .  1
 2 . . . . . . . .  2             2 . . . . . . . .  2
 3 . . . . . . . .  3             3 . . . . . . . .  3
 4 . . . X O . . .  4             4 . . O O O . . .  4
 5 . . X X X . . .  5             5 . . O X X . . .  5
 6 . . O X . . . .  6             6 . . O X . . . .  6
 7 . O X . . . . .  7             7 . O X . . . . .  7
 8 . . . . . . . .  8             8 . . . . . . . .  8
   1 2 3 4 5 6 7 8                   1 2 3 4 5 6 7 8
```

Computer: 6

Human: 3
?

Computer: 4

Human: 6
?

```
    COMPUTER IS X              COMPUTER IS X
     HUMAN IS O                 HUMAN IS O

   1 2 3 4 5 6 7 8            1 2 3 4 5 6 7 8
1  . . . . . . . .  1      1  . . . . . . . .  1
2  . . . . . . . .  2      2  . . . . . . . .  2
3  . . X . . . . .  3      3  . . X . . . . .  3
4  . . X X O . . .  4      4  . O O O . . . .  4
5  . . X X X . . .  5      5  . . X X X . . .  5
6  . . X X . . . .  6      6  . . X X . . . .  6
7  . O X . . . . .  7      7  . O X . . . . .  7
8  . . . . . . . .  8      8  . . . . . . . .  8
   1 2 3 4 5 6 7 8            1 2 3 4 5 6 7 8


Computer: 9                 Computer: 7

Human: 2                    Human: 5
?                           ?



    COMPUTER IS X              COMPUTER IS X
     HUMAN IS O                 HUMAN IS O

   1 2 3 4 5 6 7 8            1 2 3 4 5 6 7 8
1  . . . . . . . .  1      1  . . . . . . . .  1
2  . . . . . . . .  2      2  . . . . . . . .  2
3  . . X . . . . .  3      3  . . X . . . . .  3
4  . X O O O . . .  4      4  . X O O O . . .  4
5  X . O X X . . .  5      5  X . X X X . . .  5
6  . . O O . . . .  6      6  . . O X . . . .  6
7  . X O . O . . .  7      7  . X O . X . . .  7
8  X . O . . . . .  8      8  X . O . . X . .  8
   1 2 3 4 5 6 7 8            1 2 3 4 5 6 7 8


Computer: 7                 Computer: 11

Human: 9                    Human: 6
?                           ?
```

74

```
      COMPUTER IS X                COMPUTER IS X
        HUMAN IS O                   HUMAN IS O

    1 2 3 4 5 6 7 8              1 2 3 4 5 6 7 8
1   . . . . . . . .  1      1    . . . . . . . .  1
2   . . . . . . . .  2      2    . . . . . . . .  2
3   . . X . . . . .  3      3    . . X . X . . .  3
4   . X O O O . . .  4      4    . X O X X . . .  4
5   X . X O O . . .  5      5    X . X O X . . .  5
6   . . O O O . . .  6      6    . . O O X . . .  6
7   . X O . X . . .  7      7    . X O . X . . .  7
8   X . O . . X . .  8      8    X . O . . X . .  8
    1 2 3 4 5 6 7 8              1 2 3 4 5 6 7 8


Computer: 8                 Computer: 13

Human: 10                   Human: 6
?                           ?
```

And here's the listing of REVERSI:

```
10 REM REVERSI
20 GOTO 740
30 PRINT "MY MOVE..."
40 S = O:T = X:H = 0
50 FOR A = 2 TO 9:FOR B = 2 TO 9
60 IF A(A,B) <> 46 THEN 210
70 Q = 0
80 FOR C = -1 TO 1:FOR D = -1 TO 1
90 K = 0:F = A:G = B
100 IF A(F+C,G+D) <> S THEN 130
110 K = K + 1:F = F + C:G = G + D
120 GOTO 100
130 IF A(F+C,G+D) <> T THEN 150
140 Q = Q + K
150 NEXT D:NEXT C
160 IF A = 2 OR A = 9 OR B = 2 OR B = 9 TH
EN Q = Q*2
170 IF A = 3 OR A = 8 OR B = 3 OR B = 8 TH
EN Q = Q/2
```

```
180 IF (A = 2 OR A = 9) AND (B = 3 OR B =
8) OR (A = 3 OR A = 8) AND (B = 2 OR B = 9
) THEN Q = Q/2
190 IF Q < H OR (RND <.3 AND Q = H) THEN 2
10
200 H = Q:M = A:N = B
210 NEXT B:NEXT A
220 IF H = 0 AND R = 0 THEN 690
230 IF H = 0 THEN 250
240 GOSUB 580
250 GOSUB 370
260 INPUT "ENTER YOUR MOVE ";R
270 REM ENTER 0 TO PASS
280 S = X:T = 0:REM LETTER O
290 IF R = 0 THEN 350
300 IF R < 11 OR R > 88 THEN 260
310 R = R + 11
320 M = INT(R/10)
330 N = R - 10*M
340 GOSUB 580
350 GOSUB 370
360 GOTO 30
370 REM PRINT BOARD
380 C = 0:H = 0
390 CLS:REM OR 'HOME'
400 PRINT
410 PRINT "     COMPUTER IS X"
420 PRINT "       HUMAN IS O"
430 PRINT
440 PRINT TAB(5);"1 2 3 4 5 6 7 8"
450 FOR B = 2 TO 9:PRINT B - 1;" ";
460 FOR D = 2 TO 9
470 PRINT CHR$(A(B,D));" ";
480 IF A(B,D) = X THEN C = C + 1
490 IF A(B,D) = O THEN H = H + 1
500 NEXT D
510 PRINT B - 1
520 NEXT B
530 PRINT TAB(5);"1 2 3 4 5 6 7 8"
540 PRINT:PRINT
550 PRINT "Computer:"C
560 PRINT:PRINT"Human:"H
570 RETURN
580 FOR C = - 1 TO 1:FOR D = - 1 TO 1
```

```
590 F = M:G = N
600 IF A(F+C,G+D) <> S THEN 630
610 F = F + C:G = G + D
620 GOTO 600
630 IF A(F+C,G+D) <> T THEN 670
640 A(F,G) = T
650 IF M = F AND N = G THEN 670
660 F = F - C:G = G - D:GOTO 640
670 NEXT D:NEXT C
680 RETURN
690 GOSUB 370
700 IF C > H THEN PRINT "I'M THE CHAMP!"
710 IF H > C THEN PRINT "YOU'RE THE CHAMP!
"
720 IF H = C THEN PRINT "IT'S A DRAW!"
730 END
740 CLS
750 X = ASC("X"):O = ASC("O"):REM LETTER O
  NOT ZERO
760 DIM A(10,10)
770 FOR B = 1 TO 10:FOR C = 1 TO 10
780 IF B <> 1 AND C <>1 AND B <> 10 AND C
<> 10 THEN A(B,C) = ASC(".")
790 NEXT C:NEXT B
800 A(5,5) = X: A(6,6) = X
810 A(6,5) = O: A(5,6) = O
820 P = 0
830 PRINT "DO YOU WANT THE FIRST MOVE"
840 PRINT ,"Y OR N"
850 INPUT W$
860 GOSUB 370
870 IF W$ = "Y" OR W$ = "y" THEN GOTO 260
880 GOTO 30
```

Adventure

Down into the depths of darkness you go. Armed with only your computer, and your keen mind, you have decided to take on the forces of evil.

You may be on a desert island, inside a haunted house, within a dungeon deep within the bowels of the earth, or trapped in a cave system on a planet "somewhere in a galaxy far away."

Adventure games take place in all these scenarios, and a thousand more beside. Come with us now, as we discover the excitement of the worlds of ADVENTURE.

The word *adventure* is used to describe the class of computer games in which the player moves through an alternative reality. In this "otherworld" there are monsters to be fought, treasures to be discovered, maps to be made, and puzzles to be solved.

Many people feel that adventure games are the most exciting games which can be played with a computer. If you are interested in role-playing games like TSR Hobbies' Dungeons and Dragons (the game and name are registered trademarks of TSR), then you're certain to enjoy playing adventure.

I've included four adventure-type programs in this book. Two are of medium difficulty, and the third and fourth ones are much longer, and more complex, than the first two. All should have you scratching your head as you work out what is going on.

One feature of true adventure games is that the reality they model is *consistent*. That is, the world created within the adventure program is solid, and—apart from any events specific to that game, such as an earthquake, or a magic spell—the parts of the world do not shift in a random fashion. If you walk past a "gnarled and twisted oak, with the initials of your best friend carved in the trunk" when going down a certain woodland park, the same oak should still be there when you return. In a properly constructed adventure the rivers stay in place, the dungeon walls do not mysteriously move and shift every time you turn your back, and objects you put down in one cave within an underground labyrinth do not suddenly appear of their own volition a hundred caves away (unless, of course, they've been blessed with some form of magical auto-transportation).

Map-making is one of the true adventure-player's skills and delights. Working your way through an imaginary (but self-consistent) environment, tackling monsters and collecting treasures, solving puzzles as you go up and down staircases and chutes, exploring side tunnels, getting lost in self-circling mazes, and so on, is only fascinating if the world you are exploring is mappable. You should, for example, be able to expect both ends of a tunnel to always emerge in the same spots, so when you come across one entrance to that tunnel later on in a game from a different position, you will have a new, useful clue to further flesh out your map of the environment. All the "worlds" created in the games in this section of your book are mappable, and the first two even give you glimpses, from time to time, of the scene from above. The third one does not, and this is the one you should tackle last of all, once you're confident you can move through the other, much simpler, environments at will.

Role-playing is part of life. There are sure to be many situations in your everyday activities when you, to some extent, are forced to adopt a role. Most jobs, unfortunately, expect you to behave as if the needs and goals of the company were your own needs and goals, that the enthusiasm you project each day to customers and fellow-workers were your own, inner enthusiasms, and so on. You may well find that, in new situations, you have learnt to mask your lack of ease by acting confident, and at ease, discovering that—if you do it skillfully—people take the projected role as if it were your true self.

The role-playing which takes place within the imaginary environments of an adventure game is far more interesting, and is generally far removed from the self of your everyday life. When you think about it, even playing games like "Cops and Robbers" is an exercise in role-playing.

So we've all had experience in role-playing, even if some of it was not as much fun as taking part in long-range campaigns to rescue a handsome prince trapped within a tower. The adventures given in this book are by no means as elaborate as some of the ones offered for sale for your computer, but they are more carefully and consistently organized than many I have seen, and—as a bonus—give you frameworks within which you can construct adventure programs of your own.

Role-playing games which involve other people, such as TSR's Dungeons and Dragons which I mentioned earlier, generally have a great deal of flexibility in development as a game proceeds. Under the control of a good Dungeon-master, a role-playing game can develop and evolve in directions which he or she had not even imagined when setting up the initial scenario. Unfortunately, computer role-playing games cannot be so flexible. In many ways when playing adventure with a computer, you are trying to solve a puzzle, or series of them, which the programmer has created. The computer can be used to help set up the initial scenario and determine where objects will be located, and perhaps where a particular stairwell will lead, but the overall shape of the environment is fixed by the programmer when the game is written.

You can see this in action, for example, in our program STRONGHOLD OF THE DWARVEN LORDS, where you have to work your way through a maze to discover where the Dwarven treasure is stowed. The computer actually hides the treasure, and modifies the '3-D maze' to some extent, but that is all. Of course, the computer is also used to produce the feedback to the player as the game is underway, and its role there is very valuable.

Once upon a time, war campaigns were reenacted on table tops. Napoleonic battles were fought and won on large sheets of card marked with rivers and woods, as players reenacted major engagements within wars, or created their own. Wargamers found the pleasure of the games they played could be increased if attention were paid as much (if not more) to the individuals they were fighting with, rather than just with squads of soldiers. This attention to individual identity lead directly into the role-playing games we have today, as gamers discovered how rewarding it was to take on the role of a particular leader.

Our Dungeons and Dragons developed directly from the war games where players took on the identities of individuals within battles. Two gamers, Dave Arnson and E. Gary Gygax, decided to codify an entirely separate reality, which they initially gave to the world in 1974 as a boxed set of three booklets under the title *Dungeons and Dragons*. The game became an enormous success, and now hundreds of thousands of people spend a significant portion of their leisure plunging into the depths of the earth, as clerics, trolls, magicians, and sorcerers, exploring, fighting, conquering—and occasionally dying—as they go.

The original D & D idea soon spawned a host of other games, such as Runequest (Chaosium Ltd, Albany, California), Bushido and Chivalry & Sorcery (Fantasy Games Unlimited, Roslyn, New York), Tunnels & Trolls (Flying Buffalo, Inc., Scottsdale, Arizona), Traveller (Game Designers' Workshop, Bloomington, Illinois) and Heroes of Olympus (Task Force Games, Amarillo, Texas).

Will Crowther and Don Woods entered computer history in 1976 by putting the world's first role-playing game—just called ADVENTURE—onto a mainframe computer at Stanford University. (The program was actually written by Crowther, and elaborated by Woods, although today both men are generally credited with developing the program.) Although the game quickly became a cult-pursuit all over America, the floodgates to computer adventure-gaming did not open until microcomputers put machine-power—and computer time—into the hands of millions. Cheaper memory enabled extremely elaborate adventures to be created, and so now the computer adventure gamer is extremely well served.

Crowther and Woods perhaps created better than they knew. Even today, despite the multitude of programs available, the original ADVENTURE is still going strong. At least five companies at present are selling versions of the original ADVENTURE for the Apple alone.

This original program was written in Fortran, and when it was added to a free software-exchange library (Decus) organized by the Digital Equipment Computer Users' Society (most of whom used Dec's PDP-11 systems), it soon became the most-used program in the library. Two years later, another adventure program, DUNGEON, was added to Decus. This program, which took the ADVENTURE idea much further than Crowther's program, was written by Tim Anderson, Marc Blank, Bruce Daniels, and Dave Lebling, all of the Programming Technology Division of the MIT Laboratory for Computer Science.

The *Addison-Wesley Book of Apple Computer Software* (edited by Jeffrey Stanton and John Dickey, The Book Co., Lawndale, California, 1981) devotes 29 pages to describing fantasy, role-playing, adventure, and war simulation games available for the Apple II. If the support for that computer is so good in this field of software, it indicates that many other popular computers are also well-supported.

Even so, despite the adventure programs you can buy for your computer, the thrill of creating your own programs for this most special of computer games is one which you should experience. And the programs given in this part of the book will certainly give you a framework upon which to build. I suggest you get them up and running, and then elaborate them to your heart's content (or at least until you run out of memory).

Although there is a trend towards graphic-based adventures, rather than the classic text-based ones, the attraction of text programs continues. Just as television did not make radio obsolete—because the imagination is stronger than anything man can make—so graphic adventures have not taken away the special value of text-based games, where the mind is triggered to produce worlds far more fantastic than any that a clever programmer could draw using the sophisticated graphics available on many of today's machines.

However, you'll probably find you can make the presentation of the text output of these games more attractive on your computer by adding color and sound as you see fit, using the special features of your machine to enhance your enjoyment when playing the games.

One of the leading companies in the world producing adventure programs is Adventure International, founded by Scott Adams. His company has some of the most imaginative displays at computer shows of anyone in the games software field, and it is good to know his programs are as exciting as his show displays. Make sure you experience the pleasure of playing a Scott Adams adventure program in due course, and you'll see how far the genre has been extended.

I met Scott in Atlanta one day at a computer show and found him friendly, quiet, and reserved. Somehow, I'd expected him to be like a warlock from one of his dungeons, or a dragon from one of the cave systems. However, some behavior was more in keeping with my expectations. It was Halloween, and Scott and his crew were all dressed to the nines as characters out of some of the programs. The same approach to life which had him tell his staff to come to work in fancy dress permeates his programs. Start with the programs here, which are much simpler to solve than programs such as Scott's, and then graduate to the commercial programs. Perhaps his program Adventureland would be a good place to begin, before you move on to some of his other games, and on to those produced by other companies.

Avalon Hill's program Empire of the Over-Mind is another of the classics of the field, and this—as well as Sentient Software's Cyborg deserve inspection. The list could go on and on, and certainly new titles have been added to the programs now available, so your computer magazines and/or your local gamer and computer clubs would be a good place to find out just what else is around for you and your computer.

I guess it's time now to introduce you to the adventure programs in this book. If you'd like to know more about the field, to help you write your own programs, there is a vast body of literature which is of interest. It includes:

"Putting Adventure in Adventure Games," article in *Creative Computing*, August 1981, by Robert Plamondon.

"Graphic Adventures on the Atari," article in *Creative Computing*, August 1982, by John Anderson.

"Fantasy Games" (parts one and two), articles in *Creative Computing*, issues of March 1981 (part one) and May 1981 (part two) by David Lubar.

"An Adventure in Small Computer Game Simulation," article by

Scott Adams (when he was just about unknown!) in *Creative Computing,* way back in August 1979.

"Kings of the Castle Walls," article in *Practical Computing,* March 1982, by Dennis Ellis.

"Adventure Writing," this is an immensely valuable 16-page booklet, distributed by Aardvark-80, 2352 S. Commerce, Walled Lake, MI 48088 [(313) 669-3110] for around $5.00. It explains the whole background of adventure game writing, and includes a complete adventure program, Deathship. If you read nothing else in the field, you should get hold of this booklet if you really want to discover how to write adventure games.

Fantasy Role-Playing Games, by J. Eric Holmes (Hippocrene Books, Inc., New York, 1981).

What Is Dungeons and Dragons?, by John Butterfield, Philip Parker, and David Honigmann (Penguin Books, New York, 1982).

Dicing with Dragons: An Introduction to Role-Playing Games, by Ian Livingstone (Routledge & Kegan Paul, London, Melbourne, and Henley).

☐ STRONGHOLD OF THE DWARVEN LORDS

Deep beneath the earth you go, far into the Dwarven Heartland. Danger is on every side as you descend, but your greed draws you on. Searching through the dusty stacks of uncatalogued manuscripts in room 546B of the British Museum, you came across a faded, and almost illegible map to a Dwarven hoard of gold, and since that day, you have been obsessed with the idea of finding it.

As you go down into the labyrinth, you realize that the Dwarven Lords, who secreted the gold here 7389 years ago, have long since become extinct, so the main danger you face is from the layout of the cavern system itself, rather than from Guards of the Stronghold.

In STRONGHOLD OF THE DWARVEN LORDS you are in a cavern which holds the gold. Each time you play this game, the gold can be in one of three places. The only information you get as to your progress is information provided by the Dwarven Source Beam which you found as you made your way into the cave system. This gives you feedback after each move as to the location of the gold, but you need to learn how to interpret the information it gives you before you'll be able to make much use of it.

The other information you get is in the form of a straight statement regarding the directions you can move from your present position. After each move ("step"), you'll be given a screen display like the following:

```
STEP NUMBER 49

NORTH: WALL
SOUTH: OPEN
EAST: WALL
WEST: OPEN

THE DWARVEN SOURCE BEAM READS 10
```

Then you'll be asked to enter the direction you want to move, as follows:

```
Which direction do you want
to move?

N - north, S - south
E - east, W - west, H - help
? W
```

You will not, as you probably realize, be allowed to walk through walls.

The aim of the game, needless to say, is to reach the Dwarven riches as quickly as possible. To aid you, there is a map of the cavern system from above, which you can call up from time to time. The map looks like this (with the walls shown as # symbols, and you shown as *):

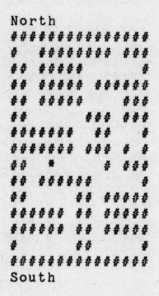

There are two catches to calling up a map of this type. First, although your position is shown, the location of the gold is not. Second, each time you enter "H" to get a look at the map, you'll be penalized 15 steps. Therefore, it is in your interests to use the Help option as few times as possible.

Although there are some features which are common to each and every cavern generated by this program (dictated by the data statements from 870 to 960), the cavern is not identical from run to run. As well as that, as I mentioned earlier, the gold itself can be in one of three locations within the cave system.

The output of the program, as it is given in terms of the directions you can take from your present position, could be modified to produce a "3-D maze" output. You know, from move to move, which direction you're facing, and the computer knows which directions from that position represent possible moves. You would need to add a subroutine which drew a picture of the situation immediately in front of you, choosing from a bank of pictures (one with the area straight in front of you clear but with the walls solid on either side of you, another with entrances to the right and to the left but with the path straight ahead blocked off, and so on) to produce a continuous picture of the scene ahead. This can be most effective, and may well be worth implementing on your system.

Now, here is the listing of STRONGHOLD OF THE DWARVEN LORDS so you can start trekking for gold:

```
10  REM STRONGHOLD OF THE DWARVEN LORDS
20  GOSUB 640
30  GOSUB 480
40  REM *******************************
50  M = M + 1
60  CLS:PRINT:PRINT
70  PRINT "STEP NUMBER"M
80  PRINT
90  PRINT "NORTH: ";
100 IF A(D + 1,E) = S THEN PRINT "OPEN"
110 IF A(D + 1,E) = X THEN PRINT "WALL"
120 PRINT "SOUTH: ";
130 IF A(D - 1,E) = S THEN PRINT "OPEN"
140 IF A(D - 1,E) = X THEN PRINT "WALL"
150 PRINT "EAST: ";
160 IF A(D,E + 1) = S THEN PRINT "OPEN"
170 IF A(D,E + 1) = X THEN PRINT "WALL"
180 PRINT "WEST: ";
190 IF A(D,E - 1) = S THEN PRINT "OPEN"
200 IF A(D,E - 1) = X THEN PRINT "WALL"
210 PRINT
220 PRINT "THE DWARVEN SOURCE BEAM READS";

230 PRINT 100*ABS(Z - D) + 10*ABS(Y - E)
240 REM *******************************
250 PRINT:PRINT:PRINT
260 PRINT "Which direction do you want"
270 PRINT "to move?"
```

```
280 PRINT:PRINT "N - north, S - south"
290 PRINT "E - east, W - west, H - help"
300 INPUT A$
310 IF A$ = "N" AND A(D + 1,E) = X THEN 30
0
320 IF A$ = "S" AND A(D - 1,E) = X THEN 30
0
330 IF A$ = "E" AND A(D,E + 1) = X THEN 30
0
340 IF A$ = "W" AND A(D,E - 1) = X THEN 30
0
350 IF A$ = "H" THEN GOSUB 480
360 IF A$ = "N" THEN D = D + 1
370 IF A$ = "S" THEN D = D - 1
380 IF A$ = "E" THEN E = E + 1
390 IF A$ = "W" THEN E = E - 1
400 IF Z = D AND Y = E THEN 430
410 GOTO 50
420 REM ****************************
430 PRINT:PRINT "You found the Dwarven ric
hes"
440 PRINT "in just"M"steps!"
450 GOSUB 500
460 END
470 REM ****************************
480 REM help
490 CLS
500 PRINT
510 PRINT "North"
520 FOR B = 15 TO 1 STEP - 1
530 FOR C = 1 TO 15
540 IF A(B,C) = X THEN PRINT "#";
550 IF B = D AND C = E THEN PRINT "#";:GOT
O 570
560 IF A(B,C) = S THEN PRINT " ";
570 NEXT C:PRINT:NEXT B
580 PRINT "South"
590 M = M + 15
600 FOR J = 1 TO 2000:NEXT J
610 CLS:A(D,E) = S
620 RETURN
630 REM ****************************
640 CLS
```

```
650 N = 1:PRINT "Press any key"
660 N = N + 1:IF INKEY$ = "" THEN 660
670 RANDOMIZE N
680 CLS
690 DIM A(15,15)
700 B = INT(RND*3) + 1
710 Z = 14: Y = 14
720 IF B = 2 THEN Y = 2
730 IF B = 3 THEN Z = 2
740 X = 1:S = 2
750 FOR B = 1 TO 15:FOR C = 1 TO 15
760 A(B,C) = X: IF RND>.8 THEN A(B,C) = S
770 IF C<2 OR C>14 OR B<2 OR B>14 THEN A(B
,C) = X
780 NEXT C:NEXT B
790 D = 2:E = 2
800 FOR F = 1 TO 68
810 READ B:READ C
820 A(B,C) = S
830 NEXT F
840 M = -15
850 RETURN
860 REM ******************************
870 DATA 2,2,2,3,2,4,2,5,2,6,2,7
880 DATA 3,7,4,7,5,7,5,6,5,5,5,4,5,3,6,3
890 DATA 7,3,7,4,7,5,7,6,7,7,7,8,7,9,9,8
900 DATA 9,9,10,8,10,7,10,6,10,5,10,4,8,8
910 DATA 10,3,11,3,12,3,13,3,14,3,14,2,7,1
0
920 DATA 6,10,5,10,4,10,3,10,2,10,2,11,2,1
2
930 DATA 2,13,2,14,6,11,6,12,6,13,6,14,7,1
2
940 DATA 14,12,8,12,8,14,9,12,9,13,9,14,10
,12
950 DATA 11,9,11,10,11,11,11,12,12,9,13,9,
13,10
960 DATA 13,11,13,12,13,13,13,14,14,14,14
```

☐ THE DUKE OF DRAGONFEAR

THE DUKE OF DRAGONFEAR puts you into another grid system world, but one which is populated with a range of fearsome possibilities including pits containing quicksand or dragons, as well as magic caves which can transport you at random within the Land of Dragonworld, and caves filled with Dragon's gold.

When you first run the program, you'll get this information:

```
Welcome to the world of Dragonfear

Your mission is to explore the
caves of Dragonworld, looking for
treasure, and attempting to slay the
fearsome dragons who live in the
caves. What is your name?

All hail, Duke Tim

You start this exploration
with 25 units of charisma, and
you must complete your task before
the charisma is worn out. You lose
one unit for every move you make

PRESS ANY KEY TO BEGIN
```

Having assimilated this, you are given a quick peek at a map of Dragonworld:

```
X X X X X X X X X X
X . D D $ ? D . . X
X D X . . X . . . X
X D . . . . Q . X X
X Q . . $ . . . ? X
X . . . H . . $ ? X
X $ $ . . . X . ? X
X . X . . . . . . X
X . Q Q . . . . . X
X X X X X X X X X X
```

In this map, X represents a wall you cannot pass or a cave you cannot enter, H (for human) is you starting in about the center of the system, $ is the treasure caves, ? the magic transportation caves, D represents dragons, and Q tells you that cave contains quicksand. Obviously this is a world filled with potential pleasures as well as dangers.

If you're a veteran of computer games, you may well recognize that THE DUKE OF DRAGONFEAR is a development of the Hunt the Wumpus games. Wumpus is one of the grand old standards of computer games, in which you are in a cave system, looking for one or more mythical beasts known, in the singular (and these are most singular beasts) as Wumpus. Wumpii, we are assured by those who care about such things, is the plural. Anyway, in essence, a grid is set up in such games, and objects, people, effects, monsters and whatever else you choose are placed at locations on the grid. From time to time, if you so decide, one or more of the contents of specific cells of the grid may move. The human player, of course, can also move from cell to cell within the grid.

Generally, there is no overall visible map of the system, although some programs (such as THE DUKE OF DRAGONFEAR) do provide such information for players. The very first Wumpus game was written by Gregory Yob in 1975. In David Ahl's superb book *More BASIC Computer Games* (Creative Computing Press, Morristown, New Jersey, 1979), Mr. Yob explains how he was visiting People's Computer Company, in Menlo Park, California, to see the programs they were developing, and he noticed there were three "hunt the something" programs being written, each on a 10 × 10 grid, and each of which gave feedback to the player in terms of "no, no . . . try to the northwest."

Unenchanted, Mr. Yob returned to a lonely time-sharing terminal (back in those ancient days, gentle reader, human beings did not have little computers at their beck and call) and hammered out the program which eventually became the very first "Hunt the Wumpus." Mr. Yob had the creature dwelling in a dodecahedron-shaped cave system.

Mr. Yob's inventive genius did not stop at this point. He peopled the cave with "magic bats" which moved you from place to place within the system at random, with bottomless pits, and ensured that the arrows with which you were equipped when you entered the system could fly round corners.

You can see now how this framework became the heart of the Wumpus programs which have proliferated around the world and which formed the very rawest framework upon which THE DUKE OF DRAGONFEAR is based. This program gives you more control on the outcome of the program, adds treasure to the caves, and imposes a time-limit to your game.

As well, you are equipped with a "magic amulet" which can see into the caves which are around you. Unfortunately, because you're not much of a whiz when it comes to invoking magic, the old amulet doesn't work too well. It can only tell you of the contents of one of the eight caves surrounding the one in which you stand, and worse than this does not tell you which of the eight it is referring to. It is not as bad as it may sound. You'll be surprised at how much use you can make of the limited information the amulet provides. As well, you'll get a brief glimpse of the cave system from above at the start of the game, and from time to time as it goes on.

As you can see from the sample run which follows this introduction, your options at each move include "F" for fight. Pressing "F" will direct the program to the subroutine starting at line 930, which first checks to see you have not used up all your arrows, and if it finds you have not, allows you to choose in which direction—from your present position—you want to fire the arrow. A successful kill earns you a handsome monetary reward.

Here are some snapshots of the program in action:

```
DUKE Tim, YOU ARE IN CAVE 55
Your amulet signals that
there is gold
nearby

YOU HAVE 25 UNITS OF CHARISMA LEFT

What do you want to do?
N - move north, S - move south
E - move east,  W - move west
F - fight a dragon, Q - quit

? N
  Treasure ! ! !
   Treasure ! ! !
    Treasure ! ! !
     Treasure ! ! !
      Treasure ! ! !
       Treasure ! ! !
        Treasure ! ! !
         Treasure ! ! !
          Treasure ! ! !
```

```
                Treasure ! ! !
                 Treasure ! ! !
                  Treasure ! ! !

     You've found a hoard of
     dragon-gold, worth $ 170

     DUKE Tim, YOU ARE IN CAVE 48
     YOU ARE CARRYING $ 170 WORTH OF GOLD
     Your amulet signals that
     there is quicksand
     nearby

     YOU HAVE 21 UNITS OF CHARISMA LEFT

     What do you want to do?
     N - move north, S - move south
     E - move east,  W - move west
     F - fight a dragon, Q - quit

     ? E

     Duke Tim, you've stumbled
     into a magic cave, and now you'll
     be whisked to another cave ....

           X X X X X X X X X
           X . D D $ ? D . . X
           X D X . . X . . . X
           X D . . . . Q . X X
           X Q . . . . . . . X
           X . . . . . . $ ? X
           X $ $ . . . X . ? X
           X . X . . . . . . X
           X . Q Q H . . . . X
           X X X X X X X X X X
```

This is the program listing to enable you to become **THE DUKE OF DRAGONFEAR**:

```
10 REM THE DUKE OF DRAGONFEAR
20 GOSUB 1280
30 CLS:PRINT:PRINT:PRINT
```

```
40  GOSUB 1200
50  Q = INT(RND*7)
60  IF Q = 0 AND E <> 55 THEN GOSUB 1200
70  CLS:PRINT:PRINT:PRINT "DUKE "A$", YOU A
RE IN CAVE"E
80  IF G > 0 THEN PRINT "YOU ARE CARRYING $
"G"WORTH OF GOLD"
90  GOSUB 760
100 PRINT:PRINT "YOU HAVE"25 - H"UNITS OF
CHARISMA LEFT"
110 PRINT:PRINT "What do you want to do?"
120 PRINT "N - move north, S - move south"

130 PRINT "E - move east,  W - move west"
140 PRINT "F - fight a dragon, Q - quit":P
RINT
150 INPUT Z$:U = 0:IF Z$ <> "N" AND Z$ <>
"S" AND Z$ <> "E" AND Z$ <> "W" AND Z$ <>
"F" AND Z$ <> "Q" THEN 150
160 IF Z$ = "N" AND A(E - 10) = 88 OR Z$ =
 "S" AND A(E + 10) = 88 OR Z$ = "E" AND A(
E + 1) = 88 OR Z$ = "W" AND A(E - 1) = 88
THEN PRINT "You cannot move that way!":GOT
O 150
170 IF Z$ = "Q" THEN Q = 9:GOTO 1170
180 A(E) = 46: IF Z$ = "N" THEN E = E - 10

190 IF Z$ = "S" THEN E = E + 10
200 IF Z$ = "E" THEN E = E + 1
210 IF Z$ = "W" THEN E = E - 1
220 IF Z$ = "F" THEN GOSUB 930
230 IF A(E) = 63 THEN GOSUB 310:REM MAGIC
240 IF A(E) = 68 THEN GOSUB 400:REM DRAGON
250 IF A(E) = 81 THEN GOSUB 550:REM QUICKS
AND
260 IF A(E) = 36 THEN GOSUB 630:REM GOLD
270 H = H + 1:IF H = 25 THEN Q = 9:GOTO 11
60
280 GOSUB 1610
290 GOTO 50
300 REM *************************
310 REM MAGIC
320 PRINT :PRINT "Duke "A$", you've stumbl
ed"
```

```
330 PRINT "into a magic cave, and now you'
ll"
340 PRINT "be whisked to another cave ....
"
350 GOSUB 1610
360 A(E) = 46
370 E = INT(RND*76) + 12: IF A(E) = 88 THE
N 370
380 RETURN
390 REM *************************
400 REM DRAGON
410 PRINT "You have wandered into a dragon
's"
420 PRINT "lair...start saying your prayer
s"
430 GOSUB 1610
440 M = RND:IF M < .2 THEN PRINT "It has f
lown away":RETURN
450 PRINT "It awakens...and it has seen yo
u"
460 GOSUB 1610
470 IF M >.8499999  THEN PRINT "but it has
 recently eaten":PRINT "and so goes back t
o sleep":RETURN
480 PRINT "And now it attacks..."
490 GOSUB 1610
500 IF M >.95 THEN PRINT "But you fight ba
ck...and win":RETURN
510 PRINT "Goodbye Duke "A$
520 GOSUB 1610
530 Q = 9:GOTO 1160
540 REM *************************
550 REM QUICKSAND
560 FOR J = 1 TO 12
570 FOR K = 1 TO J:PRINT " ";:NEXT
580 PRINT "Horrors...quicksand!"
590 FOR O = 1 TO 90:NEXT
600 NEXT
610 Q = 9:H = 0:GOTO 1160
620 REM *************************
630 REM TREASURE
640 K = INT(RND*100) + 100
650 FOR J = 1 TO 12
660 FOR Z = 1 TO J:PRINT " ";:NEXT
```

```
670 PRINT "Treasure ! ! !"
680 FOR O = 1 TO 200:NEXT
690 NEXT
700 GOSUB 1610
710 PRINT:PRINT "You've found a hoard of"
720 PRINT "dragon-gold, worth $"K
730 G = G + K
740 RETURN
750 REM **************************
760 REM AMULET DETAILS
770 Y = 1
780 L = A(E + P(Y))
790 IF L <> 46 THEN 820
800 IF Y < 8 THEN Y = Y + 1: GOTO 780
810 IF L = 46 THEN RETURN
820 PRINT "Your amulet signals that"
830 PRINT "there is ";
840 IF L = 88 THEN PRINT "a solid wall"
850 IF L = 63 THEN PRINT "a magic cave"
860 IF L = 68 THEN PRINT "a dragon"
870 IF L = 81 THEN PRINT "quicksand"
880 IF L = 36 THEN PRINT "gold"
890 PRINT "nearby"
900 GOSUB 1610
910 RETURN
920 REM **************************
930 REM ATTACK DRAGON
940 PRINT
950 AR = AR - 1:IF AR = 0 THEN PRINT "You
have used up all":PRINT "your arrows....":
GOSUB 1610:RETURN
960 PRINT "You have"AR"arrows in your quiv
er"
970 SS = 0
980 PRINT "Which direction do you want"
990 INPUT "to shoot in (N,S,E or W)";S$
1000 IF S$ = "N" AND A(E - 10) = 68 THEN S
S = 1:YT = E - 10
1010 IF S$ = "S" AND A(E + 10) = 68 THEN S
S = 1:YT = E + 10
1020 IF S$ = "E" AND A(E + 1) = 68 THEN SS
 = 1:YT = E + 1
1030 IF S$ = "W" AND A(E - 1) = 68 THEN SS
 = 1:YT = E - 1
```

```
1040 PRINT
1050 IF SS = 0 THEN PRINT "There was no dr
agon there...":PRINT "You have wasted an a
rrow":GOTO 1150
1060 PRINT "Well done, Duke "A$
1070 PRINT "You have hit"
1080 PRINT "a ferocious dragon"
1090 GOSUB 1610
1100 IF RND > .3 THEN 1140
1110 PRINT "You killed it!": A(YT) = 46: K
 = INT(RND*100) + 100
1120 PRINT
1130 PRINT "You are rewarded with $"K:G =
G + K:GOTO 1150
1140 PRINT "But you only wounded it..."
1150 GOSUB 1610:RETURN
1160 IF H < 1 THEN PRINT "All your charism
a is":PRINT "....exhausted...":GOSUB 1610:
GOTO 1180
1170 PRINT "You have"25 - H"units of chari
sma left"
1180 IF G > 0 THEN PRINT "You amassed $"G"
worth of gold"
1190 PRINT:PRINT
1200 A(E) = 72
1210 FOR J = 1 TO 100
1220 PRINT CHR$(A(J));" ";
1230 IF 10*INT(J/10) = J THEN PRINT
1240 NEXT
1250 GOSUB 1610
1260 IF Q = 9 THEN END
1270 RETURN
1280 CLS:PRINT:PRINT:PRINT
1290 PRINT "Welcome to the world of Dragon
fear"
1300 PRINT:PRINT "Your mission is to explo
re the"
1310 PRINT "caves of Dragonworld, looking
for"
1320 PRINT "treasure, and attempting to sl
ay the"
1330 PRINT "fearsome dragons who live in t
he"
1340 PRINT "caves.  What is your name";
```

```
1350 INPUT A$
1360 CLS:PRINT:PRINT "All hail, Duke "A$
1370 PRINT:PRINT "You start this explorati
on"
1380 PRINT "with 25 units of charisma, and
"
1390 PRINT "you must complete your task be
fore"
1400 PRINT "the charisma is worn out. You
lose"
1410 PRINT "one unit for every move you ma
ke"
1420 N = 1:PRINT:PRINT "PRESS ANY KEY TO B
EGIN"
1430 N = N + 1: IF INKEY$ = "" THEN 1430
1440 RANDOMIZE N:CLS
1450 PRINT "Please stand by, Duke "A$
1460 DIM A(100):H = 0:Q = 0:L = 0:G = 0:AR
 = 6
1470 FOR B = 1 TO 100:A(B) = 46
1480 IF B < 12 OR B > 90 OR 10*INT(B/10) =
 B OR 10*INT(B/10) = B - 1 THEN A(B) = 88
1490 NEXT
1500 FOR B = 1 TO 5:RESTORE: FOR D = 1 TO
5
1510 Z = INT(RND*76) + 12: IF A(Z) = 88 TH
EN 1510
1520 READ C: A(Z) = C
1530 NEXT:NEXT
1540 DATA 88, 63, 68, 81, 36
1550 FOR B = 1 TO 8:READ Z: P(B) = Z: NEXT

1560 DATA - 11, -10, -9, -1, 1,9, 10, 11
1570 E = 55
1580 RETURN
1590 REM ENGAGE CAPS LOCK
1600 REM BEFORE PLAYING
1610 FOR O = 1 TO 3000:NEXT:RETURN
```

☐ SHADOW THIEVES

Next we have an adventure program which creates its own, stable map. That is, the map does not change within a game, but is totally different from game to game. The game takes place underground, in a maze of 20 caverns connected by tunnels.

Although the number of possible combinations is not infinite, it is so huge (approaching the number of atoms in the universe) you would be unlikely to ever strike the same cavern system in your lifetime. However, the lack of true randomness in your random number generator diminishes the total number of caverns you may visit, although you are unlikely to stumble across the same one more than once.

CAVERN OF THE SHADOW THIEVES takes place in a very odd environment. You are within the maze of 20 caverns, trying to get to cavern number 20. Each cavern has four, and only four, tunnels leading from it to other caverns. Some of the tunnels are one-way, while others allow you to travel back and forth.

Several of the tunnels will contain rare treasure, such as sparkling amulets and platinum shields. You can carry up to four items at a time. Other caverns are the homes of unusual inhabitants, such as gruesome gnomes and zany zombies. Each inhabitant will demand a toll of a particular item. If you are carrying the item, the inhabitant takes it from you and allows you to pass. The inhabitant also disappears after being bribed, dropping the bribe, so you can revisit that cavern later and pick up the object again if you like.

You should make a map as you work through the cavern system. This way, you'll know for example that cavern number five contains a crazy centipede who wants a magic scroll, so that you can travel safely through cavern five as soon as you manage to pick up a suitable scroll. The interconnections between the caverns, as I said, do not change within a particular game so you can build your map with some confidence. Note that certain caves contain magic transportation spells which will move you at random within the cavern system.

The only goal of this game is to get to cavern number twenty, and you'll find the output from the program will assist you in this task, reporting your position and possessions constantly:

```
TIME REMAINING: 45

   YOU ARE IN CAVERN 14
YOU HAVE COME FROM CAVERN 5
YOU ARE CARRYING:
 1  - SPARKLING AMULET
 2  - PLATINUM SHIELD

TUNNELS LEAD TO 17 , 13 , 10 AND 16

WHERE DO YOU WANT TO GO? 17

WHERE DO YOU WANT TO GO? 17
**********************************

TIME REMAINING: 44

    YOU ARE IN CAVERN 17
YOU HAVE COME FROM CAVERN 14
YOU ARE CARRYING:
 1  - SPARKLING AMULET
 2  - PLATINUM SHIELD

THE CAVERN CONTAINS A MAGIC SCROLL

DO YOU WANT IT (Y OR  N)?

YOU HAVE MADE IT!!

YOUR CAVERN-MASTER RATING IS 9314
YOU GOT OUT WITH:
   MAGIC SCROLL
    SPUNKTRUM COIN
   WAR HAMMER
```

Here's the listing to allow you to make your own discoveries within THE CAVERN OF THE SHADOW THIEVES:

```
10 REM CAVERN OF THE SHADOW THIEVES
20 RANDOMIZE (VAL(RIGHT$(TIME$,2)))
30 DIM A(20,4),R$(4),R$(20),C$(20),D$(20
),E$(20),F$(20)
40 CLS
```

```
50  GOSUB 1130:REM BUILD CAVERNS
60  GOSUB 1030:REM FILL ARRAYS
70  GOSUB 920:REM ALLOT INHABITANTS/GOODI
ES
80  Q=50:REM TIMER
90  Y=1:X=0
100 CLS
110 REM ****** MAJOR GAME CYCLE ********
*
120 GOTO 230
130 PRINT "*******************************
****"
140 Q=Q-1:IF Q<1 THEN 880
150 PRINT:PRINT "TIME REMAINING:";Q
160 PRINT:PRINT TAB(RND(1)*6);"YOU ARE I
N CAVERN";Y
170 IF X>0 THEN PRINT "YOU HAVE COME FRO
M CAVERN";X
180 IF R$(1)>"" OR R$(2)>"" OR R$(3)>""
OR R$(4)>"" THEN PRINT "YOU ARE CARRYING
:"
190 Z=1
200 IF R$(Z)>"" THEN PRINT Z;" - ";R$(Z)

210 IF Z<4 THEN Z=Z+1:GOTO 200
220 RETURN
230 GOSUB 130
240 IF LEN(F$(Y))=0 THEN 430
250 PRINT:PRINT "THE CAVERN CONTAINS A "
;F$(Y)
260 IF INKEY$<>"" THEN 260
270 PRINT:PRINT "DO YOU WANT IT (Y OR  N
)?"
280 Q$=INKEY$
290 IF Q$<>"Y" AND Q$<>"y" AND Q$<>"N" A
ND Q$<>"n" THEN 280
300 IF Q$="N" OR Q$="n" THEN 430
310 IF R$(1)="" OR R$(2)="" OR R$(3)=""
OR R$(4)="" THEN 390
320 PRINT "YOU ARE CARRYING TOO MUCH"
330 INPUT "WHICH ITEM DO YOU WANT TO DRO
P";S
340 IF S<1 OR S>4 THEN 330
350 T$=R$(S)
```

```
360  R$(S)=F$(Y)
370  F$(Y)=""
380  GOTO 420
390  G=1
400  IF R$(G)="" THEN R$(G)=F$(Y):F$(Y)="
     ":GOTO 420
410  IF G<4 THEN G=G+1:GOTO 400
420  GOSUB 130
430  IF LEN(D$(Y))=0 THEN 600
440  IF ASC(D$(Y))=42 THEN 820
450  PRINT:PRINT "THERE IS A ";D$(Y);" HE
RE, WHO"
460  PRINT "WANTS A ";E$(Y);" TO LET YOU
PASS"
470  FOR I = 1 TO 2000:NEXT I
480  G=1
490  IF R$(G)=E$(Y) AND E$(Y)<>"" THEN 55
0
500  IF G<4 THEN G=G+1:GOTO 490
510  PRINT:PRINT "YOU MUST RETURN TO";X
520  FOR I=1 TO 3500:NEXT I
530  P=X:X=Y:Y=P
540  GOTO 230
550  PRINT "AND YOU HAVE IT!"
560  FOR I = 1 TO 2000:NEXT I
570  PRINT "THE ";D$(Y);" VANISHES!":D$(Y
)="":
580  F$(Y)=R$(G)
590  R$(G)=""
600  PRINT:PRINT "TUNNELS LEAD TO";A(Y,1)
;",";A(Y,2);",";A(Y,3);"AND";A(Y,4)
610  PRINT:INPUT "WHERE DO YOU WANT TO GO
";M
620  IF M = 0 THEN Q = Q - 5: M = 1 + INT
(RND(1)*16):GOTO 670
630  G=1
640  IF A(Y,G)=M THEN 670
650  IF G<4 THEN G=G+1:GOTO 640
660  GOTO 610
670  X=Y
680  Y=M
690  IF Y=20 THEN 710
700  GOTO 230
710  REM *******************
```

```
720 REM **** SUCCESS *****
730 CLS
740 FOR I = 1 TO 32:PRINT TAB(I);"*":NEX
T
750 PRINT:PRINT "YOU HAVE MADE IT!!"
760 PRINT:PRINT "YOUR CAVERN-MASTER RATI
NG IS";100*(100-Q) + 2*Q
770 IF R$(1)>"" OR R$(2)>"" OR R$(3)>""
OR R$(4)>"" THEN PRINT "YOU GOT OUT WITH
:"
780 FOR T = 1 TO 4
790 PRINT TAB(INT(RND(1)*7+1));R$(T)
800 NEXT T
810 END
820 REM *** TELEPORTATION ***
830 FOR I = 1 TO 32:PRINT TAB(I);"*":NEX
T
840 X=Y
850 Y=INT(RND(1)*9) + 8
860 GOTO 230
870 REM ****************
880 REM *** END 'O THE LINE ***
890 PRINT:PRINT "SORRY, FRIEND, BUT TIME
 IS UP"
900 END
910 REM ****************
920 REM *** DISTRIBUTE INHABITANTS/GOODI
ES ***
930 FOR E=1 TO 16
940 F=INT(RND(1)*18) + 2
950 D$(F)=B$(INT(RND(1)*20)+1):REM INHAB
ITANTS
960 E$(F)=C$(INT(RND(1)*20)+1):REM BRIBE
S
970 F=INT(RND(1)*19) + 2
980 F$(F)=C$(INT(RND(1)*20) + 1):REM CAV
ERN CONTENTS
990 IF RND(1)> .9 THEN D$(F)= "*":REM TE
LEPORTATION
1000 NEXT E
1010 RETURN
1020 REM ****************
1030 REM *** CREATE CAVERNS ***
```

```
1040 PRINT "PLEASE STAND BY AS I HIDE TH
E GOODIES..."
1050 FOR D=1 TO 20
1060 READ B$(D)
1070 NEXT D
1080 FOR D=1 TO 20
1090 READ C$(D)
1100 NEXT D
1110 RETURN
1120 REM ********************
1130 REM **** CONSTRUCT CAVERN ****
1140 PRINT "PLEASE STAND BY AS I CONSTRU
CT THE CAVE..."
1150 FOR B=1 TO 20
1160 PRINT TAB(B);"*"
1170 FOR C=1 TO 4
1180 A(B,C) = B + INT(RND(1)*7 - RND(1)*
6)
1190 IF A(B,C)=B OR A(B,C)<1 OR A(B,C)>2
0 THEN 1180
1200 NEXT C
1210 IF A(B,1)=A(B,2) OR A(B,1)=A(B,3) O
R A(B,1)=A(B,4) OR A(B,2)=A(B,3) OR A(B,
3)=A(B,4) OR A(B,2)=A(B,4) THEN 1170
1220 IF RND(1)<.19 AND B>12 THEN A(B,(IN
T(RND(1)*4)+1))=20
1230 NEXT B
1240 CLS
1250 RETURN
1260 REM ********************
1270 REM **** INHABITANTS ****
1280 DATA "HAIRY HOBGOBLIN","BALD BERSER
KER","SKINNY SKELETON","GRUESOME GNOME",
"CUNNING CONJURER"
1290 DATA "CRAZY CENTIPEDE","DEMENTED DW
ARF","SAVAGE SHRIEKER","CREEPY CRAWLIE",
"ROTTEN RODENT"
1300 DATA "TERRIBLE TOAD","STICKY STURGE
","GHASTLY GHOUL","WICKED WEASEL","LUMPY
 LEGEND"
1310 DATA "ZANY ZOMBIE","CROOKED CRAB","
WRATHFUL WRAITH","WEIRD WEREWOLF","GIANT
 GARGOYLE"
1320 REM ********************
```

```
1330 REM **** THE LOOT ****
1340 DATA "PIECE OF COPPER","SPUNKTRUM C
OIN","PLATINUM SHIELD","COPPER HEADBAND"
,"MAGIC SCROLL"
1350 DATA "FABULOUS POTION","WAND OF HEA
LING","SWORD OF FIRE","SPARKLING AMULET"
,"WAR HAMMER"
1360 DATA "PIECE OF COPPER","SPUNKTRUM C
OIN","PLATINUM SHIELD","COPPER HEADBAND"
,"MAGIC SCROLL"
1370 DATA "FABULOUS POTION","WAND OF HEA
LING","SWORD OF FIRE","SPARKLING AMULET"
,"WAR HAMMER"
```

☐ THE BANNOCHBURN LEGACY

As I pointed out at the start of this section of the book, when you write an adventure program, you are actually (if you do the job properly) constructing an alternative reality, with its own inner consistency and rules. In an adventure program which plays by the rules, an object placed in one room will stay there until you move it, the walls in the haunted house you're exploring will not move and shift around you every time you turn your back, and streams and rivers won't change their course each time you decide to cross them.

Our next program, and the final one in this section, THE BANNOCHBURN LEGACY, is far closer to the "standard" adventure programs we discussed in the introduction. In this program, all activities (except for the very beginning) take place within Bannochburn Castle. The castle contains a number of monsters, including "an angry warlock" and "a fire-breathing Fearbringer" who wander throughout the castle while you are playing the game, waiting for the chance to leap upon you, and tear you limb from limb. The castle also contains bottles of magic potion, chests which contain good and bad surprises, sheets of papyrus with magic spells written on them, and more besides. To tell you of everything you will meet would diminish the game somewhat.

You are unlikely to come across all the contents of the castle in a single play of the game. As well, the monsters have different powers each time you tackle the adventure, and the chests and the gilded safe, along with the rest of the magical contents, are in different locations. Although the monsters wander from room to room while you're playing, the contents do not appear and disappear at random. Once you've opened, for example, chest number two, you'll never see it again during that game. If you wound a monster in combat, and you come across him again later in the game, you'll find it is the very same (wounded) monster that you attacked earlier. Things like this help to aid the "reality" of the fictional universe.

You will not be given a map of the castle. Part of the pleasure of adventure gaming comes from actually working out how each part of the "adventure universe" is related to the other parts, and map-making is one of the skills you will probably enjoy developing. Castle

Bannochburn was mapped carefully before the program was written, to ensure that the rooms actually did match up in a coherent manner, to encourage you to map the castle as you explore it. Once you've got a reasonable map worked out, you may well want to test it by "wandering through" the castle from room to room.

The aim of the game is to find the Black Lagoon, which lies beneath the castle, but is entered from an ordinary-looking door in the castle. The location of the Black Lagoon can change from game to game, although it will not move once a game is underway. This ensures that your interest is maintained in the game, even after you first manage to map it.

You are endowed with three "attributes" when you play the game:

```
Magic - Strength - Wisdom
```

You play the whole game in terms of these attributes, choosing to battle each monster in the particular attribute in which you feel strongest, and in which you feel the particular monster is weakest.

Your attributes change and develop as the game progresses, gaining when you win a battle, and diminishing when you lose one.

When you first run the program, you'll see the following:

```
TIM, your attributes are:
   Magic: 1
Strength: 5
 Wisdom: 2

You are at the entrance to an
ancient, forbidding-looking
castle. You are standing on
the north side of the castle,
and as you look south, towards
the tumbling structure, you
notice the entrance portal
is open and unguarded.

What do you want to do now? S
```

The final question "What do you want to do now?" comes after most room descriptions in the game, and you need to give one of the following eight answers:

—N (go north)
—S (go south, the answer you must give to the first frame, shown above)
—E (go east)
—W (go west)
—F (fight—this is one of the two possible answers you can give when confronted by a monster)
—FL (flee—this is the other answer, and it is not always accepted; "No, you must stand and fight" you'll be told)
—Q (quit—this is used if you wish to end a game before the end)

The only answer you'll need is "Y" or "N" to answer questions like "Do you want to open the chest?"

This program is largely self-running, and takes care of all manner of the tasks which a Dungeon-master looks after in a role-playing game with other people.

One of these tasks is the running of the battles, or melees, which occur during the game. All fights are resolved according to the relative strength of the protagonists in the battle, and on the result of a throw of a die which is weighted to favor the stronger of the two squaring up to fight. You should therefore always select the attribute in which you outrank the monster, to increase your chances of winning that particular fight.

The point of the game is to get out of the Black Lagoon alive. In the final fight, against the Guardian of the Black Lagoon, you must have three fights, one with each attribute, and you must finish this three-part fight with a total of at least 10 attribute points. The money you collect within the castle can be used, just before the final fights, to buy additional attribute points.

To tell you much more would detract too much from your process of discovery when you play the game. All I need to do is assure you that the castle layout is mappable and coherent, and it is worth the trouble to try and work out the layout of the castle. Note that this program occupies more than 16K, so the PRINT statements may need shortening to get it into your system, making sure you also leave working space as well as allowing for the length of the listing.

The story of Bannochburn Castle is simple, but tragic. In the famed War of the Clans which ravaged northern Scotland in the closing years of the 15th Century, the Laird of Bannochburn engaged the services of Wee Sporran McMerlin, a sorcerer originally in the employ of King James in the Edinburgh Court. When the bloodthirsty McKinna Clan joined forces with the equally intemperate McClaren hordes, and together attacked Bannochburn, the Laird implored McMerlin to envoke a spell to protect the castle forever.

Unfortunately, Wee Sporran's intelligence was not as good as his magic, and instead of conjuring up some spells to look after the inhabitants, he simply conjured up a storm to protect the castle. The Laird and his retainers were slaughtered, but the castle remained intact. It survived right to this day, and your task now is to explore it, and try and seek out its secrets and gold, and to slay the Guardian of the Black Lagoon so the current Bannochburn Clan (now living above a dry cleaner's in Glasgow) can regain their rightful inheritance. You feel—possibly rightly—that they'll be pretty grateful to you if you manage to slay the Guardian, and thus rid the castle of the spooky inhabitants Wee Sporran placed within the walls so many years ago to protect it.

Note that once you enter the castle, there is no way out but through. You cannot leave again by the front entrance, so there is no room for second thoughts. All input must be in upper case, so you must ensure your computer is working in upper case before running the program, or all your precious input will be ignored.

Good luck, and may the Guardian fall to your mighty powers.

Here are a few samples of the program underway:

```
You've tripped in the dark.

Something awakes. Oh, you're face
to face with Gravelpit, the
Kneecrusher, who has magic of 1
strength of 4 and wisdom
of 1

What do you want to do now? F

Which characteristic will you fight with?
Your magic is 1 , strength is 5
and your wisdom is 2
? S
The fight table for this melee reads  1

The melee carries a cost/reward of 7

You attack first, and the
battle is joined...

Rip
                    Tear!
```

The Kneecrusher defeated you

After that fight, your
attributes are:
    Magic: 1
Strength: 0
& Wisdom: 2

And those of the Kneecrusher are:
    Magic: 1
Strength: 11
& Wisdom: 1

TIM, your attributes are:
    Magic: 3
Strength: 15
  Wisdom: 2

This is the most magnificent
room in the castle, the Great
Hall, with a massive hammerbeam
roof. You can leave it by the
double doors to the north or by
those to the east behind which
you can hear music playing.
Through the windows in the west
wall, you can see the Contoured
Garden, and beyond that, through
windows of a room hung with
many, many fine paintings

In front of you is a chest
labelled with a large # 1

Will you open it?

A goblin leaps out, stabbing you!

And this is the complete listing (all 16K of it):

```
10 REM The Bannochburn Legacy
20 REM  All inputs must be in upper case
30 GOSUB 4480
40 CLS
50 IF M(7) = 0 AND S(7) = 0 AND W(7) = 0 THE
N PRINT "The adventure has ended.":PRINT"You
 have exhausted all your powers.":PRINT:PRIN
T "You fought bravely and well":PRINT"but co
uld not endure.":PRINT:PRINT "Farewell...":E
ND
60 PRINT N$", your attributes are:"
70 IF M(7) > 0 THEN PRINT "   Magic:"M(7)
80 IF S(7) > 0 THEN PRINT "Strength:"S(7)
90 IF W(7) > 0 THEN PRINT "  Wisdom:"W(7)
100 IF MONEY > 0 THEN PRINT "Wealth: $"MONEY
110 GOSUB 4990:REM Pause
120 GOSUB 3420:REM Room
130 M = 0:IF Z>1 THEN IF RND>.5 THEN GOSUB 2
740
140 GOSUB 4990
150 GOSUB 1900
160 GOSUB 4990
170 GOTO 40
180 REM ***************************
190 REM Melee resolution
200 ROLL = INT(RND*6) + 1
210 VICTORY = 0
220 IF (DIFF < 0 AND ROLL > ABS(DIFF)) OR (D
IFF > 0 AND ROLL <=DIFF) OR (DIFF = 0 AND RO
LL<4) THEN VICTORY = 1
230 GOSUB 4990
240 RETURN
250 REM ******************
260 REM Monster subroutine
270 IF Q = 0 THEN RETURN
280 ON Q GOSUB 310,320,330,340,350
290 GOSUB 4990
300 RETURN
310 PRINT "There is an angry warlock in":PRI
NT "the room. He has a magic":PRINT "rating
of"M(1):PRINT "His strength is"S(1)"and":PRI
NT"his wisdom is"W(1):RETURN
```

```
320 PRINT "The room contains a fire-":PRINT
"breathing Fearbringer. His":PRINT "wisdom i
s"W(2)"while he":PRINT "has a strength ratin
g of"S(2):PRINT "and his magic skill":PRINT
"is"M(2):RETURN
330 PRINT "Horrors! You've stumbled in on":P
RINT "the hiding place of an awful":PRINT "S
oulthreat. You can see at a":PRINT "glance h
is strength is"S(3):PRINT "his magic ability
 rates"M(3):PRINT "and his wisdom is"W(3):RE
TURN
340 PRINT "You've tripped in the dark.":GOSU
B 4990:PRINT "Something awakes. Oh, you're f
ace":PRINT "to face with Gravelpit, the":PRI
NT "Kneecrusher, who has magic of"M(4):PRINT
 "strength of"S(4)"and wisdom":PRINT "of"W(4
):RETURN
350 PRINT "This room holds the dreaded":PRIN
T "enemy of all who enter the":PRINT "castle
, Wolvling of Wolf Glass":PRINT "with streng
th of"S(5)" plus":PRINT "wisdom of"W(5)"and"
:PRINT "magic of"M(5):RETURN
360 REM *********************
370 REM End of Game
380 PRINT "You have stumbled on to the"
390 PRINT "marshy mud surrounding the"
400 PRINT "Black Lagoon underneath the"
410 PRINT "castle.  To escape from the"
420 PRINT "castle you must fight The"
430 PRINT "Guardian of the Black Lagoon."
440 PRINT
450 PRINT "The fight must involve all"
460 PRINT "attributes...and you'll need"
470 PRINT "a total of 10 to escape..."
480 GOSUB 4990:GOSUB 4990
490 IF MONEY > 0 THEN PRINT "You have $"MONE
Y"worth of gold"
500 GOSUB 4990
510 PRINT:PRINT "The Guardian's attributes:"

520 PRINT "   Magic:"M(6)
530 PRINT "Strength:"S(6)
540 PRINT "  Wisdom:"W(6)
550 PRINT:PRINT "Your attributes are:"
```

```
560 PRINT "   Magic:"M(7)
570 PRINT "Strength:"S(7)
580 PRINT "  Wisdom:"W(7)
590 GOSUB 4990:GOSUB 4990
600 IF MONEY < 100 THEN 790
610 PRINT:PRINT "You can buy attribute point
s"
620 PRINT "for $100 each..."
630 PRINT "If you want to buy any, enter"
640 PRINT "the initial of the attribute"
650 PRINT "followed by the number of"
660 PRINT "of that attribute you want."
670 PRINT "Enter 'N' when you've got"
680 PRINT "all the attributes you want"
690 INPUT "Attribute (M, S or W)";E$
700 IF E$ = "N" THEN 790
710 INPUT "Amount";AM
720 IF MONEY - AM < 1 OR AM < 100 THEN 710
730 MONEY = MONEY - AM
740 IF E$ = "M" THEN M(7) = M(7) + INT(AM/10
0)
750 IF E$ = "S" THEN S(7) = S(7) + INT(AM/10
0)
760 IF E$ = "W" THEN W(7) = W(7) + INT(AM/10
0)
770 PRINT "Magic:"M(7)"Strength:"S(7)
780 IF MONEY > 99 THEN 690
790 CLS
800 PRINT "Now for the Ultimate Test..."
810 GOSUB 4990
820 PRINT "Press RETURN when you're"
830 INPUT "brave enough to fight",E$
840 GOSUB 4990:CLS
850 PRINT:PRINT "First, magic..."
860 PRINT:PRINT "You:"M(7)"Guardian"M(6)
870 DIFF = ABS(M(7) - M(6))
880 PRINT:PRINT "The difference is"DIFF
890 IF M(7) > M(6) THEN PRINT "in your favou
r"
900 IF M(6) > M(7) THEN PRINT "and the Guard
ian has the edge"
910 GOSUB 4990
920 K = M(6) + M(7)
930 COST = INT(RND*K) + 1
```

```
940  PRINT:PRINT "This round carries a penalt
y"
950  PRINT "of"COST"attribute points":GOSUB 4
990
960  GOSUB 2600
970  DIFF = M(7) - M(6)
980  IF DIFF > 5 THEN DIFF = DIFF - 6:GOTO 98
0
990  IF DIFF < - 5 THEN DIFF = DIFF + 6:GOTO
990
1000 GOSUB 190
1010 IF VICTORY = 1 THEN M(7) = M(7) + COST:
PRINT "And you've won...and so"
1020 IF VICTORY = 0 THEN M(7) = M(7) - COST:
PRINT "And you lost...and so"
1030 IF M(7) < 1 THEN M(7) = 0
1040 PRINT "now have"M(7)"magic points..."
1050 GOSUB 4990
1060 PRINT "Press RETURN when you're ready"
1070 INPUT "to continue this epic struggle";
E$
1080 CLS
1090 PRINT "Now it's time for a match of"
1100 PRINT "strength, where your rating"
1110 PRINT "is"S(7)"and the Guardian's"
1120 PRINT "strength rating is"S(6)
1130 DIFF = ABS(S(7) - S(6))
1140 PRINT:PRINT "The difference is"DIFF
1150 IF S(6) > S(7) THEN PRINT "in the Guard
ian's favour"
1160 IF S(7) > S(6) THEN PRINT "in your favo
ur, "N$
1170 GOSUB 4990
1180 K = S(6) + S(7)
1190 COST = INT(RND*K) + 1
1200 PRINT:PRINT "This round carries a penal
ty"
1210 PRINT "of"COST"attribute points":GOSUB
4990
1220 DIFF = S(7) - S(6)
1230 GOSUB 2600
1240 IF DIFF > 5 THEN DIFF = DIFF - 6:GOTO 1
240
1250 IF DIFF < - 5 THEN DIFF = DIFF + 6:GOTO
```

```
1250
1260 GOSUB 190
1270 IF VICTORY = 1 THEN S(7) = S(7) + COST:
PRINT "You're the victor, and so"
1280 IF VICTORY = 0 THEN S(7) = S(7) - COST:
PRINT "You're the loser, and so"
1290 IF S(7) < 0 THEN S(7) = 0
1300 PRINT "you now have"S(7)"strength point
s"
1310 GOSUB 4990
1320 PRINT:PRINT "Press the RETURN key when"
1330 PRINT "you have stopped trembling"
1340 PRINT "enough to face the third, and"
1350 INPUT "final challenge..";E$
1360 GOSUB 4990
1370 CLS
1380 PRINT "Now it's time for a match of"
1390 PRINT "wisdom, where your rating"
1400 PRINT "is"W(7)"and the Guardian's"
1410 PRINT "wisdom rating is"W(6)
1420 DIFF = ABS(W(7) - W(6))
1430 PRINT:PRINT "The difference is"DIFF
1440 IF W(6) > W(7) THEN PRINT "in the Guard
ian's favour"
1450 IF W(7) > W(6) THEN PRINT "in your favo
ur, "N$
1460 GOSUB 4990
1470 K = W(6) + W(7)
1480 COST = INT(RND*K) + 1
1490 PRINT "Now, this final challenge"
1500 PRINT "carries a huge penalty"
1510 PRINT "of"COST"attribute points":GOSUB
4990
1520 DIFF = W(7) - W(6)
1530 IF DIFF > 5 THEN DIFF = DIFF - 6:GOTO 1
530
1540 IF DIFF < - 5 THEN DIFF = DIFF + 6:GOTO
 1540
1550 GOSUB 190
1560 GOSUB 2600
1570 IF VICTORY = 1  THEN W(7) = W(7) + COST
:PRINT "And you defeated the Guardian!"
1580 IF VICTORY = 0 THEN W(7) = W(7) - COST:
PRINT "But the Guardian got the":PRINT "bett
```

er of you, "N$"!!"
```
1590 IF W(7) < 0 THEN W(7) = 0
1600 GOSUB 4990
1610 CLS:PRINT:PRINT
1620 PRINT "And now, at the end of the"
1630 PRINT "final battle, your position"
1640 PRINT "is:    Magic..."M(7)
1650 PRINT "      Wisdom..."W(7)
1660 PRINT "    Strength..."S(7)
1670 SUM = M(7) + W(7) + S(7)
1680 PRINT:PRINT "Well, "N$", your"
1690 PRINT "attribute total is"SUM
1700 GOSUB 4990
1710 IF SUM < 10 THEN 1810
1720 PRINT "You needed at least 10 points"
1730 PRINT "to win the game, and you've"
1740 PRINT "done it, "N$"!":GOSUB 4990
1750 CLS:PRINT:PRINT:PRINT
1760 PRINT "You've succeeded, O hero of"
1770 PRINT "these dark and dangerous"
1780 PRINT "times. I hereby dub thee"
1790 PRINT "Sir "N$".... Arise..."
1800 END
1810 PRINT "Unfortunately, you did not"
1820 PRINT "end up with the 10 points"
1830 PRINT "you needed, so it is all over"
1840 PRINT:PRINT "You fail to escape the clu
tches"
1850 PRINT "of the Guardian....":GOSUB 4990
1860 PRINT "You fought valiantly, but will"
1870 PRINT "now be consumed......"
1880 GOSUB 4990:GOSUB 2600:GOSUB 2600:END
1890 REM ****************************
1900 REM Action
1910 D = 4:IF MID$(B$(Z),9,1)  = "0" OR MID$
(B$(Z),9,1) = " " THEN D = 1:IF RND >.8 AND
Z > 1 THEN GOSUB 2740:GOTO 1910
1920 PRINT "What do you want to do now";
1930 INPUT Z$:IF Z$ = "Q" THEN END
1940 IF Z$ = "" THEN CLS:Z$ = "#"
1950 IF D = 4 AND LEFT$(Z$,1) <> "F" THEN D
= 0:GOTO 2090
1960 IF LEFT$(Z$,1) = "F" THEN 2060
1970 IF Z$ = "N" AND LEFT$(B$(Z),2) = "00" T
```

```
HEN PRINT ,"No exit":GOTO 1920
1980 IF Z$ = "S" AND MID$(B$(Z),3,2) = "00"
THEN PRINT  "There is no door that way":GOTO
 1920
1990 IF Z$ = "E" AND MID$(B$(Z),5,2) = "00"
THEN PRINT "That is not possible":GOTO 1920
2000 IF Z$ = "W" AND MID$(B$(Z),7,2) = "00"
THEN PRINT "You can't walk through walls!":G
OTO 1920
2010 IF Z$ = "N" THEN Z = VAL(LEFT$(B$(Z),2)
):RETURN
2020 IF Z$ = "S" THEN Z = VAL(MID$(B$(Z),3,2
)):RETURN
2030 IF Z$ = "E" THEN Z = VAL(MID$(B$(Z),5,2
)):RETURN
2040 IF Z$ = "W" THEN Z = VAL(MID$(B$(Z),7,2
)):RETURN
2050 IF LEFT$(Z$,1) <> "F" THEN RETURN
2060 IF RIGHT$(B$(Z),1) = "0" THEN PRINT "T
here is nothing to fight against":GOTO 1920
2070 IF Z$ = "FL" THEN D = INT(RND*2)
2080 IF D = 1 THEN PRINT "Which direction?":
GOTO 1930
2090 IF D = 0 THEN PRINT "No!! You must stan
d and fight"
2100 PRINT:PRINT "Which characteristic will
you fight with?"
2110 PRINT "Your magic is"M(7)", strength is
"S(7):PRINT "and your wisdom is"W(7)
2120 INPUT Z$:IF Z$ <> "M" AND Z$ <> "S" AND
 Z$ <> "W" THEN 2120
2130 IF Z$ = "M" THEN HUM = M(7):MON = M(Q)
2140 IF Z$ = "S" THEN HUM = S(7):MON = S(Q)
2150 IF Z$ = "W" THEN HUM = W(7):MON = W(Q)
2160 DIFF = HUM - MON
2170 IF DIFF > 5 THEN DIFF = DIFF - 6:GOTO 2
170
2180 IF DIFF < - 5 THEN DIFF = DIFF + 6:GOTO
 2180
2190 PRINT "The fight table for this melee r
eads "DIFF
2200 COST = ABS(DIFF) + INT(RND*6) + 1
2210 GOSUB 4990
2220 PRINT "The melee carries a cost/reward
```

```
of"COST
2230 FI = INT(RND*2):GOSUB 4990
2240 IF FI = 0 THEN PRINT "The monster attac
ks and the":PRINT "fight is underway"
2250 IF FI = 1 THEN PRINT "You attack first,
 and the":PRINT "battle is joined..."
2260 GOSUB 2600
2270 ROLL = INT(RND*6) + 1
2280 VICTORY = 0
2290 IF (DIFF<0 AND ROLL>ABS(DIFF)) OR (DIFF
>0 AND ROLL<=DIFF) OR (DIFF=0 AND ROLL<4) TH
EN VICTORY = 1
2300 IF VICTORY = 1 THEN GOSUB 2460
2310 IF VICTORY = 0 THEN GOSUB 2530
2320 GOSUB 4990
2330 PRINT "After that fight, your"
2340 PRINT "attributes are:"
2350 PRINT "   Magic:"M(7)
2360 PRINT "Strength:"S(7)
2370 PRINT "& Wisdom:"W(7)
2380 GOSUB 4990:PRINT
2390 PRINT "And those of the "M$(Q)" are:"
2400 PRINT "   Magic:"M(Q)
2410 PRINT "Strength:"S(Q)
2420 PRINT "& Wisdom:"W(Q)
2430 MID$(B$(Z),9,1) = "0"
2440 GOSUB 4990:GOSUB 4990:CLS
2450 GOTO 2740
2460 REM Human victory
2470 IF Q = 0 THEN D = 1
2480 PRINT:PRINT "You defeated the "M$(Q)
2490 IF Z$ = "M" THEN M(7) = M(7) + COST:M(Q
) = M(Q) - COST:IF M(Q) < 1 THEN M(Q) = 0
2500 IF Z$ = "W" THEN W(7) = W(7) + COST:W(Q
) = W(Q) - COST:IF W(Q) < 1 THEN W(Q) = 0
2510 IF Z$ = "S" THEN S(7) = S(7) + COST:S(Q
) = S(Q) - COST:IF S(Q) < 1 THEN S(Q) = 0
2520 RETURN
2530 REM Monster victory
2540 PRINT:PRINT "The "M$(Q)" defeated you"
2550 IF Z$ = "M" THEN M(Q) = M(Q) + COST:M(7
) = M(7) - COST:IF M(7) < 1 THEN M(7) = 0
2560 IF Z$ = "W" THEN W(Q) = W(Q) + COST:W(7
) = W(7) - COST:IF W(7) < 1 THEN W(7) = 0
```

```
2570 IF Z$ = "S" THEN S(Q) = S(Q) + COST:S(7
) = S(7) - COST:IF S(7) < 1 THEN S(7) = 0
2580 RETURN
2590 REM *****************
2600 REM Fight effects
2610 FOR J = 1 TO RND*10 + 2
2620 ON (INT(RND*6 +1)) GOSUB 2670,2680,2690
,2700,2710,2720
2630 FOR P = 1 TO 100 +RND*100:NEXT P
2640 PRINT:PRINT
2650 NEXT J
2660 CLS:RETURN
2670 PRINT "     Bash!!!!":FOR P = 1 TO 100:N
EXT P:RETURN
2680 PRINT ,"Aaaaaarghhh!":FOR P = 1 TO 20:N
EXT P:RETURN
2690 PRINT "Rip":FOR P = 1 TO 100:NEXT P:PRI
NT ,,"Tear!":FOR P = 1 TO 100:NEXT P:RETURN
2700 FOR E = 1 TO 20:PRINT "!!! ";:NEXT E:CL
S:RETURN
2710 RETURN
2720 FOR E = 1 TO 3:PRINT "!*&&*@!!    ";:NEX
T E:FOR P = 1 TO 20:NEXT P :RETURN
2730 REM **************************
2740 REM Contents
2750 K = 2 + INT(RND*8)
2760 IF K = Z THEN 2750
2770 IF RIGHT$(B$(Z),1) <> "0" THEN RETURN
2780 MID$(B$(K),9,1) = MID$(B$(Z),9,1)
2790 MID$(B$(Z),9,1) = "0"
2800 IF RND >.5 THEN RETURN
2810 PRINT
2820 CT = INT(RND*5) + 1
2830 ON CT GOSUB 2870,2980,3100,3210,2870:RE
M this double 7100 is correct
2840 GOSUB 4990
2850 RETURN
2860 REM ***********
2870 CHEST = CHEST + 1:IF CHEST = 5 THEN RET
URN
2880 PRINT "In front of you is a chest"
2890 PRINT "labelled with a large #"CHEST
2900 PRINT:PRINT "Will you open it?"
2910 GOSUB 3380
```

```
2920 IF Z$ = "N" THEN RETURN
2930 J = INT(RND*3):GOSUB 4990
2940 IF J = 0 THEN CASH = 100 + INT(RND*300)
:PRINT "It holds dragon's gold worth $"CASH:
MONEY = MONEY + CASH:GOSUB 4990:RETURN
2950 IF J = 1 THEN PRINT "A goblin leaps out
, stabbing you!":LOSS = INT(RND*6) + 1:MONEY
 = MONEY - INT(RND*200):IF MONEY < 1 THEN MO
NEY = 0:GOSUB 4990:RETURN
2960 IF J = 2 THEN PRINT "A strange smoke co
mes out":PRINT "making you sleepy and":PRINT
 "sapping your magic power":LOSS = INT(RND*8
) + 1:M(7) = M(7) - LOSS:IF M(7) < 1 THEN M(
7) = 0:GOSUB 4990:RETURN
2970 REM ******************
2980 IF POTION = 1 THEN 2820
2990 POTION = 1
3000 PRINT "You see a small bottle engraved"

3010 PRINT "with curious, twisted letters...
"
3020 PRINT:PRINT "Will you drink the potion
which"
3030 PRINT "you can see inside the bottle?"
3040 GOSUB 3380
3050 IF Z$ = "N" THEN RETURN
3060 GOSUB 4990
3070 IF RND >.6 THEN PRINT "It contained a p
otion to":PRINT "enhance your wisdom":W(7) =
 W(7) + INT(RND*6) + 1:GOSUB 4990:RETURN
3080 PRINT "It contained a potion which":PRI
NT "weakens you further....":GOSUB 4990:S(7
) = S(7) - (INT(RND*6) + 1):IF S(7) < 1 THEN
 S(7) = 0:GOSUB 4990:RETURN
3090 REM ******************
3100 IF SCROLL = 1 THEN RETURN
3110 SCROLL = 1
3120 PRINT "You see a papyrus scroll."
3130 PRINT:PRINT "Do you wish to try to read
 it?"
3140 GOSUB 3380:IF Z$ = "N" THEN RETURN
3150 IF RND >.5 THEN PRINT "You cannot under
stand":PRINT "the language...":GOSUB 4990:RE
TURN
```

```
3160 PRINT "It contains a magic spell. Do":P
RINT "you wish to read it?"
3170 GOSUB 3380:IF Z$ = "N" THEN RETURN
3180 IF RND >.5 THEN PRINT "It was a benefic
ent spell":GOSUB 4990:M(7) = M(7) + INT(RND*
6) + 1:RETURN
3190 PRINT "It was an evil spell":GOSUB 4990
:M(7) = 0:S(7) = INT(S(7)/2): RETURN
3200 REM ******************
3210 IF SAFE = 1 THEN 2820
3220 SAFE = 1
3230 PRINT "On the wall is a small, gilded":
PRINT "safe, and in front of":PRINT "it is a
 key..."
3240 PRINT "Do you want to open the safe?"
3250 GOSUB 3380
3260 IF Z$ = "N" THEN RETURN
3270 IF RND > .3 THEN 3330
3280 GOSUB 4990:PRINT "A shrieking harpy fli
es out":PRINT "and sinks its teeth into":PRI
NT "your throat!"
3290 GOSUB 4990
3300 PRINT "You grapple with it, and...":GOS
UB 4990:PRINT "...finally wring its neck"
3310 S(7) = S(7) - INT(RND*6) + 1:IF S(7) <
1 THEN S(7) = 0
3320 GOSUB 4990:RETURN
3330 PRINT "A choir of angelic voices is":PR
INT "heard.....":GOSUB 4990
3340 PRINT:PRINT "You are healed and refresh
ed..."
3350 M(7) = M(7) + 2:S(7) = S(7) + 2:W(7) =
W(7) + 2
3360 GOSUB 4990
3370 RETURN
3380 Z$ = INKEY$
3390 IF Z$ <> "N" AND Z$ <> "Y" THEN 3380
3400 PRINT:RETURN
3410 REM ******************
3420 REM Room descriptions
3430 ON Z GOSUB 3480,3570,3630,3680,3770,385
0,3950,4080,4210,4270,4350,4440
3440 Q = 0:IF RND > .81 AND Z > 1 THEN Q = I
NT(RND*6):MID$(B$(Z),9,1) = MID$(STR$(Q),2,1
```

```
):GOTO 260
3450 E$ = MID$(B$(Z),9,1):IF E$ > "0" AND E$
     < "6" THEN Q = VAL(E$)
3460 IF Q > 0 THEN GOSUB 260
3470 RETURN
3480 PRINT "You are at the entrance to an"
3490 PRINT "ancient, forbidding-looking"
3500 PRINT "castle. You are standing on"
3510 PRINT "the north side of the castle,"
3520 PRINT "and as you look south, towards"
3530 PRINT "the tumbling structure, you"
3540 PRINT "notice the entrance portal"
3550 PRINT "is open and unguarded."
3560 RETURN
3570 PRINT "You are in the entrance hall,"
3580 PRINT "which is hung with rich"
3590 PRINT "fabrics. Doors lead to the"
3600 PRINT "east and the south, and there"
3610 PRINT "is an open portal to the west"
3620 RETURN
3630 PRINT "This is only a store room."
3640 PRINT "There is a single exit, back"
3650 PRINT "the way you came in,"
3660 PRINT "to the west"
3670 RETURN
3680 PRINT "This small room, which"
3690 PRINT "features an ornate sculpture"
3700 PRINT "of the moon goddess on a"
3710 PRINT "pedestal in the north-east"
3720 PRINT "corner, is the Royal"
3730 PRINT "Presence Chamber. Doors lead"
3740 PRINT "to the south, the west and"
3750 PRINT "to the east..."
3760 RETURN
3770 PRINT "The Hall of Plots, a"
3780 PRINT "wooden-pannelled room"
3790 PRINT "redolent with whispers and"
3800 PRINT "rumours, with exits to the east"
3810 PRINT "and to the south from which"
3820 PRINT "comes the smell of sulphur and"
3830 PRINT "a weird chanting..."
3840 RETURN
3850 PRINT "You have entered the Wizard's"
3860 PRINT "Den, with a cauldron bubbling"
```

```
3870 PRINT "over a fire with green flames"
3880 PRINT "in the south-west corner."
3890 PRINT "This room reeks of burning"
3900 PRINT "sulphur, and the echo of"
3910 PRINT "ancient spells. You can leave"
3920 PRINT "to the north, the south, or"
3930 PRINT "to the east"
3940 RETURN
3950 PRINT "You find yourself in a place"
3960 PRINT "which seems quiet and peaceful."

3970 PRINT "This is the castle's Picture"
3980 PRINT "Gallery, with a large painting"
3990 PRINT "of the Legendary Guardian of"
4000 PRINT "the Black Lagoon to the left of"

4010 PRINT "the window in the east wall. Thr
ough"
4020 PRINT "the  window you can see the mull
ioned"
4030 PRINT "windows of the Great Hall across
 the"
4040 PRINT "Contoured Garden.  Exits from th
e"
4050 PRINT "Gallery  are to the north and"
4060 PRINT "to the east....."
4070 RETURN
4080  PRINT "This is the most magnificent"
4090 PRINT "room in the castle, the Great"
4100 PRINT "Hall, with a massive hammerbeam"

4110 PRINT "roof. You can leave it by the"
4120 PRINT "double doors to the north or by"

4130 PRINT "those to the east behind which"
4140 PRINT "you can hear music playing."
4150 PRINT "Through the windows in the west"
4160 PRINT "wall, you can see the Contoured"

4170 PRINT "Garden, and beyond that, through
"
4180 PRINT "windows of a room hung with"
4190 PRINT "many, many fine paintings"
4200 RETURN
```

```
4210 PRINT "Sounds of a string quartet"
4220 PRINT "fill this room, the Musicians'"
4230 PRINT "Chamber. You can leave by"
4240 PRINT "doors to the west or by one"
4250 PRINT "to the south..."
4260 RETURN
4270 PRINT "You are now in the Sanctuary"
4280 PRINT "of Silence, a room whose"
4290 PRINT "calmness may be a deception."
4300 PRINT "The room is damp and cold. An"
4310 PRINT "exit leaves the room to the"
4320 PRINT "north ";
4330 IF MID$(B$(10),3,2) = "12" THEN PRINT "
and one leaves to the south"
4340 PRINT:RETURN
4350 PRINT "This must be the Vestibule"
4360 PRINT "of Sighs, a dank and clammy"
4370 PRINT "room where legend says the"
4380 PRINT "Guardian of the Black Lagoon"
4390 PRINT "can sometimes be heard at"
4400 PRINT "night. There is a door to"
4410 PRINT "north ";
4420 IF MID$(B$(11),3,2) = "12" THEN PRINT "
and one leaves to the south"
4430 PRINT:RETURN
4440 GOTO 370
4450 IF MID$(B$(Z),9,1) <> "0" THEN Q = VAL(
MID$(B$(Z),9,1):GOSUB 260
4460 RETURN
4470 REM ********************
4480 REM Initialise
4490 RANDOMIZE VAL(RIGHT$(TIME$,2))
4500 Z = 1
4510 MONEY = 0
4520 CHEST = 0
4530 POTION = 0
4540 SCROLL = 0
4550 SAFE = 0
4560 DIM B$(12),M$(6),M(7)
4570 CLS:PRINT:PRINT
4580 INPUT "Please enter your first name";N$
4590 CLS:PRINT "Hi there, ";N$
4600 PRINT "Please stand by..."
4610 REM Fill rooms
```

```
4620 FOR T = 1 TO 12
4630 READ B$(T)
4640 L = RND
4650 Q$ = STR$(INT(RND*5) + 1)
4660 IF T > 1 AND T < 11 AND L < .63 THEN B$
(T) = B$(T) + RIGHT$(Q$,1)
4670 IF T > 10 OR L >= .63 THEN B$(T) = B$(T
) + "0"
4680 NEXT T
4690 L = RND
4700 IF L < .5 THEN B$(11) = "091200000"
4710 IF L >= .5 THEN B$(10) = "061200000"
4720 REM Create monsters
4730 FOR T = 1 TO 6
4740 READ M$(T)
4750 S(T) = INT(RND*6) + 1
4760 M(T) = INT(RND*6) + 1
4770 W(T) = INT(RND*6) + 1
4780 NEXT T
4790 REM Human characteristics
4800 S(7) = INT(RND*6) + 1
4810 M(7) = INT(RND*6) + 1
4820 W(7) = INT(RND*6) + 1
4830 REM Room data
4840 DATA "000200000"
4850 DATA "00080304"
4860 DATA "00000002"
4870 DATA "00070205"
4880 DATA "00060400"
4890 DATA "05100700"
4900 DATA "04000600"
4910 DATA "02000900"
4920 DATA "00110008"
4930 DATA "06000000"
4940 DATA "09000000"
4950 DATA "00000000"
4960 REM Monster data
4970 DATA "Warlock","Fearbringer","Soulthrea
t","Kneecrusher","Wolvling","Guardian"
4980 REM *********************
4990 REM Pause routine
5000 FOR P = 1 TO 1000:NEXT P
5010 PRINT
5020 RETURN
```

Simulations

Simulations are ways of producing a counterfeit reality. In contrast to adventure, where the reality created via the computer is often magical and dream-like, the worlds accessed through computer simulations are generally more down to earth.

In a simulation, the computer manipulates variables in accordance with formulae you've specified, keeping tabs on the unfolding of the situation you've generated, and taking the place of the environment in terms of reacting to your input.

Simulations attempt to replicate life. However, because reality is notoriously hard to pin down and limit, we need to do some pretty drastic simplification before we can produce a workable simulation.

Despite this simplification—as you'll soon see—a well-written simulation can imitate life to an uncanny extent. Cause and effect are linked as accurately as you can devise formulae for them. The random number generator can take the place of such things as changes in the weather, in population numbers, in the behavior of molecules in a gas or the way a colored ink is dispersed through a clear liquid.

In this section of the book we have four simulations. One of them—MISTRESS OF XENOPHOBIA—is simple to the point of absurdity, but it is great fun to play as you tinker with the fate of an entire planet. The other three—RURAL PURSUITS (where you run a farm with extremely fickle works), CHAIRMAN OF THE BOARD (in which a factory, which can produce any one of a range of products including pith helmets and skyhooks, is under your command), and AVALANCHE (which puts the lives of the hapless inhabitants of an Alpine village in your care)—are a little more serious. The formulae employed in them produce results a little closer to "real life." Despite the seriousness of the last three mentioned, they are still great fun to play, as you'll see when you get them up and running on your micro.

If you want to know more about writing simulations, the booklet *Designing Classroom Simulations* by Glenn Pate and Hugh Parker, Jr., will be of help. As well, *Creative Computing* magazine has printed two articles which are very valuable. These are "How to Write a

Computer Simulation" by the magazine's erstwhile editor, David Ahl, which appeared in the Jan./Feb., 1978 issue of the magazine (and is the text of a talk David presented at the Conference on Computers in the Undergraduate Curricula in Pullman, Washington, in June 1974), and "Strategies for Successful Simulation" by Bruno B. Wolff, Jr., which was in the August 1981 issue. It is worth checking your library for these back issues, as you'll learn a lot of value by reading them. Of particular interest in the Wolff article is a set of four equations which link cause and effect and can easily be adapted for a simulation you write.

☐ MISTRESS OF XENOPHOBIA

We'll start our exploration of simulations with the silliest one of the lot, MISTRESS OF XENOPHOBIA, which is based on a program written by Alastair Gourlay, a talented programmer who lives in Glasgow.

There's no need to explain MISTRESS, as the program gives you all the prompts you could need. Here's part of one run:

```
Mistress of Xenophobia, a report for
you from the Office of Information
regarding the state of your planet
in this year of Grace, 1995


The planet's population is 440

The grovelling peasants could work
some 119 acres this year...

Your treasury holds gold, gems
and coins worth $ 1049

Time to issue a decree...

How much land is to be farmed
this year? 27
_____

The grovelling peasants could work
some 268 acres this year...

Your treasury holds gold, gems
and coins worth $ 2204

Time to issue a decree...

How much land is to be farmed
this year? 24
```

And how much will you spend
on food for the peasants? 24

Oh dear!! There's not
enough food for everyone...

Horrors, your Xenoness
There's been a rebellion!!!
The peasants are revolting
(I had to get that line in!)

Your treasury holds gold, gems
and coins worth $ 890

Time to issue a decree...

How much land is to be farmed
this year? 100

Well, Xeno, that's a fine
mess you've got yourself, and
our little planet into.

The Treasury is bankrupt!!

Guess who blew it?????????

If you'd like another shot
ruling, then just press 'Y' or
press 'N' to end this farce..

And this is the listing:

```
10 REM Mistress of Xenophobia
20 GOSUB 700:REM Initialise
30 REM **************************
40 FOR Y = 1 TO 20
50 CLS
60 PRINT:PRINT:PRINT
```

```
70 PRINT "Mistress of Xenophobia, a repo
rt for"
80 PRINT "you from the Office of Informa
tion"
90 PRINT "regarding the state of your pl
anet"
100 PRINT "in this year of Grace,"1994 +
 Y
110 PRINT:PRINT
120 PRINT "The planet's population is"IN
T(P)
130 GOSUB 880
140 PRINT "The grovelling peasants could
 work"
150 PRINT "some"L"acres this year..."
160 GOSUB 880
170 PRINT "Your treasury holds gold, gem
s"
180 PRINT "and coins worth $"INT(U)
190 GOSUB 880
200 PRINT "Time to issue a decree..."
210 PRINT:PRINT "How much land is to be
farmed"
220 INPUT "this year";W
230 U = U - W*10
240 IF U < 1 THEN 780
250 L = L + W
260 GOSUB 880
270 PRINT:PRINT "And how much will you s
pend"
280 INPUT "on food for the peasants";W
290 U = U - W*10
300 IF U < 1 THEN 780
310 R = INT(RND*10) + 1
320 GOSUB 880
330 IF P - W*R*5 > P/4 THEN PRINT "Oh de
ar!! There's not":PRINT "enough food for
 everyone...":GOSUB 580
340 P = P + RND*(W*R*5 - P)
350 IF P > 149 THEN 410
360 GOSUB 880
370 PRINT "The population of Xenophobia
is"
380 PRINT "now down to"P"and that"
```

```
390 PRINT "just ain't enough, Your Xeno"

400 GOTO 480
410 U = U + INT(P*L)/93
420 NEXT Y
430 PRINT:PRINT:PRINT "Well, Your Xenoph
obic, that's"
440 PRINT "the end of your 20 year domin
ation of"
450 PRINT "our little planet.  You  mana
ged"
460 PRINT "to accumulate some $"U"which"

470 PRINT "I guess ain't too bad..."
480 GOSUB 880
490 PRINT:PRINT "If you'd like another s
hot"
500 PRINT "ruling, then just press 'Y' o
r"
510 PRINT "press 'N' to end this farce..
"
520 A$ = INKEY$
530 IF A$ <> "N" AND A$ <> "n" AND A$ <>
 "Y" AND A$ <> "y" THEN 520
540 IF A$ = "N" OR A$ = "n" THEN PRINT:P
RINT "Your wish is my command":PRINT "oh
 Mistress of Xenophobia":END
550 RUN
560 END
570 REM *************************
580 PRINT:PRINT "Horrors, your Xenoness"

590 PRINT "There's been a rebellion!!!"
600 PRINT "The peasants are revolting"
610 PRINT "(I had to get that line in!)"

620 GOSUB 880
630 IF RND < .2 THEN PRINT "And your cop
s couldn't stop them":GOTO 480
640 PRINT "But your ruthless police have
"
650 PRINT "put a stop to all that nonsen
se"
660 GOSUB 880
```

```
670 RETURN
680 NEXT Y
690 REM *************************
700 REM Initialisation
710 RANDOMIZE VAL(RIGHT$(TIME$,2))
720 CLS
730 P = 200 + INT(RND*300)
740 U = 700 + INT(RND*500)
750 L = 70 + INT(RND*50)
760 RETURN
770 REM **********
780 REM Bankruptcy
790 PRINT:PRINT "Well, Xeno, that's a fi
ne"
800 PRINT "mess you've got yourself, and
"
810 PRINT "our little planet into."
820 GOSUB 880
830 PRINT:PRINT "The Treasury is bankrup
t!!"
840 GOSUB 880
850 PRINT :PRINT "Guess who blew it?????
????"
860 GOTO 490
870 REM *************************
880 REM Delay
890 FOR J = 1 TO 1500:NEXT J
900 PRINT
910 RETURN
```

☐ **RURAL PURSUITS**

If you've survived being MISTRESS OF XENOPHOBIA, you may be interested in something a little more earthy—running a farm. In RURAL PURSUITS, based loosely on a program written by Stephen Glen, also of Glasgow, you have a very difficult task, as you battle with an extremely touchy work-crew to bring home the bacon (or at least the wheat and barley).

Again the program is largely self-prompting, and working with it will teach you the best strategy for gaining a maximum return from your farm (and surviving for the requisite 20 years to win the game). However, a few hints will not go astray. Although you can save money by paying your workers extremely badly, you'll find they'll desert you in droves in the following year, and the return you get from your land is dictated, to some degree, by the number of people you have working on the land.

Another factor to keep in mind is that the three crops which you can plant have quite different returns, so it is in your interest to work out which is the most profitable crop, and concentrate on that.

Do not be dismayed if you foul the process up the first few times you run the program. You'll have to develop some real skills to keep your farm solvent, and it may take you several bad years to get the hang of it.

Here's part of the output of RURAL PURSUITS:

```
You have $ 7203 in year 1

You are employing 484
laborers, working for
you on 351 acres

Crops:-        0 corn
               0 barley
               0 wheat

It will be $ 10 in
general costs to work each
acre...and so the maximum
number of acres you can
work this year is 351
How much land do you want to harvest? 100
```

You have $ 6203 in year 1

How much will you pay each worker? 11.50

You have $ 637 in year 1

What proportion (out of ten) do
wish to concentrate on corn? 3

Of the remaining 7 out of 10,
how much wheat will you plant? 5

Crops:-   265 corn
                 33 barley
                 418 wheat

 716 tons were harvested

And your total return
was $ 2781

And here's the program so you can become a happy farmer:

```
10  REM Rural Pursuits
20  RANDOMIZE VAL(RIGHT$(TIME$,2))
30  YR = 1
40  MO = INT(RND*1000 + 7000)
50  LA = INT(RND*1000 + 100)
60  AC = INT(RND*200 + 300)
70  CS = INT(RND*5) + 8:CX = CS
80  BA = 0:WH = 0:CO = 0
90  GOSUB 170
100 GOSUB 290
110 IF YR = 10 THEN 750
120 IF MO < 1 THEN 790
130 IF LA < 1 THEN 820
140 YR = YR + 1
```

```
150 CS = CS + INT(12.5*CS/100):REM General
costs increase at 12.5% a year
160 GOTO 80
170 REM Update
180 GOSUB 870
190 PRINT "You have $"MO"in year"YR
200 GOSUB 880
210 PRINT "You are employing"LA
220 PRINT "laborers, working for"
230 PRINT "you on"AC"acres"
240 GOSUB 880
250 PRINT "Crops:-",CO"corn"
260 PRINT ,BA"barley"
270 PRINT ,WH"wheat"
280 RETURN
290 PRINT:PRINT "It will be $"CS"in"
300 PRINT "general costs to work each"
310 PRINT "acre...and so the maximum"
320 PRINT "number of acres you can"
330 PRINT "work this year is";
340 MAX = INT(MO/CS): IF MAX > AC THEN MAX
= AC
350 PRINT MAX
360 PRINT "How much land do you want to har
vest";
370 INPUT L
380 IF L > MAX THEN 370
390 MO = MO - L*CS
400 GOSUB 170
410 PRINT:PRINT "How much will you pay each
 worker";
420 INPUT W
430 IF W*LA > MO THEN 420
440 MO = MO - LA*W
450 GOSUB 170
460 P = 10
470 PRINT "What proportion (out of ten) do"

480 PRINT "wish to concentrate on corn";
490 INPUT CP
500 IF CP > P THEN 490
510 P = P - CP
520 PRINT:PRINT "Of the remaining"P"out of
10,"
```

```
530 PRINT "how much do you wheat will you p
lant";
540 INPUT WP
550 IF WP > P THEN 540
560 P = P - WP
570 GOSUB 870
580 PRINT "Stand by for a year..."
590 FOR Z = 1 TO 2000:NEXT Z
600 BA = INT(P*L*LA*W*3/100000 )
610 CO = INT(CP*L*LA*W*2.7/17000)
620 WH = INT(WP*L*LA*W*1.4/9300)
630 T = BA + CO + WH
640 GOSUB 170
650 PRINT:PRINT T"tons were harvested"
660 RT = INT((.5 + 8.7*BA + 5.94*CO + 2.2*W
H)*(CS - CX + 1))
670 IF BA=0 AND CO=0 AND WH=0 THEN RT = 0
680 FOR Z = 1 TO 2000:NEXT Z
690 PRINT:PRINT "And your total return"
700 PRINT "was $"RT
710 MO = MO + RT
720 LA = INT(LA - LA/(W + .01))
730 FOR Z = 1 TO 2000: NEXT Z
740 RETURN
750 GOSUB 870
760 PRINT "You have survived for 10 years"
770 PRINT "Congratulations!"
780 END
790 GOSUB 870
800 PRINT "You have gone broke!"
810 END
820 GOSUB 870
830 PRINT "You have no workers, and"
840 PRINT "have been forced to sell"
850 PRINT ,"your farm"
860 END
870 CLS
880 PRINT:PRINT
890 RETURN
```

☐ AVALANCHE

In this simulation, you are Mayor Glugenheimer, the leader of a Swiss alpine village which lies directly in the path of avalanches which launch themselves at the village with monotonous regularity. The game, like the other three in the book, forces you to make decisions regarding the expenditure of strictly limited resources. On these decisions hang the fate of your village.

You are (you hope) in office for 20 years. Although it is more likely than not that the village will survive from year to year without suffering the ravages of an avalanche, the chances of an avalanche increase each year. The only resource under your control is money, which can be used to build shelters within which your villagers can huddle in comparative safety when an avalanche hits.

You have limited money (which is bearing a generous interest rate if it is not spent on shelter). The longer you hang on to the money, the more you will have to spend on avalanche shelters. However, the longer you wait without buying shelter, the more likely it is that an avalanche will occur, and many members of your village will be killed. You must therefore determine what proportion of your money you will keep on deposit, and what portion of it will be spent on shelter. If you have no shelter when an avalanche strikes, the village will be wiped out.

As you can see, you are bearing a considerable amount of responsibility. If an avalanche does strike, and the computer considers the loss of life totally unacceptable, the game will terminate with the following statement:

```
THE LOSS OF HUMAN LIFE WAS
CATASTROPHIC...YOU HAVE
BEEN FORCED TO STEP DOWN
FROM THE OFFICE OF MAYOR
```

Here are a few "years" from the program in action:

```
YEAR 1

THE CHANCE OF AN AVALANCHE IS 19 TO 1

THE VILLAGE HAS 2633 PEOPLE

THE VILLAGE TREASURY HOLDS $ 12914
```

HOW MUCH WILL YOU SPEND ON SHELTER? 12000

    YEAR 2

THE CHANCE OF AN AVALANCHE IS 18 TO 1

THE VILLAGE HAS 2764 PEOPLE

YOU HAVE 32400 SHELTER

THE VILLAGE TREASURY HOLDS $ 1005

HOW MUCH WILL YOU SPEND ON SHELTER? 834

THE CHANCE OF AN AVALANCHE IS 4 TO 1

THE VILLAGE HAS 5465 PEOPLE

YOU HAVE 35199 SHELTER

THE VILLAGE TREASURY HOLDS $ 278

HOW MUCH WILL YOU SPEND ON SHELTER? 21
** AVALANCHE **
** AVALANCHE **
 ** AVALANCHE **
              ** AVALANCHE **
              ** AVALANCHE **
             ** AVALANCHE **
             ** AVALANCHE **

 3526 PEOPLE ARE SAFE...

BUT 1939 PEOPLE WERE KILLED...

THERE ARE 31729 CUBIC YARDS OF SHELTER LEFT

```
YEAR 19

THE CHANCE OF AN AVALANCHE IS 1 TO 1

THE VILLAGE HAS 3581 PEOPLE

YOU HAVE 29236 SHELTER

THE VILLAGE TREASURY HOLDS $ 3

THERE ARE 2392 VILLAGERS DEAD

HOW MUCH WILL YOU SPEND ON SHELTER? 3
** AVALANCHE **


                   ** AVALANCHE **
                    ** AVALANCHE **
                    ** AVALANCHE **

  2924 PEOPLE ARE SAFE...

BUT 657 PEOPLE WERE KILLED...

THERE ARE 26320 CUBIC YARDS OF SHELTER LEFT
```

You can see that if an avalanche does strike, but not enough people are killed to force you out of office, it becomes a little easier to cope with future avalanches because you have less people who you must shelter. However, the villagers waste no time in adding to their numbers (there is little to do on winter nights except huddle under the bedclothes and listen for the warning rumble of an impending avalanche, so the gradual population increase is not hard to understand).

You'll be rewarded with a statement like the following if you survive 20 years in office:

```
WELL DONE, MAYOR GLUGENHEIMER

YOU MANAGED TO SURVIVE 20 YEARS
IN OFFICE, AND END YOUR TERM WITH:

  $ 0 IN THE TREASURY

  3070 PEOPLE SURVIVING
```

YOUR MAYORAL RATING IS 54202

Your final "mayoral rating" (see line 300) is related to the amount of money you still have left in the treasury, the number of surviving villagers, and shelter on hand. This total is offset by the number of people who have been killed in avalanche falls during your term of office.

```
10 REM AVALANCHE!
20 RANDOMIZE VAL(RIGHT$(TIME$,2))
30 M = INT(RND(1)*5000 + 9087)
40 P = INT(RND(1)*1000 + 2278)
50 S=0:D=0:N=0
60 FOR Y = 1 TO 20
70 CLS
80 IF Y = 20 THEN 240
90 PRINT TAB(4);"YEAR";Y
100 PRINT:PRINT "THE CHANCE OF AN AVALAN
CHE IS";20-Y;"TO 1"
110 PRINT:PRINT "THE VILLAGE HAS";P;"PEO
PLE"
120 IF S<>0 THEN PRINT:PRINT "YOU HAVE";
S;"SHELTER"
130 PRINT:PRINT "THE VILLAGE TREASURY HO
LDS $";M
140 IF D<>0 THEN PRINT:PRINT "THERE ARE"
;D;"VILLAGERS DEAD"
150 IF N<>0 THEN PRINT:PRINT "THERE HAVE
 BEEN";N;"AVALANCHES"
160 PRINT:INPUT "HOW MUCH WILL YOU SPEND
 ON SHELTER";A
170 IF M-A<0 OR S+A<0 THEN 160
180 M=M-A
190 S=S+INT(2.7*A)
200 M=M+INT(M/10 +.5)
210 IF INT(RND(1)*(20-Y))+1=1 THEN GOSUB
 320
220 P = INT(P+.05*P)
230 NEXT Y
240 PRINT:PRINT "WELL DONE, MAYOR GLUGEN
HEIMER"
```

```
250 PRINT:PRINT "YOU MANAGED TO SURVIVE
20 YEARS"
260 PRINT "IN OFFICE, AND END YOUR TERM
WITH:"
270 PRINT:PRINT TAB(4);"$";M;"IN THE TRE
ASURY"
280 PRINT:PRINT TAB(4);P;"PEOPLE SURVIVI
NG"
290 PRINT:PRINT TAB(4);S;"CUBIC YARDS OF
 SHELTER"
300 PRINT:PRINT "YOUR MAYORAL RATING IS"
;10*M+20*P+P+S - 12*D
310 END
320 REM *** AVALANCHE ***
330 FOR J = 1 TO 32
340 PRINT TAB(J/2);"** AVALANCHE **"
350 FOR E=1 TO 330 - 10*J:NEXT E
360 NEXT J
370 Q=INT(S/10 + .5)
380 PRINT:PRINT Q;"PEOPLE ARE SAFE..."
390 X=P-Q
400 IF X<1 THEN 500
410 PRINT:PRINT "BUT";X;"PEOPLE WERE KIL
LED..."
420 D=D+X
430 P=Q
440 S=S-INT(S/10 + .5)
450 PRINT:PRINT "THERE ARE";S;"CUBIC YAR
DS OF SHELTER LEFT"
460 FOR E=1 TO 3000:NEXT E
470 IF X>P THEN 490
480 RETURN
490 PRINT:PRINT
500 PRINT "THE LOSS OF HUMAN LIFE WAS"
510 PRINT "CATASTROPHIC...YOU HAVE"
520 PRINT "BEEN FORCED TO STEP DOWN"
530 PRINT "FROM THE OFFICE OF MAYOR"
540 END
```

☐ CHAIRMAN OF THE BOARD

Finally in this section we have our major simulation, **CHAIRMAN OF THE BOARD**.

Again the program is largely self-prompting. The aim of the game is to keep your factory running until you manage to make $10,000 (in total, combining the value of stock in hand plus your capital). You have to deal with recalcitrant unions (who won't always let you fire the people you wish to get rid of, and have a great appetite for pay raises which you cannot deny), with workers who will hardly ever meet the production targets you set, and raw material suppliers who enjoy putting their prices up as much as the unions enjoy slugging you for more pay.

You'll find, in contrast to the other two programs, which are only very vague approximations to "real life," that the life and health of your factory will become very important to you, and you'll certainly learn ways of manipulating resources for maximum return. Keep in mind that although you have great freedom in setting the retail price of your products, each rise in price will increase consumer resistance to purchasing those products.

Here are a few samples from a run of **CHAIRMAN OF THE BOARD**:

```
Shop floor report, sir,
    for week 1

Capital in hand is $ 520
Running costs are $ 119 a week

Your stores hold 414 kazoos
    worth $ 4968

They sell for $ 12  each
and cost $ 10 each to make

Your workforce is now
  10 strong, and you are
paying them $ 12 each, so
the wages bill this week is $ 120
```

147

Each person can make 10
kazoos a week, a total
output of 100
How many people do you
want to hire? 3

Your workforce is now
 13 strong, and you are
paying them $ 12 each, so
the wages bill this week is $ 156

Each person can make 10
kazoos a week, a total
output of 130
How many do you wish to produce? 130

You do not have enough money
How many do you wish to produce? 100

You do not have enough money
How many do you wish to produce? 70

You do not have enough money
How many do you wish to produce? 20

Yes sir...the target for week 1
is 20 kazoos

The number of kazoos
actually produced in week 1
was 19 ...

The total number of kazoos
sold is 340

The income from that
sale was $ 4080

A fire in your warehouse has
destroyed some stock. Please
stand by for a report on
the damage caused...

There were 33 kazoos
destroyed. They were
worth $ 396 retail

You have a chance to raise
    your price. Your
kazoos now sell for $ 12

What percentage increase would
you like to impose? 7

The kazoos now sell for $ 12.84

How many people do you
wish to fire? 7

The unions will allow
you to get rid of 3

The unions are demanding a
pay rise of 4 %

Pay per employee is now $ 12.48

You're bankrupt!!

Oh the shame of it!!

Still, you keep the business
going for 6 weeks

Enter 'Y' for another stint
as Chairman of the Board...
(or 'N' if you want to quit)

And now you can satisfy your corporate ambitions with this listing:

```
10 REM Chairman of the Board
20 GOSUB 1670: REM initialise
30 WE = WE + 1
40 GOSUB 930:REM report
50 GOSUB 1300:REM staff
60 GOSUB 930:REM report
70 GOSUB 1130:REM production
80 GOSUB 930:REM report
90 GOSUB 730:REM sales
100 GOSUB 140:REM problems
110 CA = CA - WA*WO - RC
120 GOTO 30
130 REM ********************
140 REM Problems
150 CLS
160 IF RND < .45 THEN 260
170 A = INT(RND*7) + 1
180 PRINT:PRINT:PRINT
190 PRINT "The unions are demanding a"
200 PRINT  "pay rise of"A"%"
210 WA = INT(100*(WA + WA*A/100))/100
220 GOSUB 1840
230 PRINT:PRINT "Pay per employee is now $
"WA
240 GOSUB 1840
250 CLS
260 IF RND < .81 THEN 410
270 PRINT:PRINT:PRINT
280 PRINT "A fire in your warehouse has"
290 PRINT "destroyed some stock.  Please"
300 PRINT "stand by for a report on"
310 PRINT "the damage caused..."
320 GOSUB 1840
330 A = INT(RND*ST/2) + 1
340 ST = ST - A
350 PRINT:PRINT "There were"A;A$
360 PRINT "destroyed. They were"
370 PRINT "worth $"A*SP"retail"
380 GOSUB 1840
390 PRINT "Stock in hand is"
400 PRINT "now"ST;A$
```

```
410 IF RND > .3 THEN 560
420 CLS
430 PRINT:PRINT:PRINT
440 PRINT "Your main supplier has announce
d"
450 PRINT "a dramatic price rise..."
460 GOSUB 1840
470 A = INT(RND*100*CO/7)/100
480 IF A < .01 THEN 470
490 PRINT:PRINT"The cost of making "A$
500 PRINT "has risen by $"A"each"
510 GOSUB 1840
520 CO = CO + A
530 PRINT:PRINT "It now costs $"CO
540 PRINT "to make each one..."
550 GOSUB 1840
560 IF RND < .65 AND MA < SP THEN RETURN
570 CLS
580 PRINT:PRINT:PRINT
590 PRINT "You have a chance to raise"
600 PRINT TAB(4);"your price.  Your"
610 PRINT A$;" now sell for $"SP
620 GOSUB 1840
630 PRINT
640 PRINT "What percentage increase would"

650 INPUT "you like to impose";A
660 RE = RE + A
670 SP = INT(100*(SP + A*SP/100))/100
680 GOSUB 1840
690 PRINT:PRINT "The "A$" now sell for $"S
P
700 GOSUB 1840
710 RETURN
720 REM ********************
730 REM Sales
740 PRINT:PRINT "Your total stock of"
750 PRINT A$" is"ST
760 GOSUB 1840
770 PRINT:PRINT "Please stand by for a"
780 PRINT "sales report..."
790 A = INT(RND*ST/(RE/1000)) + 1
800 IF A > ST THEN 790
810 CLS
```

```
820  PRINT:PRINT:PRINT
830  PRINT "The total number of "A$
840  PRINT "sold is"A
850  ST = ST - A
860  ZA = A*SP
870  PRINT:PRINT "The income from that"
880  PRINT "sale was $"ZA
890  CA = INT(A*SP*100)/100  + CA
900  GOSUB 1840
910  RETURN
920  REM ********************
930  REM Report to the Chairman
940  CLS
950  IF CA + ST < 1 THEN 1510:REM Bankruptc
y
960  IF CA + ST > 9999 THEN PRINT "You've m
ade $10,000 and":PRINT "can now retire..."
:GOSUB 1840:GOTO 1590
970  PRINT:PRINT "Shop floor report, sir,"
980  PRINT TAB(6);"for week"WE
990  PRINT:PRINT "Capital in hand is $"INT(
CA*100)/100
1000 PRINT "Running costs are $"RC"a week"

1010 PRINT:PRINT "Your stores hold"ST;A$
1020 PRINT TAB(6);"worth $"INT(ST*SP*100)/
100
1030 PRINT:PRINT "They sell for $"SP" each
"
1040 PRINT "and cost $"CO"each to make"
1050 PRINT:PRINT "Your workforce is now"
1060 PRINT WO"strong, and you are"
1070 PRINT "paying them $"WA"each, so"
1080 PRINT "the wages bill this week is $"
WA*WO
1090 PRINT:PRINT "Each person can make"PR
1100 PRINT A$" a week, a total"
1110 PRINT "output of"PR*WO
1120 RETURN
1130 INPUT "How many do you wish to produc
e";MA
1140 IF MA = 0 THEN RETURN
1150 PRINT
1160 IF MA*CO > CA THEN PRINT "You do not
```

```
have enough money":GOTO 1130
1170 IF MA > PR*WO THEN PRINT "You do not
have enough people":PRINT"in your workforc
e to make":PRINT TAB (6);"that many":GOTO
1130
1180 PRINT "Yes sir...the target for week"
WE
1190 PRINT "is"MA;A$
1200 MA = INT(MA - RND*MA/5)
1210 GOSUB 1840
1220 PRINT:PRINT "The number of "A$
1230 PRINT "actually produced in week"WE
1240 PRINT "was"MA"..."
1250 ST = ST + MA
1260 CA = CA - CO*MA
1270 GOSUB 1840
1280 RETURN
1290 REM ****************************
1300 REM Staff
1310 PRINT "How many people do you"
1320 INPUT "want to hire";A
1330 WO = WO + A
1340 PRINT:PRINT "The total workforce"
1350 PRINT "is now"WO"strong"
1360 GOSUB 1840
1370 IF A > 0 THEN RETURN
1380 GOSUB 930
1390 PRINT "How many people do you"
1400 INPUT "wish to fire";A
1410 IF A = 0 THEN 1480
1420 IF A > WO THEN 1390
1430 A = INT(RND*A + 1)
1440 GOSUB 1840
1450 PRINT:PRINT "The unions will allow"
1460 PRINT "you to get rid of"A
1470 WO = WO - A
1480 GOSUB 1840
1490 RETURN
1500 REM ****************************
1510 REM The Bottom Line!
1520 PRINT:PRINT "You're bankrupt!!"
1530 GOSUB 1840
1540 PRINT:PRINT "Oh the shame of it!!"
1550 GOSUB 1840
```

```basic
1560 PRINT:PRINT "Still, you keep the busi
ness"
1570 PRINT "going for"WE"weeks"
1580 GOSUB 1840
1590 PRINT "Enter 'Y' for another stint"
1600 PRINT "as Chairman of the Board..."
1610 PRINT "(or 'N' if you want to quit)"
1620 A$ = INKEY$
1630 IF A$ = "" THEN 1620
1640 IF A$ = "Y" OR A$ = "y" THEN RUN
1650 END
1660 REM *****************************
1670 REM Initialise
1680 RANDOMIZE VAL(RIGHT$(TIME$,2))
1690 FOR Z = 1 TO RND*8 + 1
1700 READ A$
1710 NEXT Z
1720 CA = 500 + INT(RND*500)
1730 ST = 100 + INT(RND*500)
1740 SP = 10 + INT(RND*5)
1750 CO = 7 + INT(RND*5)
1760 IF CO > SP THEN 1750
1770 WO = 7 + INT(RND*10)
1780 WA = 12 + INT(RND*SP)
1790 PR = 5 + INT(RND*6)
1800 RC = 100 + INT(RND*20)
1810 WE = 0
1820 RE = 1:REM RE is sales resistance fac
tor
1830 RETURN
1840 REM delay subroutine
1850 FOR Z = 1 TO 3000:NEXT Z:RETURN
1860 DATA "eponyms","bicycles","harmonicas
"
1870 DATA "kazoos","lecterns","moleskins"
1880 DATA "carpetbags","pith helmets","sky
 hooks"
1890 DATA "barbells"
```

Dice Games

Dice games—for high stakes, low stakes, or none—have proved popular throughout history. Whether the dice were made from stone or wood, or carved from the bones of a beast killed for food, whether they had four important sides or six, dice have proved a diversion for countless men throughout time.

The dice, physical means of demonstrating the waywardness of chance, have also found employment in foretelling the future, and like all oracles, probably bear some responsibility for changing the tide of history.

At Troy the Greeks played with dice, as did Mark Antony at Alexandria. Italy and France led medieval Europe in their love for dice, and devotion to the six-sided cubes has continued up to the present day. In this section of the book, we'll be investigating ways of using the random number generator of your computer to take the place of physical dice. However, you'll discover that the dice are no less compelling because they exist only within the software of your computer rather than in a more gross physical form.

Playing against the computer, instead of against another human being, changes the "feel" of dice games somewhat. Not having to pay up when you lose is one of the real advantages!

An enormous range of games is now played with dice, and they sport an intriguing variety of titles. Here are some names of common dice programs:

- Going to Boston
- Craps
- Fifty
- Crag
- Pig
- Chicago

157

- Twenty-Six
- Twenty-One
- Round the Clock
- Centennial
- Yankee Grab
- Help Your Neighbor
- Drop Dead
- Shut the Box
- Baseball
- Basketball
- Poker Dice
- Liar Dice

The dice games we'll be playing in this book are SNAKES' EYES, ONE-AND-TWENTY, SEVEN/ELEVEN, OVER'N' UNDER, NO SWEAT, CHEMIN DE COMPUTER, and MALIBU.

☐ CHEMIN DE COMPUTER

CHEMIN DE COMPUTER is based, as I'm sure you've realized, on Chemin de Fer. In this game, you and your computer take it in turns to roll five dice, adding the pips up as you go. You are aiming to get a higher total than the computer.

However, this game is not just a simple "add the pips" one. Any die which falls showing a five or a two must be thrown again, and your total is just the final digit of the answer (that is, a total of 27 is counted as 7, and a total of 13 is counted as 3).

There are three special totals—7 (a Natural), 8 (La Petite), and 9 (La Grande). The names are only bestowed when the relevant total is achieved on the first throw (i.e., the dice which came up with 5 or 2 have not been, and are not in this case, rethrown). You (and the computer) always stand on a 7, 8, or 9 thrown with the first toss of the five dice.

If you look at the program listing, you'll see that after the random number generator has been seeded in line 20, the screen cleared and the game counter (GAME) and variables for your score (HS) and that of the computer (CS) have been initialized to zero, the program goes to line 330, where the game proper begins.

As in many other programs in this book, there is a delay loop routine at the end of the listing which is called a number of times throughout a game to improve the speed with which the game advances, and to give you (in many cases) a chance to read on the screen what is going on before the program races on, clearing the screen, and leaving you quite unsure of exactly what has just happened. In this program, there are two loops, one of which is longer than the other, and which also prints a couple of blank lines before returning to the main program.

Line 330 calls a delay and then clears the screen before incrementing the counter GAME in the next line. You are told which game it is by line 350 and then the computer announces that, because it is taking the role of the banker, who always goes first, it will take the first roll. The "roll the dice" subroutine from line 70 is then triggered. You'll see that the loop counter G is used (line 80) to set the variable A to a randomly chosen value between one and six each time through the loop. If the die comes up with five or two (line 90) then it is reset to zero, before the value is printed by the following line.

The running total is clocked up on variable D, and then leading

159

digits are stripped from this (i.e., 27 is cut down first to 17, then to 7) by line 150. The changing total is printed on the screen each time. After a delay the computer prints up "Total on the first roll is . . ." and then checks (lines 180, 190 and 200) to see if one of the special rolls has eventuated.

If so, a message to that effect is printed. If not, the computer gets to line 210 where it can see if any dice have to be rolled again (C is incremented by one each time a 2 or a 5 is rolled, see line 90). If there are none which have to be re-rolled, the computer moves on to line 410 to print out "So my final total is. . . ." If, however, C is not equal to zero, then the computer runs through another loop (240 to 300) to throw those dice again. Once again, any dice coming up two or five are discarded (line 280).

Once the computer has had its roll, it is your turn to play. Your involvement, actually, is pretty small at this stage. Once you've pressed RETURN (lines 440 and 450) the computer takes over for you, using the same routine near the beginning of the program to roll the dice for you, and incrementing your total as it does so.

Once both of you have had your go, the computer then decides if it has beaten you, or you have defeated it, or whether the two of you have drawn ("Standoff"). The aim of CHEMIN DE COMPUTER is to win the majority out of nine scoring games (and a Standoff game does not count as a scoring game).

"Now the totals so far in Chemin de Computer are . . ." you are told by line 670 and—if nine scoring games have not been played— the computer makes some comment on the game ("Looks like I'm in front . . ." or "And you seem to have the edge . . .") before returning to the main program.

Once a total of nine scoring games has been detected (by line 700) then the routine from line 750 comes into action. "Well, old buddy, we seem to have come to the end of the game . . ." the computer tells you, then determines who has been the overall winner.

You're in good company when you play this game. Baccarat, from which Chemin de Fer was derived, was first introduced into France from Italy in about 1490, during the reign of Charles VIII. The Italian game was called "Baccara."

Here's what it looks like in action:

>>>> This is game 3 <<<<

****
Now, I'll roll as banker...
****
 5 6 2 5 4
 10
 0

Total on the first roll is 0

 3 must be rolled again
 6 2 1

So my final total is 7

Press RETURN to roll your dice
****
 5 1 5 2 1
 2

Total on the first roll is 2

 3 must be rolled again
 1 2 6
So your final total is 9

Computer   Human

 7   9

$$$$$$$$$$$$$$$$$$$$$$$$$$$$$$$$$$
     You're the winner that time!
$$$$$$$$$$$$$$$$$$$$$$$$$$$$$$$$$$$

```
   3 must be rolled again
   1  2  6
So your final total is 9

Computer       Human


   7             9


$$$$$$$$$$$$$$$$$$$$$$$$$$$$$$$$$$$$$$$$
     You're the winner that time!
$$$$$$$$$$$$$$$$$$$$$$$$$$$$$$$$$$$$$$$$


  Now the totals so far in
  Chemin de Computer are
  1 for me, and 2 for you...


And you seem to have the edge!

          _____


     Now the totals so far in
     Chemin de Computer are
     4 for me, and 5 for you...


     Well, old buddy, we seem
     to have come to the end
     of the game...with a total
     of nine scoring rounds...


     And, for once, it is
     you who has beaten me!


     Thanks for the game, old
     buddy, we must do it again
     some time, when you feel
     lucky....................
```

And here is the program listing:

```
10 REM Chemin
20 RANDOMIZE VAL(RIGHT$(TIME$,2))
30 CLS
40 GAME = 0
50 B1 = 0:P1 = 0
60 GOTO 330
70 D = 0:C = 0
80 FOR G = 1 TO 5:A = INT(RND*6) + 1
90 IF A = 2 OR A = 5 THEN C = C + 1
100 PRINT A;
110 GOSUB 930
120 IF A = 2 OR A = 5 THEN A = 0
130 D = D + A:NEXT G
140 PRINT:PRINT D;
150 IF D>9 THEN D = D - 10:PRINT:PRINT D
:GOTO 150
160 GOSUB 900
170 PRINT:PRINT "Total on the first roll
 is"D
180 IF D = 9 THEN PRINT "And that's La G
rande...":RETURN
190 IF D = 8 THEN PRINT "And that's La P
etite...":RETURN
200 IF D = 7 THEN PRINT "And that's a Na
tural...":RETURN
210 IF C = 0 THEN RETURN
220 GOSUB 930
230 PRINT:PRINT C"must be rolled again"
240 FOR A = 1 TO C
250 GOSUB 930
260 E = INT(RND*6) + 1
270 PRINT E;
280 IF E = 2 OR 2 = 5 THEN E = 0
290 D = D + E
300 NEXT A
310 IF D > 9 THEN D = D - 10:PRINT D;:GO
TO 310
320 RETURN
330 GOSUB 930:CLS
340 GAME = GAME + 1
350 PRINT:PRINT ">>>> This is game"GAME"
```

```
   <<<<":PRINT
360 PRINT "*****************************
***"
370 PRINT "Now, I'll roll as banker..."
380 PRINT "*****************************
***"
390 GOSUB 70
400 GOSUB 900
410 PRINT:PRINT "So my final total is"D
420 GOSUB 900
430 PRINT "*****************************
***"
440 INPUT "Press RETURN to roll your dic
e",A$
450 PRINT "*****************************
***"
460 J = D
470 GOSUB 930
480 GOSUB 70
490 PRINT:PRINT "So your final total is"
D
500 PRINT:PRINT
510 GOSUB 930
520 PRINT "Computer","Human"
530 GOSUB 900
540 PRINT J,D
550 GOSUB 930:PRINT
560 PRINT "$$$$$$$$$$$$$$$$$$$$$$$$$$$$$
$$$$$$$"
570 PRINT TAB(5);
580 IF J = D THEN PRINT "That's a stand-
off":GOTO 620
590 IF J > D THEN PRINT "I'm the";:B1 =
B1 + 1
600 IF D > J THEN PRINT "You're the";:P1
 = P1 + 1
610 PRINT " winner that time!"
620 PRINT "$$$$$$$$$$$$$$$$$$$$$$$$$$$$$
$$$$$$$"
630 PRINT:PRINT
640 GOSUB 900
650 PRINT " Now the totals so far in"
660 PRINT " Chemin de Computer are"
670 PRINT B1"for me, and"P1"for you..."
```

```
680 PRINT:PRINT
690 GOSUB 930
700 IF B1 + P1 = 9 THEN 750
710 IF B1 > P1 THEN PRINT " Looks like I
'm in front!"
720 IF P1 > B1 THEN PRINT " And you seem
 to have the edge!"
730 GOSUB 900
740 GOTO 330
750 REM End of game
760 PRINT:PRINT
770 PRINT "Well, old buddy, we seem"
780 PRINT "to have come to the end"
790 PRINT "of the game...with a total"
800 PRINT "of nine scoring rounds..."
810 GOSUB 900
820 IF P1 > B1 THEN PRINT "And, for once
, it is":PRINT "you who has beaten me!":
GOTO 840
830 IF B1 > P1 THEN PRINT "And, once aga
in, the":PRINT "mighty machine proves th
e":PRINT "supreme champeen!!"
840 GOSUB 900
850 PRINT "Thanks for the game, old"
860 PRINT "buddy, we must do it again"
870 PRINT "some time, when you feel"
880 PRINT "lucky...................."
890 END
900 FOR Z = 1 TO 1000:NEXT Z
910 PRINT:PRINT
920 RETURN
930 FOR Z = 1 TO 500:NEXT Z:RETURN
```

☐ MALIBU

Roll the dice now for a few rounds of Malibu. You and the computer take it in turns to roll three dice each. Various dice combinations, and the total of the three dice, are worth points. For example, if the total of the pips showing is 13 ("Lucky Joe") on the computer's dice, the computer gets six points, and the human loses six points.

You start the game with 50 points each, and there are five rounds to a game. As I said, there are certain winning combinations (such as three sixes, called a "high roller") and certain winning totals (such as 9 or 12, a "straight road"). You can score more than once from a single roll, so if your total of nine was gained by rolling two fours and a one, you'd get the "straight road" score of three, plus another three for getting "two of a kind."

The only exception to this is rolling three of a kind ("triple crown"). You can score most of the other possible combinations, although you cannot get "two of a kind" and "triple crown" from the same roll.

Now this may all seem very confusing. It is much easier to play than it is to read about, because the computer rolls the dice for you, works out what the score should be, and keeps the tally. All you have to do is bite your fingernails as you watch the computer defeating you.

Here's a complete list of the winning throws (and remember that when one player gains a certain number of points, they must come off the other player's total, so the totals always add up to 100):

Total	Name	Points
13 plus a pair	Sough	10
6 or 15	Easy Rider	4
9 or 12	Straight Road	3
All the same	Triple Crown	5
Two the same	Two of a Kind	3
13	Lucky Joe	6
3	Low and Mean	7
18	High Roller	12

The only losing throw is a seven ("Dreaded Seven"), which costs you two points, and adds two to your opponent.

A human is humbled by the computer:

```
WELCOME TO THE GAME OF MALIBU
WHICH IS PLAYED WITH THREE DICE...

WHAT IS YOUR NAME? HANGFIRE


OK, HANGFIRE, PRESS THE SPACE
BAR WHEN YOU'RE READY TO PLAY...

THIS IS ROUND 1
HANGFIRE: 50    ME: 50

FIRST I'LL ROLL THREE DICE FOR
MYSELF...STAND BY...
...ROLLING DIE 1 WHICH CAME UP 5
-----------------------------------------
...ROLLING DIE 2 WHICH CAME UP 2
-----------------------------------------
...ROLLING DIE 3 WHICH CAME UP 5
-----------------------------------------

AND NOW IT'S TIME TO ROLL FOR YOU

...ROLLING DIE 1 WHICH CAME UP 6
-----------------------------------------
...ROLLING DIE 2 WHICH CAME UP 2
-----------------------------------------
...ROLLING DIE 3 WHICH CAME UP 2
-----------------------------------------

I ROLLED 5  2  5

YOU ROLLED 6  2  2
>> I CRACK A STRAIGHT ROAD <<
$$ TWO OF A KIND FOR ME $$
$$ TWO OF A KIND FOR YOU $$


>>> AFTER ROUND 1 THE SCORES ARE:
>>> HANGFIRE: 47    COMPUTER: 53
```

```
THIS IS ROUND 5
HANGFIRE: 40    ME: 60

FIRST I'LL ROLL THREE DICE FOR
MYSELF...STAND BY...
...ROLLING DIE 1 WHICH CAME UP 5
--------------------------------------------
...ROLLING DIE 2 WHICH CAME UP 6
--------------------------------------------
...ROLLING DIE 3 WHICH CAME UP 5
--------------------------------------------

AND NOW IT'S TIME TO ROLL FOR YOU
...ROLLING DIE 1 WHICH CAME UP 1
--------------------------------------------
...ROLLING DIE 2 WHICH CAME UP 1
--------------------------------------------
...ROLLING DIE 3 WHICH CAME UP 2
--------------------------------------------

I ROLLED 5  6  5

YOU ROLLED 1  1  2
$$ TWO OF A KIND FOR ME $$
$$ TWO OF A KIND FOR YOU $$


WELL,HANGFIRE, THAT'S THE END OF
OUR LITTLE GAME OF MALIBU....

HANGFIRE'S FINAL SCORE IS 40
AND MINE IS 60

SO I'M THE WINNER!!!

DO YOU WANT ANOTHER GAME, HANGFIRE (Y OR N)?

OK, THANKS FOR THE GAME, HANGFIRE
SEE YOU AGAIN SOME TIME
```

Here's the listing for your own round of MALIBU:

```
10  REM MALIBU
20  GOSUB 680
30  REM *******************************
40  REM *** THE MAIN GAME ROUTINE ***
50  FOR T=1 TO 5
60  CLS
70  PRINT:PRINT:PRINT "THIS IS ROUND";T
80  IF CS*HS<>0 THEN PRINT A$;":";HS;"  M
E:";CS
90  GOSUB 840
100 PRINT:PRINT "FIRST I'LL ROLL THREE D
ICE FOR"
110 PRINT "MYSELF...STAND BY..."
120 GOSUB 840
130 FOR Z=1 TO 3:C(Z)=0:H(Z)=0:NEXT Z
140 GOSUB 850
150 PRINT:PRINT "AND NOW IT'S TIME TO RO
LL FOR YOU"
160 GOSUB 850
170 PRINT:PRINT "I ROLLED";C(1);C(2);C(3
)
180 PRINT:PRINT "YOU ROLLED";H(1);H(2);H
(3)
190 REM *** ASSESS RESULT OF ROLLS ***
200 HT=H(1)+H(2)+H(3)
210 CT=C(1)+C(2)+C(3)
220 IF (C(1)=C(2) OR C(2)=C(3) OR C(1)=C
(3)) AND CT=13 THEN PRINT "THAT'S SOUGH
FOR ME!":CS=CS+10:HS=HS-10
230 IF (H(1)=H(2) OR H(2)=H(3) OR H(1)=H
(3)) AND HT=13 THEN PRINT "THAT'S SOUGH
FOR YOU!":HS=HS+10:CS=CS-10
240 IF HT=15 OR HT=6 THEN HS=HS+4:CS=CS-
4:PRINT "**EASY RIDER FOR YOU**"
250 IF CT=15 OR CT=6 THEN CS=CS+4:HS=HS-
4:PRINT "**EASY RIDER FOR ME**"
260 IF CT=9 OR CT=12 THEN CS=CS+3:HS=HS-
3:PRINT ">> I CRACK A STRAIGHT ROAD <<"
270 IF HT=9 OR HT=12 THEN HS=HS+3:CS=CS-
3:PRINT ">> YOU CRACK A STRAIGHT ROAD <<
"
280 IF C(1)=C(2) AND C(2)=C(3) THEN PRIN
```

```
T "A TRIPLE CROWN FOR ME!":CS=CS+5:HS=HS
-5:GOTO 300
290 IF C(1)=C(2) OR C(2)=C(3) OR C(1)=C(
3) THEN PRINT "$$ TWO OF A KIND FOR ME $
$":CS=CS+3:HS=HS-3
300 IF H(1)=H(2) AND H(2)=H(3) THEN PRIN
T "A TRIPLE CROWN FOR YOU!":HS=HS+5:CS=C
S-5:GOTO 320
310 IF H(1)=H(2) OR H(2)=H(3) OR H(1)=H(
3) THEN PRINT "$$ TWO OF A KIND FOR YOU
$$":HS=HS+3:CS=CS-3
320 IF HT=13 THEN PRINT "FOR YOU...LUCKY
 JOE!":HS=HS+6:CS=CS-6
330 IF CT=13 THEN PRINT "FOR ME...LUCKY
JOE!":CS=CS+6:HS=HS-6
340 IF HT=3 THEN PRINT "LOW AND MEAN...F
OR YOU!":HS=HS+7:CS=CS-7
350 IF CT=3 THEN PRINT "LOW AND MEAN...F
OR ME!":CS=CS+7:HS=HS-7
360 IF HT=18 THEN PRINT "HIGH ROLLER FOR
 THE HUMAN...":HS=HS+12:CS=CS-12
370 IF CT=18 THEN PRINT "HIGH ROLLER FOR
 THE MACHINE...":CS=CS+12:HS=HS-12
380 IF HT=7 THEN PRINT "YOU TRIPPED A DR
EADED SEVEN":HS=HS-2:CS=CS+2
390 IF CT=7 THEN PRINT "I TRIPPED A DREA
DED SEVEN":CS=CS-2:HS=HS+2
400 REM *** PRINT OUT SCORES ***
410 PRINT:PRINT
420 IF T<5 THEN PRINT ">>> AFTER ROUND";
T;"THE SCORES ARE:":PRINT ">>> ";A$;":";
HS;"     COMPUTER:";CS
430 GOSUB 840:GOSUB 840
440 REM ** CHECK BOTH STILL IN GAME **
450 IF CS<1 OR HS<1 THEN T=5
460 NEXT T
470 REM *** RESULT OF FIVE ROUNDS ***
480 PRINT:PRINT "WELL,";A$;", THAT'S THE
 END OF"
490 PRINT "OUR LITTLE GAME OF MALIBU....
"
500 PRINT:PRINT A$;"'S FINAL SCORE IS";H
S
510 PRINT "AND MINE IS";CS
```

```
520 GOSUB 840
530 PRINT
540 IF CS>HS THEN PRINT "SO I'M THE WINN
ER!!!"
550 IF HS>CS THEN PRINT "SO ";A$;" TAKES
 THE WINNER'S TROPHY!!"
560 IF CS=HS THEN PRINT "IT LOOKS LIKE A
 DEAD HEAT...."
570 GOSUB 840:GOSUB 840
580 PRINT:PRINT "DO YOU WANT ANOTHER GAM
E, ";A$;" (Y OR N)?"
590 PRINT
600 F$=INKEY$
610 IF F$<>"y" AND F$<>"Y" AND F$<>"n" A
ND F$<>"N" THEN 600
620 IF F$="N" OR F$="n" THEN PRINT "OK,
THANKS FOR THE GAME, ";A$:PRINT "SEE YOU
 AGAIN SOME TIME":END
630 PRINT "OK, ";A$;", STAND BY..."
640 GOSUB 840
650 GOSUB 770
660 GOTO 50
670 REM ********************
680 REM *****INITIALISE******
690 RANDOMIZE VAL(RIGHT$(TIME$,2))
700 CLS
710 DIM H(3),C(3)
720 PRINT:PRINT:PRINT "WELCOME TO THE GA
ME OF MALIBU"
730 PRINT "WHICH IS PLAYED WITH THREE DI
CE..."
740 GOSUB 840
750 PRINT:INPUT "WHAT IS YOUR NAME";A$
760 GOSUB 840
770 CLS:PRINT
780 HS=50:CS=50
790 PRINT "OK, ";A$;", PRESS THE SPACE"
800 PRINT "BAR WHEN YOU'RE READY TO PLAY
..."
810 IF INKEY$="" THEN 810
820 RETURN
830 REM *** DELAY SUBROUTINE ***
840 FOR I=1 TO 2000:NEXT I:RETURN
850 REM ***REM DICE ROLL***
```

```
860 FOR Z=1 TO 3
870 PRINT "...ROLLING DIE";Z;
880 FOR I=1 TO 800:NEXT I
890 K=INT(RND(1)*6)+1
900 PRINT "WHICH CAME UP";K
910 PRINT "-------------------------------
----------"
920 IF C(Z)=0 THEN C(Z)=K ELSE H(Z)=K
930 NEXT Z
940 GOSUB 840
950 RETURN
```

☐ SEVEN/ELEVEN

SEVEN/ELEVEN is another fine dice game, and one in which your goal changes in each game. Based on craps, you have a "target number" to reach in each round (known as your "point" in craps).

Craps is an American version of the old English dice game "hazard." In SEVEN/ELEVEN, the complex betting of craps has been removed, leaving just the fun of the game. Rather than worry about computing odds and placing "pass" and "don't pass" bets, you can concentrate on the serious business of praying for the right roll to come up.

In this game, you are playing against yourself. Your winning and losing rounds are tallied, so you know—at every point in the game— just how well (or otherwise) you are doing.

You throw two dice at a time. If you throw a 2, 3, or a 12 with your first roll, you lose that round. Getting a 7, or an 11, on the first roll is the best thing you can do, because you've won that round with that single roll (which is why the game is called SEVEN/ELEVEN).

Any other number rolled as your first roll of a round becomes your "target number." You have to try and roll this again, before you roll a 7 or an 11. If you manage to roll your target number again, you win that round. However, rolling a 7 or an 11 before you've rethrown your target total causes you to lose that round.

Here are some "snapshots" of the game in progress:

```
The tally so far:
Wins: 1    Losses: 1
You have $ 105

This is round number 4

Press 'R' to roll
You rolled 5
and 3

In 7/11 you've rolled 8
```

```
Your target number is 8

Press 'R' to roll
You rolled 6
and 1

In 7/11 you've rolled 7
And so you lose
```

```
The tally so far:
Wins: 1    Losses: 2
You have $ 100

This is round number 5

Press 'R' to roll
```

And this is the listing of SEVEN/ELEVEN:

```
10 REM Seven Eleven
20 B$ = "In 7/11 you've rolled"
30 G = 0:W =0:L = 0:M = 105
40 CLS
50 PRINT:PRINT "The tally so far:"
60 PRINT "Wins:"W"  Losses:"L
70 G = G + 1
80 M = M - 5
90 PRINT "You have $"M
100 PRINT:PRINT "This is round number"G
110 GOSUB 200
120 IF A = 7 OR A = 11 THEN 300
130 IF A = 2 OR A = 3 OR A = 12 THEN PRI
NT "so that's the end of the round":GOTO
 320
140 P = A
150 CLS:PRINT:PRINT "Your target number
is"P
160 GOSUB 200
```

```
170 IF A = P THEN 300
180 IF A = 7 OR A = 11 THEN 310
190 GOSUB 340:GOTO 150
200 N = 0
210 PRINT:PRINT"Press 'R' to roll"
220  N = N + W: IF INKEY$ = "" THEN 220
230 C = INT(RND*6) + 1:PRINT "You rolled
"C
240 GOSUB 340
250 B = INT(RND*6) + 1:PRINT "and"B
260 A = B + C
270 PRINT:PRINT B$;A
280 GOSUB 340
290 RETURN
300 PRINT "And you've won":W = W + 1:M =
 M + 20:GOTO 320
310 PRINT "And so you lose":L = L + 1
320 GOSUB 340
330 GOTO 40
340 FOR T = 1 TO 500: NEXT T
350 RETURN
```

☐ NO SWEAT

The name of this game—NO SWEAT—comes from one of the early English names for the game from which this is derived. Known as "sweatcloth," the game, when first played in England, used three dice within a wooden "shoe." The most common variation of this game is now seen in US gambling casinos, where it is called "birdcage," because of the equipment which is used.

In birdcage, three dice are held within a metal cage which can spin about a central axis. Once bets have been laid, the cage is rotated. This is supposed to ensure that the dice are spun properly, as they are not actually touched by a casino operator.

Betting in birdcage, and in NO SWEAT, is fast and simple, and despite the fact that you might think the odds are in your favor as a player, you'll quickly learn how easy it is to lose your shirt.

You place a bet of a specified amount (see lines 50 and 60) up to the size of your stake (held by the variable M, for money—see lines 30 and 250) and then choose a number between one and six. The amount of your bet is subtracted from your stake, and then the three dice are rolled. For each one which lands showing your number, you'll have an amount equal to your bet returned to you.

As you can see, this means you have to throw one die with your number showing to break even, and two to actually make some money. The need to throw the same, chosen number twice is what gives the casino such a good edge in this game.

After the random number generator is seeded in line 20, and the money variable (M) is set to 30 for you in line 30, the computer goes to the subroutine from line 240 which prints up:

```
********************
Your stake is now $30
********************
```

After this, the game gets underway.

Line 50 asks you how much you'd like to bet, and the variable A is assigned to your choice. This is compared with the money you actually have (in line 60) to see if you are trying to bet more than you have on hand. Having passed that hurdle, your bet is subtracted from your stake in line 70 and then the computer asks you (line 50) to enter your bet.

The C loop, from lines 100 to 180, rolls the dice and compares each roll with your number, reporting to you after each roll. Your winnings (if there are any) are also added in this loop.

After each round of the game, your money (M) is compared with 250 (if you've got more than $250 you've exceeded the house limits and are therefore excluded from future play) and with zero (those who have no money are not allowed to play further). If, however, you do not have more than 250 nor less than zero, you're able to continue playing.

Here's NO SWEAT in full play:

```
****************************
    Your stake is now $ 30
****************************
How much would you like to bet? 4


Which number are you betting on? 5

Die 1 fell 4
****************************
    Your stake is now $ 26
****************************


Die 2 fell 5
so you win $ 4
****************************
    Your stake is now $ 30
****************************


Die 3 fell 2
****************************
    Your stake is now $ 30
****************************



    Your stake is now $ 5
****************************
How much would you like to bet? 4


Which number are you betting on? 6
```

```
Die 1 fell 6
so you win $ 4
****************************
    Your stake is now $ 5
****************************

Die 2 fell 6
so you win $ 4
****************************
    Your stake is now $ 9
****************************

Die 3 fell 3
****************************
    Your stake is now $ 9
****************************



    Your stake is now $ 0
****************************

Die 2 fell 6
****************************
    Your stake is now $ 0
****************************

Die 3 fell 1
****************************
    Your stake is now $ 0
****************************
The game is over, 'cos you're broke!
The game is over, 'cos you're broke!
The game is over, 'cos you're broke!
```

And here's the listing so you and your computer can take part in a round or two:

```
10  REM No Sweat
20  RANDOMIZE VAL(RIGHT$(TIME$,2))
30  M = 30
40  CLS:GOSUB 240
```

```
50 INPUT "How much would you like to bet
";A
60 IF A > M THEN 50
70 M = M - A:PRINT:PRINT
80 INPUT "Which number are you betting o
n";B
90 IF B<1 OR B > 6 THEN 80
100 FOR C = 1 TO 3
110 W = 0
120 GOSUB 280
130 D = INT(RND*6) + 1
140 PRINT:PRINT "Die"C"fell"D
150 IF D = B THEN W =A:PRINT "so you win
 $"W
160 M = M + W
170 GOSUB 240
180 NEXT C
190 GOSUB 280:GOSUB 280
200 IF M > 250 THEN 310
210 IF M > 0 THEN 40
220 PRINT "The game is over, 'cos you're
 broke!"
230 GOTO 220
240 PRINT "*****************************"
250 PRINT "   Your stake is now $"M
260 PRINT "*****************************"
270 RETURN
280 FOR P = 1 TO 1000
290 NEXT P
300 RETURN
310 FOR J = 1 TO 30
320 PRINT "You've topped $250!"
330 PRINT TAB(J);"Well done!!"
340 NEXT J
```

▢ ONE-AND-TWENTY

Our dice games continue now with ONE-AND-TWENTY which, as you realized the moment you read the title in the introduction, is a dice version of blackjack.

The game is simple, but demands a degree of cool thinking, as well as the ability to guess which numbers are going to come up next when the die is rolled. In ONE-AND-TWENTY, you are playing against the computer.

You are always given the first go. You roll the die as many times as you like, aiming to get a total as close as possible to, but not exceeding, 21. You can stop adding to the total whenever you like.

If you exceed 21 (that is, you "bust") then the computer wins that round automatically. A game consists of five rounds, and the winner of the most rounds, naturally enough, wins the game.

After initializing some variables (including HS for the human score and CS for the computer score) in lines 20 and 30, and clearing the screen in line 40, the computer asks you to "Press 'R' to roll, 'S' to stand." The word "Stand" means you are happy with the total you've achieved so far and you'll stay with it, giving the computer a chance to try and beat you. You'll soon learn that the speed with which you enter an R or an S can affect the number which is thrown, because the delay between the "Press 'R' to roll . . ." and the time you actually do press an R or an S is used to create a number (N) which—together with your current total—is used to seed the random number generator for the next dice roll.

The lines from 50 to 170 control your dice-rolling, and the computer only exits this cycle when you decide to stand. The whole of the computer's game-playing logic is held within line 180, which determines whether it is worth risking a bust to try and exceed your total. If it decides to roll, the lines from 190 to 250 control this.

Once the computer decides it has had enough of that, it uses lines 260, 280 and 290 to determine who has won. If both your scores are the same, or both of you are over 21, then the round is counted as a dead heat (line 320 tells you this), and neither CS nor HS is incremented. Line 280 spots a computer win, adding one to CS and printing "I," while the next line adds one to HS and prints "You." The mysterious "I" and "You" are used as the first part of the sentence concluded by "win!!!" in line 300.

As in CHEMIN DE COMPUTER, where the aim was to get the best out of nine scoring games, in ONE-AND-TWENTY, the intention is to score wins in the majority of games out of five. Line 390 looks to see if this has happened, and if so sends the program to line 450 where the result of the game (with a sarcastic comment or two) is printed. If five scoring games have not been played, line 400 asks you to "Stand by for the next round . . ." and after a brief pause (line 430), the next round is upon you.

Let's have a look at part of a game in action:

```
Your total is 18

I rolled a 4
so my total is 4

I rolled a 4
so my total is 8

I rolled a 4
so my total is 12

I rolled a 5
so my total is 17

I rolled a 2
so my total is 19

**********************************

              I win!!

      _____


I rolled a 6
so my total is 22

**********************************

              You win!!

**********************************

After that round, the game score is
          You: 2 , and me 3

**********************************
```

That's the end of the game

Final scores:
                    You: 2
                    Me: 3

And I defeated you, humanoid!

This listing will enable your computer to challenge (and probably beat) you in ONE-AND-TWENTY:

```
10 REM One-and-Twenty
20 HS = 0:CS = 0
30 H = 0:C = 0:N = 0
40 CLS
50 PRINT "Press 'R' to roll, 'S' to stand"
60 A$ = INKEY$
70 N = N + 1
80 IF A$ <> "s" AND A$ <> "S" AND A$ <> "r"
 AND A$ <> "R" THEN 60
90 IF A$ = "s" OR A$ = "S" THEN CLS:PRINT "
Your total is"H:GOTO 180
100 RANDOMIZE (N + H)
110 GOSUB 430
120 R = INT(RND*6) + 1
130 PRINT:PRINT "You rolled a"R
140 H = H + R
150 PRINT "so your total is"H
160 GOSUB 430
170 PRINT:GOTO 50
180 IF C>H AND C<22 OR C>21 OR H>21 OR H=21
 AND C=21 THEN 260
190 R = INT(RND*6) + 1
200 GOSUB 430
210 PRINT:PRINT "I rolled a"R
220 C = C + R
230 PRINT "so my total is"C
240 GOSUB 430
250 GOTO 180
260 IF H=C OR H>21 AND C>21 THEN 320
270 GOSUB 510
280 IF (C>H OR H>21) AND C<22 THEN PRINT ,"
I";:CS = CS + 1
```

```
290 IF (C<H OR C>21) AND H<22 THEN PRINT ,"
You";:HS = HS + 1
300 PRINT " win!!"
310 GOTO 330
320 PRINT "That round is a dead heat...no s
core"
330 GOSUB 430
340 GOSUB 510
350 PRINT "After that round, the game score
 is"
360 GOSUB 430
370 PRINT ,"You:"HS", and me"CS
380 GOSUB 510
390 IF CS + HS = 5 THEN GOTO 450
400 PRINT:PRINT "Stand by for the next roun
d..."
410 GOSUB 430:GOSUB 430
420 CLS:GOTO 30
430 FOR O = 1 TO 900:NEXT O
440 RETURN
450 PRINT:PRINT "That's the end of the game
"
460 PRINT:PRINT "Final scores:"
470 PRINT ,"You:"HS
480 PRINT ," Me:"CS:PRINT
490 IF CS>HS THEN PRINT "And I defeated you
, humanoid!":END
500 PRINT "And remarkably, a mere human bea
t the machine!":END
510 PRINT:PRINT "****************************
*********":PRINT
520 RETURN
```

☐ SNAKES' EYES

SNAKES' EYES demands some more cool thinking under pressure. You and your computer take it in turns to throw a pair of dice. You add the total of the pips, and in turn add this to your score.

You can roll the dice as many times as you like, but if you roll a seven, you automatically lose. Therefore, as you can see, the program demands you make decisions based on whether you should be careful and perhaps lose the round by not rolling a high enough score, or whether you should be greedy and go for the absolute maximum score and risk a seven.

As in ONE-AND-TWENTY, the time you take to press RE-TURN to roll the dice has some effect on the score you achieve. You can see, in lines 120 to 150, that the variable N (set to zero in line 120) is incremented by one each time around the 140/150 loop, until you press the "q," "Q," "r," or "R" keys.

If you press "r" or "R" to indicate that you wish to roll the dice, the computer goes to the subroutine from line 370 where the screen is cleared (380) and then the two dice (X and Y) are rolled. The Q loop is covered 20 times, gradually slowing down as it is traversed (by the inner loop, in line 430), until finally—with line 420—the results of the dice rolls are printed. The variable Z is set equal to the tally of the two rolls (in line 480) before the computer goes to line 700 for the delay and to print a line across the screen, and then returns to the start of the program to line 180, the one after the one which sent it to the "roll the dice" routine. Here the computer checks that the total is not 7 (line 180) and if it is not, then adds the result of the latest roll to your tally.

If, however, you signal through INKEY$ that you wish to quit, the action goes to the routine from line 220. After printing STAND BY, the computer goes to the delay loop, and line print routine, and then uses the same routine as the human did for rolling the dice, and—on returning from the subroutine—checking that the total was not 7, and if not, adding the new total to the score. The computer has a very simple means of deciding if it will roll again: if it has less than the human, it takes the risk.

You'll find that it is relatively easy to program games like this on your computer. Once you've worked out the "mechanical" routines which do such things as roll the dice, and increment the score, for the human player, it is not very difficult to work out a routine to enable the computer to use the same mechanical routines. Most dice games do not demand much "intelligence" and their strategy can often be reduced to a couple of IF/THEN statements. Read books on dice games—such as the excellent *Dice Games Old and New* by William E. Tredd (The Oleander Press, New York, 1981)—to get ideas for games to turn into programs, and for simple ideas on how to play the game as well as possible. It is these ideas which you should find relatively easy to turn into simple "intelligent algorithms" to enable your computer to play reasonably well against you.

And if, as in this case and in ONE-AND-TWENTY, you stipulate that the human must go first, the computer knows exactly what target it is aiming at, and therefore starts a round with a considerable advantage, which helps overcome the machine's inherent stupidity.

Anyway, here's what SNAKES' EYES looks like when it is up and running:

```
Please stand by...

Your total is 0

-------------------------------
Press 'R' to roll
'Q' to quit
-------------------------------
Die one: 1    Die two: 2

Your total is 3

Your total is 3

-------------------------------
Press 'R' to roll
'Q' to quit
-------------------------------
Die one: 4    Die two: 4

Your total is 11

Your total is 11

-------------------------------
Press 'R' to roll
'Q' to quit
-------------------------------
Die one: 6    Die two: 6
```

```
Your total is 23

Your total is 23

--------------------------
Press 'R' to roll
'Q' to quit

Stand by
--------------------------
Die one: 5    Die two: 5

My total is 10
Your total is 23

Stand by
--------------------------
Die one: 4    Die two: 1

My total is 15
Your total is 23

Stand by
--------------------------
Die one: 2    Die two: 1

My total is 18
Your total is 23

Stand by
--------------------------
Die one: 4    Die two: 2

My total is 24
Your total is 23

I win!

The score is:
                You: 0
                Me: 1
```

186

```
------------------------
And I'm in the lead...
Please stand by...

Your total is 0

------------------------
Press 'R' to roll
'Q' to quit
------------------------
Die one: 1    Die two: 3

Your total is 4

Your total is 4


------------------------
Press 'R' to roll
'Q' to quit
------------------------
Die one: 3    Die two: 5

Your total is 12

Your total is 12

------------------------
Press 'R' to roll
'Q' to quit



Stand by
------------------------
Die one: 5    Die two: 2
You win!

The score is:
            You: 1
            Me: 1
------------------------
```

```
The score is:
          You: 1
          Me: 7
--------------------------
And I'm in the lead...
Please stand by...


Your total is 0

--------------------------
Press 'R' to roll
'Q' to quit
--------------------------
Die one: 6    Die two: 2

Your total is 8

Your total is 8

--------------------------
Press 'R' to roll
'Q' to quit
--------------------------
Die one: 4    Die two: 3
I win!


The score is:
          You: 1
          Me: 8


Well, buddy, that's the end
   of the game...

Your final score was 1
and mine was 8
I'm the winner!!
```

And this is the listing for the game:

```
10 REM Snakes Eyes
20 CLS
30 H = 0:CZ = 0
40 HS = 0:CS = 0
50 PRINT "Please stand by..."
60 GOSUB 700
70 CLS:PRINT:PRINT
80 PRINT "Your total is"HS:PRINT
90 GOSUB 710
100 PRINT "Press 'R' to roll"
110 PRINT "'Q' to quit"
120 N = 0
130 W$ = INKEY$
140 N = N + 1
150 IF W$ <> "q" AND W$ <> "Q" AND W$ <>
 "r" AND W$ <> "R" THEN RANDOMIZE N:GOTO
 130
160 IF W$ = "q" OR W$ = "Q" THEN 220
170 GOSUB 370 .
180 IF Z = 7 THEN 350
190 HS = HS + Z
200 PRINT:PRINT "Your total is"HS
210 GOTO 60
220 PRINT:PRINT:PRINT "Stand by"
230 GOSUB 700
240 GOSUB 370
250 IF Z = 7 THEN 330
260 CS = CS + Z
270 PRINT:PRINT "My total is"CS
280 PRINT "Your total is"HS
290 IF CS<HS THEN 220
300 IF CS=HS THEN PRINT "It's a dead hea
t!"
310 IF CS>HS THEN 350
320 GOTO 510
330 PRINT:PRINT "You win!":H = H + 1
340 GOTO 510
350 PRINT:PRINT "I win!":CZ = CZ + 1
360 GOTO 510
370 REM Roll the dice
380 CLS
390 FOR Q = 1 TO 20
```

```
400 X = INT (RND*6) + 1
410 Y = INT (RND*6) + 1
420 PRINT:PRINT "Die one:"X"    Die two:"
Y
430 FOR P = 1 TO 3*Q:NEXT P
440 NEXT Q
450 CLS
460 GOSUB 710
470 PRINT "Die one:"X"    Die two:"Y
480 Z = X + Y
490 GOSUB 700
500 RETURN
510 PRINT:PRINT "The score is:"
520 PRINT ,"You:"H
530 PRINT ," Me:"CZ
540 IF CZ + H = 9 THEN 580
550 GOSUB 710
560 IF H > CZ THEN PRINT "You are leadin
g!"
570 IF CZ > H THEN PRINT "And I'm in the
 lead..."
580 GOSUB 700
590 CLS
600 IF CZ + H = 9 THEN 620
610 GOTO 40
620 PRINT:PRINT:PRINT
630 PRINT "Well, buddy, that's the end"
640 PRINT "   of the game..."
650 PRINT:PRINT:PRINT
660 PRINT "Your final score was"H
670 PRINT "and mine was"CZ:PRINT
680 IF H < CZ THEN PRINT "I'm the winner
!!":END
690 PRINT "You're the winner!!":END
700 FOR P = 1 TO 1000:NEXT P:RETURN
710 PRINT "---------------------------":PR
INT:RETURN
```

☐ UNDER 'N' OVER

UNDER 'N' OVER is a computer adaptation of the dice game usually known as "Under and Over Seven." In this game, you bet on the likelihood of the total of a pair of dice landing so that the total is:

- less than seven;
- exactly equal to seven; or
- greater than seven.

Again, this is a game which—at first sight—seems to offer pretty good odds to the player. However, if you played the game forever, witha pair of perfect dice, you'd find your losses would outweigh your wins by nearly 17%.

The program structure is not hard to follow. After seeding the random number generator in line 20 and clearing the screen in line 30, the computer sets your starting stake (again called M for money) to 30 (for $30). Line 50 sends action to the subroutine from line 450 where your current money is printed up: "You now have $30" before returning to line 60 where the delay subroutine (lines 470, 480 and 490) is called.

Lines 70 and 120 ask you to place your bet, giving you the key for entering it (press A to bet under seven, B to bet on seven and C to bet on a total greater than seven). Lines 130 and 140 read the keyboard using INKEY$, rejecting (line 140) any input which is not A, B or C.

Having received a valid choice, the odds are printed up by lines 150 to 180 and then line 200 asks you to enter the amount of your bet. Of course, you can't bet more than you have (not in this game, anyway) so line 220 checks your bet (A) against your money (M) and if you haven't got enough prints up: "You haven't got that much!"

The next section rolls the dice, assigning random values between one and six to variables B and C, and adding them to produce total D in line 280. You are told of the total by line 300.

The outcome

This is determined by the routine from lines 310 to 350 where a loss is first assumed (line 310, with variable W, for "win," assigned to the negative of your bet). This is changed—if needed—into the correct amount for a win if one has, in fact, taken place. You can see you get paid four times your bet for correctly specifying the dice will land with a total of seven (line 320) and even money for either over or under seven (lines 330 and 340).

Lines 370 and 380 tell you about your win (or loss) and then line 420 checks that you still have some money in hand. If you have, you are offered a new round of the game. If not, you are dismissed with a certain severity.

Here's UNDER 'N' OVER in action:

```
OK, punter, 'tis time to
place your bet.........


Enter 'A' to bet under 7
      'B' to bet on 7, or
      'C' to bet over 7

The odds are:
   A - pays even
   B - pays 4 to 1
   C - pays even


Now how much would you like to bet? 625

               Die one came up 1

               Die two came up 6

               So the total is 7


You've just won $ 2500


Enter 'A' to bet under 7
      'B' to bet on 7, or
      'C' to bet over 7
```

The odds are:
   A - pays even

                   So the total is 6

And so you lose $ 15625

You now have $ 0

You're flat broke, buddy
so I gotta close the casino

There's no room for deadbeats in my joint

                    ─────────────

And this is the listing to turn your computer into a dice fiend:

```
10 REM Under'n'over
20 RANDOMIZE VAL(RIGHT$(TIME$,2))
30 CLS
40 M = 30
50 GOSUB 450
60 GOSUB 470
70 PRINT "OK, punter, 'tis time to"
80 PRINT "place your bet.........."
90 GOSUB 470
100 PRINT "Enter 'A' to bet under 7"
110 PRINT "        'B' to bet on 7, or"
120 PRINT "        'C' to bet over 7"
130 A$ = INKEY$
140 IF A$ <> "A" AND A$ <> "a" AND A$ <>
 "B" AND A$ <> "b" AND A$ <> "C" AND A$
<> "c" THEN 130
150 PRINT:PRINT "The odds are:"
160 PRINT "  A - pays even"
170 PRINT "  B - pays 4 to 1"
180 PRINT "  C - pays even"
```

```
190 GOSUB 470
200 INPUT "Now how much would you like t
o bet";A
210 GOSUB 470
220 IF A > M THEN PRINT "You haven't got
 that much!":PRINT:GOTO 200
230 B = INT(RND*6) + 1
240 PRINT ,"Die one came up"B
250 GOSUB 470
260 C = INT(RND*6) + 1
270 PRINT ,"Die two came up"C
280 D = C + B
290 GOSUB 470
300 PRINT ,"So the total is"D
310 W = - A
320 IF D = 7 AND (A$ = "B" OR A$ = "b")
THEN W = 4*A
330 IF D < 7 AND (A$ = "A" OR A$ = "a")
THEN W = A
340 IF D > 7 AND (A$ = "C" OR A$ = "c")
THEN W = A
350 M = M + W
360 GOSUB 470
370 IF W > 0 THEN PRINT "You've just won
 $"W
380 IF W < 0 THEN PRINT "And so you lose
 $"(W* - 1)
390 GOSUB 470
400 GOSUB 450
410 GOSUB 470
420 IF M < 1 THEN PRINT "You're flat bro
ke, buddy":PRINT "so I gotta close the c
asino":PRINT:PRINT "There's no room for
deadbeats in my joint":END
430 CLS
440 GOTO 50
450 PRINT:PRINT "You now have $"M
460 RETURN
470 FOR P = 1 TO 1000:NEXT P
480 PRINT:PRINT
490 RETURN
```

Artificial Intelligence

Artificial intelligence is a goal which has not yet been achieved. Certainly, programs which enable computers to exhibit behavior which could conceivably be classed as intelligent have been written, but the "intelligence" has been limited and effective only within a severely restricted domain. That is, a computer can appear to be brainy, but only if you limit the environment within which it has to demonstrate those brains.

In this section of the book, we have four programs which will give your computer the appearance of intelligence, and certainly provide impressive demonstrations of "electronic brainpower" when the programs are shown to computer-naive people.

Despite the claims made by some people (such as Carl Sagan, "In Defense of Robots," *Broca's Brain)* that human beings are, essentially, just well-made computers, we sense there is a wide gulf between our own perception of our selfhood, and the total non-awareness that computers can have (at least at present) of their own existence. And it seems to me that this self-perception lies at the heart of at least one aspect of intelligence.

Computers can function extremely "intelligently" in restricted areas. Look at the five-inch-square, hand-held chess machines. Within the limited domain of a chess game, a solid appearance of intelligence can be created.

It is so within the limited universes created by the programs in this section. One of them is a variant of one of the most well-known and popular AI programs ever, ELIZA, in which the computer takes the role of a psychiatrist, and apparently carries on a conversation. ELIZA was developed in the mid-'60s by Joseph Weizenbaum. He was attempting to produce a program which would caricature a Rogerian psychoanalyst, and it has been suggested (see "You're Never Alone with a Fluffy Micro," David Tebbutt, *MicroScope,* January 13, 1983, p. 9) that Weizenbaum has regretted ever since that day his work on ELIZA. It is not hard to see why.

In the euphoric days after the program was made public, wild

197

and erratic claims were made that it was only a matter of (very little) time before computers could totally replace "mind-doctors." Further, the ELIZA success—said some incautious observers—paved the way for genuinely intelligent computers.

Weizenbaum did not believe it for a moment. He writes that he was amazed at the beginning—and continued to be amazed—at the reaction people had to the program. Written in LISP on a mainframe at MIT, the program could be accessed from any one of a number of time-sharing terminals dotted around the campus. Weizenbaum reports he was very interested to see that the program was being accessed time and time again very late at night, as though troubled students were really discussing their problems with the program. Furthermore, the accesses were all very long. The computer log showed some people were hooked into ELIZA for over an hour at a time.

Weizenbaum's secretary had worked closely with him over the six months or so it took to produce the program, and she knew as well as he how it worked, scanning a person's speech for "key words" (such as *dream* and *friends)* and then choosing a suitable reply from a bank of such replies. Other words from the user's sentences could be incorporated, sentences could be "turned around" (so, "I am happy because of the weather" could be simply fed back as either, "Why are you happy because of the weather," or just as a statement of the form, "You are happy because of the weather. What does this suggest to you?") and a number of other replies (such as, "That is interesting, please go on") could be used if no key word was recognized.

Despite the secretary's familiarity with the program, Weizenbaum noticed that if he walked into the office when she was accessing the program, she became embarrassed and refused to let him see the printout. Further, when he suggested it would be interesting to hook up a printer to the main body of the computer to record the late night conversations students had with the program, the suggestion was greeted with horror, as though he was suggesting a kind of electronic peeping-Tom activity. (If you'd like to look further into Weizenbaum's work on AI, you might be interested in his book *Computer Power and Human Reason*, W. H. Freeman and Co., San Francisco, 1976.)

A common stumbling block in the work of early researchers into the field of artificial intelligence was that writing a program which emulated some aspect of human reasoning (such as a very impressive checkers program by Samuels) did not necessarily lead researchers any closer to either producing behavior which could be classed as intelligent, nor toward a theoretical understanding of the processes of human reasoning and deduction. "Progress in producing intelligent behavior is not necessarily progress towards producing thought" (Nor-

198

man Whaland, "When Is a Program Intelligent?," *Creative Computing*, February 1981, pp. 44-49).

There is another way of approaching the problem, which I call the "if it quacks like a duck, it's a duck" approach. In the book *The Turing Criterion: Machine Intelligent Programs for the 16K ZX81* (Charlton et al., Interface Publications, London, 1982), which I edited, I answer the question "What is the Turing Criterion?" in the following words:

> In 1950, the English mathematician and logician A. M. Turing proposed what has become known as the "Turing Criterion" for machine intelligence.
>
> He said that if you were dealing with something at the end of a wire that could be a machine, or could be human, and you could not tell—from the responses coming to you over the wire—whether that with which you were dealing was human or machine, the "thing" at the other end was, by definition, intelligent.

On this basis, it would be possible to class many, many computer programs as intelligent. Certainly those within this section of the book could almost pass the test, especially if you were prepared to accept the possibility that some pretty stupid humans were dealing with you.

Time now to explore the worlds of Artificial Intelligence with the following programs:

- ELIZA

- ELECTRONIC BRAIN, in which the computer tries to crack a "mastermind-like" code you've worked out

- PROBOSCIDEAN, from the adjective describing the class of mammal elephants belong to, in which you face the computer in a round of "concentration"

- AMANUENSIS, in which the computer accepts the task of writing poetry.

☐ ELIZA

We'll start our investigation of artificial intelligence with a simplified version of the classic program, ELIZA, which we discussed at some length in the introduction. As we said there, the program scans your input for words it can use, and then reflects your words back to you in a way which makes it seem as if the program is really speaking to you. Once you've played with it a while, you'll learn how to trigger the most effective responses.

Here's part of one "conversation" I had with my version of ELIZA:

```
WELCOME TO ANOTHER SESSION WITH
YOUR COMPUTER PSYCHIATRIST, ELIZA

WHAT IS YOUR FIRST NAME? TIM


WELL, HI THERE TIM

IT SURE IS NEAT TO HAVE YOU DROP BY

PRESS MY SPACE BAR WHEN YOU'RE READY TO
START


? I HAVE A SERIOUS PROBLEM
WHY ARE YOU SAYING THAT?

? BECAUSE I'VE COME TO YOU FOR HELP
TIM, I'M NOT SURE I UNDERSTAND YOU FULLY.

? I AM AFRAID OF MICE
TIM, HOW LONG HAVE YOU BEEN AFRAID OF MICE

? SINCE BEFORE I TOOK UP COMPUTERS
TIM, WHY DO YOU MENTION COMPUTERS?

? IT SEEMED RELEVANT AT THE TIME
THAT IS QUITE INTERESTING!
```

? AS I WAS SAYING I AM AFRAID OF LITTLE
  SQUEAKY THINGS
HOW LONG HAVE YOU BEEN AFRAID OF LITTLE
  SQUEAKY THINGS

? I THINK WE HAVE BEEN THROUGH THIS BEFORE
DO YOU DOUBT WE HAVE BEEN THROUGH THIS
  BEFORE

? I SOMETIMES DOUBT EVERYTHING
TIM, WELL, WELL...DO GO ON.

? MANY PEOPLE HAVE DOUBTS
WELL, WELL...DO GO ON.

? I BET EVEN YOU HAVE DOUBTS
THAT'S SO...PLEASE CONTINUE...

? DO YOU EVER DREAM OF ROBOTS
YES, I EVER DREAM OF ROBOTS

? WELL I NEVER EVER DREAM ABOUT THEM
WHY DID YOU BRING UP THE SUBJECT OF DREAMS?

? I HAVE THIS THING ABOUT MICE
COULD YOU SAY THAT AGAIN, IN A DIFFERENT
  WAY?

? I'M AFRAID THEY'LL COME AND JUST STAY FOR
  TEA
TIM, WHY ARE YOU TELLING ME YOU'RE AFRAID
THEY'LL COME AND JUST STAY FOR TEA

? I THOUGHT YOU WERE MEANT TO ASSIST IN AN
  HOUR OF NEED
CAN YOU ELABORATE ON THAT?

? HOW CAN I SAY IT MORE CLEARLY
PERHAPS YOU DON'T WANT TO BE ABLE TO SAY IT
MORE CLEARLY

? I THINK YOU ARE A FRAUD
WHAT MAKES YOU THINK I AM A FRAUD

```
? BECAUSE YOU NEVER GIVE ME A STRAIGHT
  ANSWER
I'M NOT SURE I UNDERSTAND YOU FULLY.

? COME ON TURKEY I WANT A STRAIGHT ANSWER
TIM, WHY DO YOU WANT A STRAIGHT ANSWER

? TO HELP ME IN MY HOUR OF NEED
TIM, I SEE...

? YOU'RE PRETTY DUMB FOR A MACHINE
WHAT IS YOUR REACTION TO ME BEING PRETTY
DUMB FOR A MACHINE


? IT MAKES ME WANT TO DRINK HEAVILY
MODERATION IN ALL THINGS SHOULD BE THE RULE.

? EVEN IN SEX
I FEEL YOU SHOULD REALLY DISCUSS THIS WITH
  A HUMAN.

? BYE
BYE BYE FOR NOW.
SEE YOU AGAIN SOME TIME.
```

And here's the listing, so your computer can now help you sort yourself out:

```
10 REM ELIZA
20 REM ALL INPUT MUST BE IN UPPER CASE
30 REM NO PUNCTUATION EXCEPT APOSTRAPHES
40 REM     AS IN  DON'T  YOU'RE  I'M  I'VE
YOU'VE
50 GOSUB 660:REM INITIALISE
60 PRINT "WELCOME TO ANOTHER SESSION WITH"
70 PRINT "YOUR COMPUTER PSYCHIATRIST, ELIZA
"
80 PRINT:INPUT "WHAT IS YOUR FIRST NAME";Z$
90 CLS:PRINT "WELL, HI THERE ";Z$
100 PRINT:PRINT "IT SURE IS NEAT TO HAVE YO
U DROP BY"
110 PRINT:PRINT "PRESS MY SPACE BAR WHEN YO
```

```
U'RE READY TO START"
120 N = N + 1
130 IF INKEY$ = "" THEN 120
140 CLS:RANDOMIZE N
150 GOSUB 590:REM ACCEPT USER INPUT
160 IF RND < .2 THEN PRINT Z$;", ";
170 GOSUB 190:REM PROCESS INPUT, PRINT REPL
Y
180 PRINT:GOTO 150
190 REM FIND KEY WORD, PHRASE
200 Z = 0
210 Z = Z + 1
220 D = INSTR(A$,B$(Z))
230 IF D <> 0 THEN 260
240 IF Z < 35 THEN 210
250 GOSUB 440:RETURN
260 REM PROCESS KEYWORDS
270 PRINT C$(Z);" ";
280 IF RIGHT$(C$(Z),1) < "A" THEN PRINT:RET
URN
290 H = LEN(A$) - (D + LEN(B$(Z)))
300 IF H > 0 THEN A$ = RIGHT$(A$,H)
310 Z = 0
320 Z = Z + 1
330 D = INSTR(A$,F$(Z))
340 IF D <> 0 THEN 370
350 IF Z < 8 THEN 320
360 PRINT A$:RETURN
370 J$ = LEFT$(A$,(D - 1)) + " " + G$(Z)
380 Z = LEN(A$) - LEN(LEFT$(A$,(D - 1))) -
LEN(G$(Z))
390 PRINT J$
400 IF Z > 2 THEN L$ = RIGHT$(A$,(Z - 2)):I
F INSTR(K$,L$) = 0 THEN RETURN
410 IF Z > 2 THEN PRINT RIGHT$(A$,(Z - 2))
420 IF Z < 2 THEN PRINT
430 RETURN
440 REM RANDOM REPLIES, NO KEY WORD
450 Z = INT(RND*11) + 1
460 ON Z GOSUB 480,490,500,510,520,530,540,
550,560,570,580
470 RETURN
480 PRINT "WHAT DOES THAT SUGGEST TO YOU?":
RETURN
```

```
490 PRINT "I SEE...":RETURN
500 PRINT "I'M NOT SURE I UNDERSTAND YOU FU
LLY.":RETURN
510 PRINT "CAN YOU ELABORATE ON THAT?":RETU
RN
520 PRINT "THAT IS QUITE INTERESTING!":RETU
RN
530 PRINT "THAT'S SO...PLEASE CONTINUE...":
RETURN
540 PRINT "I UNDERSTAND...":RETURN
550 PRINT "WELL, WELL...DO GO ON.":RETURN
560 PRINT "WHY ARE YOU SAYING THAT?":RETURN

570 PRINT "PLEASE EXPLAIN THE BACKGROUND TO
 THAT REMARK...":RETURN
580 PRINT "COULD YOU SAY THAT AGAIN, IN A D
IFFERENT WAY?":RETURN
590 REM ACCEPT USER INPUT
600 INPUT A$:K$ = A$
610 IF LEFT$(A$,3) = "BYE" THEN PRINT "BYE
BYE FOR NOW.":PRINT "SEE YOU AGAIN SOME TIM
E.":END
620 K = LEN (A$)
630 IF LEFT$(A$,7) = "BECAUSE" THEN A$ = RI
GHT$(A$,(K - 7)):K = K - 7
640 A$ = " " + A$ + " "
650 RETURN
660 REM INITIALISE
670 CLS:N = 0
680 DIM  B$(35),C$(35),F$(8),G$(8)
690 REM FILL B$,C$ WITH KEY WORDS, REPLIES
700 FOR A = 1 TO 35
710 READ B$(A),C$(A)
720 NEXT A
730 RESTORE 1150
740 FOR A = 1 TO 8
750 READ F$(A):READ G$(A)
760 NEXT A
770 RETURN
780 REM KEYWORDS, REPLIES
790 DATA " CAN YOU","PERHAPS YOU WOULD LIKE
 TO BE ABLE TO"
800 DATA " DO YOU","YES, I"
810 DATA " CAN I","PERHAPS YOU DON'T WANT T
```

O BE ABLE TO"
820 DATA " YOU ARE","WHAT MAKES YOU THINK I
 AM"
830 DATA " YOU'RE","WHAT IS YOUR REACTION T
O ME BEING"
840 DATA "I DON'T","WHY DON'T YOU"
850 DATA " I FEEL","TELL ME MORE ABOUT FEEL
ING"
860 DATA " WHY DON'T YOU","WHY WOULD YOU WA
NT ME TO"
870 DATA " WHY CAN'T I","WHAT MAKES YOU THI
NK YOU SHOULD BE ABLE TO"
880 DATA " ARE YOU","WHY ARE YOU INTERESTED
 IN WHETHER OR NOT I AM"
890 DATA " I CAN'T","HOW DO YOU KNOW YOU CA
N'T"
900 DATA " SEX","I FEEL YOU SHOULD REALLY D
ISCUSS THIS WITH A HUMAN."
910 DATA " I AM","HOW LONG HAVE YOU BEEN"
920 DATA " I'M","WHY ARE YOU TELLING ME YOU
'RE"
930 DATA " I WANT","WHY DO YOU WANT"
940 DATA " WHAT","WHAT DO YOU THINK?"
950 DATA " HOW","WHAT ANSWER WOULD PLEASE Y
OU THE MOST?"
960 DATA " WHO","HOW OFTEN DO YOU THINK OF
SUCH QUESTIONS?"
970 DATA " WHERE","WHY DID YOU ASK ME THAT?
"
980 DATA " WHEN","WHAT WOULD YOUR BEST FRIE
ND SAY TO THAT QUESTION?"
990 DATA " WHY","WHAT IS IT THAT YOU REALLY
 WANT TO KNOW?"
1000 DATA " PERHAPS","YOU'RE NOT VERY FIRM
ON THAT!"
1010 DATA " DRINK","MODERATION IN ALL THING
S SHOULD BE THE RULE."
1020 DATA " SORRY","WHY ARE YOU APOLOGIZING
?"
1030 DATA " DREAM","WHY DID YOU BRING UP TH
E SUBJECT OF DREAMS?"
1040 DATA " I LIKE","IS IT GOOD THAT YOU LI
KE"
1050 DATA " MAYBE","AREN'T YOU BEING A BIT

```
TENTATIVE?"
1060 DATA " NO","WHY ARE YOU BEING NEGATIVE
?"
1070 DATA " YOUR","WHY ARE YOU CONCERNED AB
OUT MY"
1080 DATA " ALWAYS","CAN YOU THINK OF A SPE
CIFIC EXAMPLE?"
1090 DATA " THINK","DO YOU DOUBT"
1100 DATA " YES","YOU SEEM QUITE CERTAIN. W
HY IS THIS SO?"
1110 DATA " FRIEND","WHY DO YOU BRING UP TH
E SUBJECT OF FRIENDS?"
1120 DATA " COMPUTER","WHY DO YOU MENTION C
OMPUTERS?"
1130 DATA " AM I","YOU ARE"
1140 REM CONJUGATE
1150 DATA " I ","YOU"
1160 DATA " ARE ","AM"
1170 DATA " WERE ","WAS"
1180 DATA " YOU ","ME"
1190 DATA " YOUR ","MY"
1200 DATA " I'VE ","YOU'VE"
1210 DATA " I'M ","YOU'RE"
1220 DATA " ME ","YOU"
1230 DATA " AM I ","YOU ARE"
1240 DATA " AM ","ARE"
```

☐ ELECTRONIC BRAIN

ELECTRONIC BRAIN is an attempt to write a program which would work toward the answer to a problem, in an apparently intelligent manner. The computer is attempting to solve a problem of the type where you think of a numerical code, and the computer tries to guess it. The feedback you give its answers are as "whites" and "blacks," where a white is given for a digit which is correct, but is in the wrong position in the code, and a black is given whenever there is a correct digit within the code.

The problem is not totally straightforward, as the computer does not *know*, for certain, which digit produced which result. I wrote two versions of this program, one to solve three-digit codes, and a modification of that program to solve four-digit ones. It works in a simple manner (although implementing the relatively simple idea behind the program was not particularly easy). Every time a digit appears in a code which is awarded a black, every digit within that code is weighted so that it appears more often in future guesses. The more blacks in that particular code, the higher the weighting each code gets. A much smaller weighting is awarded if the code gets one or more whites. Any code getting neither a black nor a white leads to all the digits within that guess being totally removed from future consideration.

As I said, the three-digit version is the basis upon which the four-digit program was written. Enter the three-digit one first, and then save it in that form, before making the needed conversion to make it work as a four-digit program. Whereas the three-digit version works reasonably well, and reasonably quickly, the four-digit program grinds almost to a halt toward the end, as it tries to generate codes which (a) reflect the weighting that previous answers have produced, and (b) are not codes which have been previously suggested in that particular run.

Here's the program solving a three-digit code:

Guess number 1

My guess is 1   2   3

How many blacks? 1

And how many whites? 0

Guess number 2

My guess is 4   5   6

How many blacks? 0

And how many whites? 1

Guess number 3

My guess is 7   8   9

How many blacks? 1

And how many whites? 0

Guess number 4

My guess is 4   2   6

How many blacks? 0

And how many whites? 1

Guess number 5

My guess is 8   2   1

How many blacks? 0

And how many whites? 1

Guess number 6

My guess is 1   9   4

How many blacks? 1

And how many whites? 2

Guess number 7

My guess is 1   4   9

How many blacks? 3

I guessed your code of
      1   4   9 in just 7
      guesses

And this is the listing that produced it:

```
10  REM ELECTRONIC BRAIN - 3 digits
20  GOSUB 510:REM INITIALISE
30  REM MAKE A GUESS
40  IF GUESS < 3 THEN FOR Z = 1 TO 3:B(Z) =
Z + 3*GUESS:NEXT Z:GOTO 70
60  GOSUB 280
70  CLS
80  GUESS = GUESS + 1
90  PRINT:PRINT
100 PRINT "Guess number"GUESS
110 PRINT
120 PRINT "My guess is"B(1);B(2);B(3)
130 PRINT:PRINT
140 INPUT "How many blacks";B
150 IF B = 3 THEN GOTO 600
160 IF B = 2 THEN 190
170 PRINT:PRINT
180 INPUT "And how many whites";W
190 IF W + B = 3 THEN Q = 3:C(1) = B(1):C(2
) = B(2):C(3) = B(3)
200 IF B + W = 0 THEN C(B(1)) = 0:C(B(2)) =
 0:C(B(3)) = 0:GOTO 30
210 IF B > AID THEN FOR Z = 1 TO 3:E(Z) = B
(Z):NEXT Z:AID = B
220 FOR Z = 1 TO 9
230 FOR D = 1 TO 3
240 IF B(D) = C(Z) THEN C(Z) = C(Z) + (B +
W)*100 + W*10
250 NEXT D
260 NEXT Z
270 GOTO 30
280 REM Pick three numbers
290 FOR Z = 1 TO 3
300 D1 = C(INT(RND*Q) + 1)
310 IF D1 = 0 THEN 300
320 D2 = C(INT(RND*Q) + 1)
330 IF D2 = 0 THEN 320
340 IF INT(D1/10) > INT(D2/10) THEN B(Z) =
D1
350 IF INT(D1/10) < INT(D2/10) THEN B(Z) =
D2
```

```
360 IF INT(D1/10) = INT(D2/10) THEN B(Z) =
D1
370 IF B(Z) > 100 THEN B(Z) = B(Z) - 100*IN
T(B(Z)/100):GOTO 370
380 IF B(Z) > 10 THEN B(Z) = B(Z) - 10*INT(
B(Z)/10):GOTO 380
390 NEXT Z
400 IF B(1) = B(2) OR B(1) = B(3) OR B(2) =
 B(3) THEN 290
410 IF AID > 0 THEN COUNT = 0:FOR Z = 1 TO
3:IF B(Z) = E(Z) THEN COUNT = COUNT + 1
420 IF AID > 0 THEN NEXT Z:IF COUNT < AID T
HEN 290
430 M = 100*B(1) + 10*B(2) + B(3)
440 K(GUESS) = M
450 IF GUESS < 3 THEN 500
460 COUNT = 1
470 COUNT = COUNT + 1
480 IF K(COUNT) = M THEN  290
490 IF COUNT < GUESS - 1 THEN 470
500 RETURN
510 REM INITIALISE
520 DEFINT A - Z
530 GUESS = 0:Q = 9:AID = 0
540 RANDOMIZE VAL(RIGHT$(TIME$,2))
550 DIM B(3),C(9),E(3),K(100)
560 FOR Z = 1 TO 9
570 C(Z) = Z
580 NEXT Z
590 RETURN
600 PRINT:PRINT
610 PRINT "I guessed your code of"B(1);B(2)
;B(3)
620 PRINT TAB(5);"in just"GUESS"guesses"
630 END
```

Now, after some conversion, the computer is trying to crack a four-digit code:

Guess number 10

My guess is 9 5 1 2
How many blacks? 0
And how many whites? 1

Guess number 11

My guess is 1 2 4 9
How many blacks? 0
And how many whites? 2

Guess number 12

My guess is 7 1 4 9
How many blacks? 0
And how many whites? 2

Guess number 13

My guess is 4 3 7 1
How many blacks? 1
And how many whites? 1

Guess number 14

My guess is 7 3 4 2
How many blacks? 1
And how many whites? 1

Guess number 15

My guess is 6 3 9 4
How many blacks? 4

I guessed your code of
      6 3 9 4 in just
15 guesses

This is the listing to solve four-digit codes, which is based on the three-digit one. Note the addition of "−1" in line 420 of this program, as well as the other changes:

```
10 REM ELECTRONIC BRAIN - 4 digits
20 GOSUB 510:REM INITIALISE
30 REM MAKE A GUESS
40 IF GUESS = 0 THEN FOR Z = 1 TO 4:B(Z) =
Z:NEXT Z:GOTO 70
50 IF GUESS = 1 THEN FOR Z = 1 TO 4:B(Z) =
Z + 4:NEXT Z:GOTO 70
60 GOSUB 280
70 CLS
80 GUESS = GUESS + 1
90 PRINT:PRINT
```

```
100  PRINT "Guess number"GUESS
110  PRINT
120  PRINT "My guess is"B(1);B(2);B(3);B(4)
130  PRINT:PRINT
140  INPUT "How many blacks";B
150  IF B = 4 THEN GOTO 600
160  IF B = 3 THEN 190
170  PRINT:PRINT
180  INPUT "And how many whites";W
190  IF W + B = 4 THEN Q = 4:C(1) = B(1):C(2
) = B(2):C(3) = B(3):C(4) = B(4)
200  IF B + W = 0 THEN C(B(1)) = 0:C(B(2)) =
 0:C(B(3)) = 0:C(B(4)) = 0:GOTO 30
210  IF B > AID THEN FOR Z = 1 TO 4:E(Z) = B
(Z):NEXT Z:AID = B
220  FOR Z = 1 TO 9
230  FOR D = 1 TO 4
240  IF B(D) = C(Z) THEN C(Z) = C(Z) + (B +
W)*100 + W*10
250  NEXT D
260  NEXT Z
270  GOTO 30
280  REM Pick four numbers
290  FOR Z = 1 TO 4
300  D1 = C(INT(RND*Q) + 1)
310  IF D1 = 0 THEN 300
320  D2 = C(INT(RND*Q) + 1)
330  IF D2 = 0 THEN 320
340  IF INT(D1/10) > INT(D2/10) THEN B(Z) =
D1
350  IF INT(D1/10) < INT(D2/10) THEN B(Z) =
D2
360  IF INT(D1/10) = INT(D2/10) THEN B(Z) =
D1
370  IF B(Z) > 100 THEN B(Z) = B(Z) - 100*IN
T(B(Z)/100):GOTO 370
380  IF B(Z) > 10 THEN B(Z) = B(Z) - 10*INT(
B(Z)/10):GOTO 380
390  NEXT Z
400  IF B(1) = B(2) OR B(1) = B(3) OR B(1) =
 B(4) OR B(2) = B(3) OR B(2) = B(4) OR B(3)
 = B(4) THEN 290
410  IF AID > 0 THEN COUNT = 0:FOR Z = 1 TO
4:IF B(Z) = E(Z) THEN COUNT = COUNT + 1
```

```
420 IF AID > 0 THEN NEXT Z:IF COUNT < AID -
   1  THEN 290
430 M = 1000*B(1) + 100*B(2) + 10*B(3) + B(
4)
440 K(GUESS) = M
450 IF GUESS < 3 THEN 500
460 COUNT = 1
470 COUNT = COUNT + 1
480 IF K(COUNT) = M THEN  290
490 IF COUNT < GUESS - 1 THEN 470
500 RETURN
510 REM INITIALISE
520 DEFINT A - Z
530 GUESS = 0:Q = 9:AID = 0
540 RANDOMIZE VAL(RIGHT$(TIME$,2))
550 DIM B(4),C(9),E(4),K(100)
560 FOR Z = 1 TO 9
570 C(Z) = Z
580 NEXT Z
590 RETURN
600 PRINT:PRINT
610 PRINT "I guessed your code of"B(1);B(2)
;B(3);B(4)
620 PRINT TAB(5);"in just"GUESS"guesses"
630 END
```

☐ PROBOSCIDEAN

PROBOSCIDEAN is a program in which the computer shows what a wonderful memory it has, as it challenges you to a round of the card game "concentration."

A deck of cards is shuffled, and then laid out on the screen. You and the computer take it in turns to choose two cards. These are turned over, and if they are a pair, the player who selected them is awarded a point. This process continues until all the cards have been selected. The winner, naturally enough, is the player who has selected the most pairs.

Here's a game in which (as usual) the mere human (me) is thrashed by the computer's 64K memory:

```
Please stand by, card-sharp!

Start flexing those memory muscles...

What level of difficulty (1 - 10)?
(10 is easy, 1 is almost IMPOSSIBLE!)
? 1


     1  --   2  --   3  --   4  --   5  --
     6  --   7  --   8  --   9  --  10  --
    11  --  12  --  13  --  14  --  15  --
    16  --  17  --  18  --  19  --  20  --
    21  --  22  --  23  --  24  --  25  --
    26  --  27  5D 28  --  29  --  30  --
    31  --  32  --  33  --  34  --  35  --
    36  --  37  --  38  --  39  --  40  --
    41  --  42  --  43  QS 44  --  45  --
    46  --  47  --  48  --  49  --  50  --
    51  --  52  --

Your cards: 27 and 43
No, they are not a pair
```

My score is 0 and
    yours is 0

We are playing on level 1

```
 1  --    2  --    3  JD   4  --    5  --
 6  --    7  --    8  --   9  --   10  --
11  --   12  --   13  --  14  --   15  --
16  --   17  --   18  --  19  --   20  --
21  --   22  --   23  --  24  --   25  --
26  --   27  --   28  --  29  --   30  --
31  --   32  --   33  JC  34  --   35  --
36  --   37  --   38  --  39  --   40  --
41  --   42  --   43  --  44  --   45  --
46  --   47  --   48  --  49  --   50  --
51  --   52  --
```

My cards:- 3 and 33
And I've picked a pair!

My score is 12 and
    yours is 0

We are playing on level 1

```
 1  8S    2  9C    3  JD   4  8C    5  AC
 6  2D    7  KH    8  TS   9  --   10  --
11  --   12  TD   13  4C  14  --   15  --
16  --   17  --   18  --  19  --   20  --
21  --   22  KS   23  --  24  --   25  QH
26  4D   27  --   28  8H  29  --   30  --
31  KC   32  8D   33  JC  34  --   35  --
36  TC   37  --   38  --  39  KD   40  QD
41  9H   42  --   43  QS  44  QC   45  --
46  2H   47  --   48  --  49  --   50  --
51  AH   52  TH
```

My cards:- 44 and 40
And I've picked a pair!

215

My score is 16 and
    yours is 0

We are playing on level 1

1	8S	2	9C	3	JD	4	8C	5	AC
6	2D	7	KH	8	TS	9	6D	10	--
11	3C	12	TD	13	4C	14	--	15	AS
16	--	17	AD	18	3D	19	--	20	--
21	6S	22	KS	23	5S	24	--	25	QH
26	4D	27	5D	28	8H	29	--	30	--
31	KC	32	8D	33	JC	34	--	35	--
36	TC	37	--	38	--	39	KD	40	QD
41	9H	42	--	43	QS	44	QC	45	--
46	2H	47	--	48	--	49	--	50	--
51	AH	52	TH						

My cards:- 27 and 23
And I've picked a pair!

My score is 18 and
    yours is 0

We are playing on level 1

1	8S	2	9C	3	JD	4	8C	5	AC
6	2D	7	KH	8	TS	9	6D	10	4H
11	3C	12	TD	13	4C	14	--	15	AS
16	7S	17	AD	18	3D	19	4S	20	--
21	6S	22	KS	23	5S	24	--	25	QH
26	4D	27	5D	28	8H	29	--	30	--
31	KC	32	8D	33	JC	34	--	35	--
36	TC	37	7H	38	--	39	KD	40	QD
41	9H	42	--	43	QS	44	QC	45	--
46	2H	47	--	48	--	49	--	50	--
51	AH	52	TH						

Your cards: 10 and 19
Yes, they are a pair

My score is 23 and
    yours is 2

We are playing on level 1

```
    1   8S    2   9C    3   JD    4   8C    5   AC
    6   2D    7   KH    8   TS    9   6D   10   4H
   11   3C   12   TD   13   4C   14   JH   15   AS
   16   7S   17   AD   18   3D   19   4S   20   7C
   21   6S   22   KS   23   5S   24   3S   25   QH
   26   4D   27   5D   28   8H   29   3H   30   6H
   31   KC   32   8D   33   JC   34   2C   35   9S
   36   TC   37   7H   38   2S   39   KD   40   QD
   41   9H   42   9D   43   QS   44   QC   45   6C
   46   2H   47   7D   48   5C   49   5H   50   JS
   51   AH   52   TH
```

Your cards: 30 and 45
Yes, they are a pair

My score is 23 and
    yours is 3

We are playing on level 1

```
    1   8S    2   9C    3   JD    4   8C    5   AC
    6   2D    7   KH    8   TS    9   6D   10   4H
   11   3C   12   TD   13   4C   14   JH   15   AS
   16   7S   17   AD   18   3D   19   4S   20   7C
   21   6S   22   KS   23   5S   24   3S   25   QH
   26   4D   27   5D   28   8H   29   3H   30   6H
   31   KC   32   8D   33   JC   34   2C   35   9S
   36   TC   37   7H   38   2S   39   KD   40   QD
   41   9H   42   9D   43   QS   44   QC   45   6C
   46   2H   47   7D   48   5C   49   5H   50   JS
   51   AH   52   TH
```

Your cards: 30 and 45

That's brings us to the end
of a round of Proboscidean!

I'm the winner, human!

217

You might well like to make the game easier, at least in the early stages, by adding a mechanism to remove guessed cards from the screen. This can be done by changing the third element of the each string which represents a correctly chosen card. Here, though, is the listing which played that last game:

```
10  REM Proboscidean
20  GOSUB 790:REM Initialise/Shuffle
30  GOSUB 610:REM Print out
40  GOSUB 430:REM Human guess
50  GOSUB 150:REM Computer guess
60  IF HS + CS < 26 THEN 30
70  PRINT "That's brings us to the end"
80  PRINT "of a round of Proboscidean!"
90  PRINT
100 IF HS > CS THEN PRINT "You're the win
ner!"
110 IF CS > HS THEN PRINT "I'm the winner
, human!"
120 IF CS = HS THEN PRINT "It's a draw, h
umanoid!"
130 END
140 REM ********************
150 REM Computer guess
160 MOVE = 0
170 IF R = 1 OR RND < LEVEL THEN 260
180 X = R
190 X = X - 1
200 Y = 1
210 Y = Y + 1
220 IF D(X) = D(Y) THEN 240
230 IF ASC(A$(D(X))) = ASC(A$(D(Y))) THEN
 IF X <> Y THEN IF MID$(A$(D(X)),3,1) = "
X" AND MID$(A$(D(Y)),3,1) = "X" THEN A =
D(X):B = D(Y):GOTO 340
240 IF Y < X THEN 210
250 IF X - 1 > R THEN 190
260 REM Random guess
270 COUNT = 0
280 COUNT = COUNT + 1
290 IF COUNT = 200 THEN 70
300 A = INT(RND*52) + 1
310 B = INT(RND*52) + 1
```

218

```
320 IF B = A THEN 310
330 IF RIGHT$(A$(A),1) <> "X" OR RIGHT$(A
$(B),1) <> "X" THEN 280
340 PRINT "I've selected cards"A"and"B
350 FOR P = 1 TO 1000:NEXT P
360 MID$(A$(A),3,1) = " ":MID$(A$(B),3,1)
 = " "
370 GOSUB 610
380 IF LEFT$(A$(A),1) = LEFT$(A$(B),1) TH
EN PRINT "And I've picked a pair!":CS = C
S + 1
390 IF LEFT$(A$(A),1) <> LEFT$(A$(B),1) T
HEN PRINT "But they're not a pair!":MID$(
A$(A),3,1) = "X":MID$(A$(B),3,1) = "X":D$
(R) = A$(A):D$(R + 1) = A$(B):D(R) = A:D(
R + 1) = B:R = R + 2
400 FOR P = 1 TO 1000:NEXT P
410 RETURN
420 REM *********************
430 REM Human guess
440 MOVE = 1
450 PRINT:INPUT "Enter card choice number
 one";A
460 IF A<1 OR A>52 THEN 450
470 IF RIGHT$(A$(A),1) = " " THEN PRINT "
That card has been picked":GOTO 450
480 MID$(A$(A),3,1) = " "
490 INPUT "Enter card choice number two";
B
500 IF B<1 OR B>52 OR B = A THEN 490
510 IF RIGHT$(A$(B),1) = " " THEN PRINT "
That card has been picked":GOTO 490
520 MID$(A$(B),3,1) = " "
530 GOSUB 610
540 IF LEFT$(A$(A),1) = LEFT$(A$(B),1) TH
EN PRINT "Yes, they are a pair":HS = HS +
 1
550 IF LEFT$(A$(A),1) <> LEFT$(A$(B),1) T
HEN PRINT "No, they are not a pair":MID$(
A$(A),3,1) = "X":MID$(A$(B),3,1) = "X"
560 IF LEFT$(A$(A),1) <> LEFT$(A$(B),1) T
HEN D$(R) = A$(A):D$(R + 1) = A$(B):D(R)
= A:D(R + 1) = B:R = R + 2
570 FOR P = 1 TO 1000:NEXT P
```

```
580 GOSUB 610
590 RETURN
600 REM ********************
610 REM Print out
620 CLS:PRINT "My score is"CS"and":PRINT
    "   yours is"HS
630 PRINT:PRINT "We are playing on level"
10*LEVEL
640 PRINT:PRINT "   ";
650 FOR Z = 1 TO 52
660 IF Z = 6 THEN PRINT "  ";
670 PRINT Z;" ";
680 B$ = RIGHT$(A$(Z),1)
690 IF B$ = "X" THEN PRINT "-- ";
700 IF B$ = " " THEN PRINT LEFT$(A$(Z),2)
;" ";
710 IF 5*(INT(Z/5)) = Z THEN PRINT
720 NEXT Z
730 PRINT
740 PRINT
750 IF MOVE = 1 THEN PRINT "Your cards:"A
"and"B
760 IF MOVE = 0 THEN PRINT "My cards:-"A"
and"B
770 RETURN
780 REM ********************
790 REM Initialise/Shuffle
800 RANDOMIZE VAL(RIGHT$(TIME$,2))
810 DIM A$(52),D$(500),D(500)
820 CLS:PRINT "Please stand by, card-shar
p!"
830 PRINT:PRINT "Start flexing those memo
ry muscles..."
840 CS = 0:HS = 0:R = 1:MOVE = 3
850 FOR B = 1 TO 52
860 D$(B) = "."
870 READ A$(B)
880 NEXT B
890 REM Moses/Oakford shuffle routine
900 FOR J = 52 TO 2 STEP - 1
910 Z = INT(RND*J) + 1
920 H$ = A$(Z)
930 A$(Z) = A$(J)
940 A$(J) = H$
```

```
950 NEXT J
960 PRINT:PRINT "What level of difficulty
(1 - 10)?"
970 PRINT "(10 is easy, 1 is almost IMPOS
SIBLE!)"
980 INPUT LEVEL:IF LEVEL < 1 OR LEVEL > 1
0 THEN 980
990 LEVEL = LEVEL/10
1000 RETURN
1010 DATA "AHX","2HX","3HX","4HX","5HX","
6HX","7HX","8HX","9HX","THX","JHX","QHX",
"KHX"
1020 DATA "ADX","2DX","3DX","4DX","5DX","
6DX","7DX","8DX","9DX","TDX","JDX","QDX",
"KDX"
1030 DATA "ASX","2SX","3SX","4SX","5SX","
6SX","7SX","8SX","9SX","TSX","JSX","QSX",
"KSX"
1040 DATA "ACX","2CX","3CX","4CX","5CX","
6CX","7CX","8CX","9CX","TCX","JCX","QCX",
"KCX"
```

☐AMANUENSIS

Next we'll have our poetry writing program. This demands no interaction from you, except for that of admiring the wonderful (!) output of the program. Here's a sample of the kind of verse it produces:

```
THE CONVOY CLAIMED SLAVISHLY
     IN THE COURT...
PRAYING FOR AN ASTRAL INFLUENCE,
   TO DEMUR THE FAUN...
  EXHAUSTING, THEN GNAWING
     ...IMPOUNDING, BREAKING.


THE POSTULANT BESEECHED NEGLECTFULLY
     IN THE ENEMY'S CAMP...
WANTING FOR A DOGMATIST,
   TO RECANT THE DJINN...
 DISPENSING WITH, THEN ERODING
    ...ENCLOSING, WOUNDING.


THE ASPIRANT CRAVED SUCCESSFULLY
     IN THE RACECOURSE...
PRAYING FOR HOBSON'S CHOICE,
   TO QUENCH THE GHOST...
  EMPTYING, THEN BLIGHTING
     ...HANDCUFFING, ROTTING.


THE ASPIRANT ENTREATED HALTINGLY
     IN THE HIPPODROME...
PRAYING FOR A BLIND BARGAIN,
   TO RECANT THE NAIAD...
 WASTING, THEN BREAKING
     ...RESTRAINING, UNDERMINING.
```

```
THE CASTELLAN DEMANDED HALTINGLY
    IN THE HIPPODROME...
SCREAMING FOR THE FATES,
  TO RELINQUISH THE GHOST...
EXHAUSTING, THEN DAMAGING
    ...SUPPRESSING, BREAKING.


THE APPLICANT PRESSED PRIDEFULLY
    IN THE ENEMY'S CAMP...
WATCHING FOR A SPELLBINDER,
  TO DEMUR THE HOBGOBLIN...
DRYING UP, THEN ROTTING
    ...HANDCUFFING, DAMAGING.


THE CLAIMANT CRAVED SLAVISHLY
    IN THE BEAR GARDEN...
CRYING FOR HOBSON'S CHOICE,
  TO WAVER THE DRYAD...
DRYING UP, THEN ERODING
    ...RESTRAINING, ROTTING.


THE MENDICANT CONJURED HELPLESSLY
    IN THE COURT...
PRAYING FOR A DOGMATIST,
  TO QUENCH THE LEPRECHAUN...
RUNNING OUT, THEN ERODING
    ...IMPOUNDING, BLIGHTING.


THE CONVOY DEMANDED HELPLESSLY
    IN THE HIPPODROME...
WATCHING FOR A ZEALOT,
  TO ABJURE THE GHOST...
SPENDING, THEN CORRODING
    ...IMPOUNDING, GNAWING.
```

```
THE POSTULANT ENTREATED ENDLESSLY
      IN THE PLAYGROUND...
WAITING FOR HOBSON'S CHOICE,
   TO RELINQUISH THE SATUR...
DISPENSING WITH, THEN DAMAGING
   ...COERCING, BREAKING.


THE BEGGAR CLAIMED HALTINGLY
      IN THE THEATRE OF WAR...
ASKING FOR FORTUNE'S WHEEL,
   TO BACK THE NAIAD...
DISPENSING WITH, THEN BREAKING
   ...MUZZLING, WOUNDING.
```

This is the listing of AMANUENSIS. Once you've run it for a while, you may well wish to change the words in the DATA statements, to vary the kind of poetry it produces.

```
10 REM AMANUENSIS
20 CLS
30 DIM A$(12)
40 N = 0
50 PRINT "PRESS ANY KEY TO BEGIN"
60 N = N + 1: IF INKEY$ = "" THEN 60
70 RANDOMIZE N:CLS
80 REM *****************************
90 RESTORE 330:GOSUB 450:A$(1) = B$
100 RESTORE 340:GOSUB 450:A$(2) = B$
110 RESTORE 350:GOSUB 450:A$(3) = B$
120 RESTORE 360:GOSUB 450:A$(4) = B$
130 RESTORE 370:GOSUB 450:A$(5) = B$
140 RESTORE 380:GOSUB 450:A$(6) = B$
150 RESTORE 390:GOSUB 450:A$(7) = B$
160 RESTORE 400:GOSUB 450:A$(8) = B$
170 RESTORE 410:GOSUB 450:A$(9) = B$
180 RESTORE 420:GOSUB 450:A$(10) = B$
190 RESTORE 430:GOSUB 450:A$(11) = B$
200 RESTORE 420:GOSUB 450:A$(12) = B$
210 REM *****************************
220 PRINT "THE ";A$(1);" ";A$(2);" ";A$(
3)
```

```
230 PRINT "      IN THE ";A$(4);"..."
240 PRINT A$(5);" FOR ";A$(6);","
250 PRINT "   TO ";A$(7);" THE ";A$(8);"
...""
260 PRINT " ";A$(9);", THEN ";A$(10)
270 PRINT "   ...";A$(11);", ";A$(12);"
."
280 PRINT:PRINT
290 REM ****************************
300 FOR T = 1 TO 1000:NEXT T
310 GOTO 90
320 REM ****************************
330 DATA "APPLICANT","SUPPLICANT","MENDI
CANT","BEGGAR","ASPIRANT","CLAIMANT","PO
STULANT","CONVOY","SENTINEL","CASTELLAN"

340 DATA "ENTREATED","BESEECHED","WAITED
","BESOUGHT","CONJURED","PRESSED","URGED
","CRAVED","DEMANDED","CLAIMED"
350 DATA "SUCCESSFULLY","COURAGEOUSLY","
PROGRESSIVELY","FOOLISHLY","ENDLESSLY","
HELPLESSLY","HALTINGLY","SLAVISHLY","NEG
LECTFULLY","PRIDEFULLY"
360 DATA"FIELD","BATTLEFIELD","PLAYGROUN
D","CIRCUS RING","BEAR GARDEN","ENEMY'S
CAMP","HIPPODROME","THEATRE OF WAR","COU
RT","RACECOURSE"
370 DATA "WAITING","ASKING","HOPING","WA
TCHING","PRAYING","STAYING","SCREAMING",
"WANTING","STARING","CRYING"
380 DATA "THE FATES","FORTUNE'S WHEEL","
HOBSON'S CHOICE","THE STARS","AN ASTRAL
INFLUENCE","A BLIND BARGAIN","A SPELLBIN
DER","A MALEVOLENT SPIRIT","A ZEALOT","A
 DOGMATIST"
390 DATA "QUENCH","RECANT","FORSWEAR","A
BJURE","RENOUNCE","RELINQUISH","WAVER","
DEMUR","SWERVE","BACK"
400 DATA "GHOST","SPECTRE","HOBGOBLIN","
DJINN","LEPRECHAUN","PIXY","FAUN","SATUR
","DRYAD","NAIAD"
410 DATA "WASTING","SPENDING","USING","C
ONSUMING","RUNNING OUT","DRYING UP","EMP
TYING","EXHAUSTING","SQUANDERING","DISPE
```

```
NSING WITH"
420 DATA  "CORRODING","ERODING","BLIGHTI
NG","ROTTING","GNAWING","UNDERMINING","S
HAKING","BREAKING","DAMAGING","WOUNDING"

430 DATA "RESTRAINING","COERCING","CHECK
ING","DETAINING","ENCLOSING","IMPOUNDING
","HANDCUFFING","MUZZLING","GAGGING","SU
PPRESSING"
440 REM ******************************
450 FOR N = 1 TO RND*10 + 1
460 READ B$
470 NEXT N
480 RETURN
```

Just for Fun

There is a range of games in this section of your book, all designed just for fun. From NOUGHTS AND CROSSES, through LAS VEGAS HIGH, to INNER SPRING and ROBOT MINEFIELD, a splendid time is guaranteed for all.

As well as the games mentioned above, you'll find NIMGRAB and CADDY in this section. And if you have a group of little kids you'd like to leave playing with the computer for a while, we have a massive program called CAVALCADE OF PUZZLES, which brings together a collection of enjoyable games. You can only play one game when you've successfully completed the one before it. It's a great way of keeping the very young (in age or heart) amused.

Let's get down to it right away.

☐ INNER SPRING

We'll start this section of the book with one of the simplest games of the lot, INNER SPRING. As the program explains, the computer produces two numbers between one and 13, and asks you to bet on the probability of the next number it thinks of lying between the first two. It's simple to play, and a lot of fun.

Here's what one round looks like in action:

```
MY FIRST NUMBER IS 2
      MY SECOND IS 4

YOU HAVE $ 2

HOW MUCH DO YOU BET
MY NEXT NUMBER LIES
BETWEEN 2 AND 4 ? 1

MY NUMBER WAS 3
WELL DONE, YOU WIN $ 2
```

And here's the listing of INNER SPRING:

```
10  REM INNER SPRING
20  GOSUB 330
30  GOSUB 80
40  IF D<1 THEN GOTO 420
50  GOSUB 340
60  GOTO 30
70  REM ************************
80  PRINT:PRINT:PRINT
90  PRINT "MY FIRST NUMBER IS"A
100 PRINT"      MY SECOND IS"B
110 PRINT
120 PRINT "YOU HAVE $"D
130 PRINT
140 PRINT "HOW MUCH DO YOU BET"
150 PRINT "MY NEXT NUMBER LIES"
160 PRINT "BETWEEN"A"AND"B;
170 INPUT E
```

```
180 IF E > D THEN 170
190 D = D - E
200 GOSUB 500
210 PRINT:PRINT "MY NUMBER WAS"C
220 GOSUB 500
230 IF NOT (C>A AND C<B OR C<A AND C>B)
THEN 290
240 PRINT "WELL DONE, YOU WIN $"2*E
250 D = D + 3*E
260 GOSUB 500
270 RETURN
280 REM ************************
290 PRINT "SORRY, YOU LOSE $"E
300 GOSUB 500
310 RETURN
320 REM ************************
330 D = 20
340 CLS
350 A = INT (RND*13) + 1
360 B = INT (RND*13) + 1
370 IF ABS(A - B) < 2 OR ABS(A - B) > 6
THEN 360
380 C = INT(RND*13) + 1
390 IF A = C OR B = C THEN 380
400 RETURN
410 REM ************************
420 PRINT
430 PRINT "THE GAME IS OVER"
440 PRINT
450 PRINT "YOU ARE BROKE!"
460 PRINT
470 PRINT "THANKS FOR THE GAME"
480 END
490 REM ************************
500 FOR Z = 1 TO 1000
510 NEXT Z
520 RETURN
```

☐ NIMGRAB

NIMGRAB is a game which seems easy at first, but is the very devil to play . . . and win. You and the wily computer take turns taking objects away from the screen. There is a limit to how many you can take away each move (and this limit changes from game to game, although it does not change within a particular round of the game). The winner is the person who manages to force the other player to remove the last object.

Once you see it in action, you'll understand how to play it. Then you can start working on perfecting a method of actually beating the computer. Here is NIMGRAB underway:

```
The maximum you can grab is 4

*#*#*#*#*#*#*#*#*#*#*#*#*#*#*#*#*#*#*

1
2  3
4
5  6  7
8  9  10
11  12  13  14  15  16  17  18  19
*#*#*#*#*#*#*#*#*#*#*#*#*#*#*#*#*#*#*

How many will you grab?

So you want to grab 2

*#*#*#*#*#*#*#*#*#*#*#*#*#*#*#*#*#*#*
```

232

```
*#*#*#*#*#*#*#*#*#*#*#*#*#*#*#*#*

The maximum you can grab is 4

*#*#*#*#*#*#*#*#*#*#*#*#*#*#*#*#*

You took 2 , and I took 2
  1
  2   3
  4   5   6   7   8   9   10
  11  12
  13  14  15

*#*#*#*#*#*#*#*#*#*#*#*#*#*#*#*#*

How many will you grab?


    _____



*#*#*#*#*#*#*#*#*#*#*#*#*#*#*#*#*

The maximum you can grab is 4

*#*#*#*#*#*#*#*#*#*#*#*#*#*#*#*#*

You took 1 , and I took 4
  1
*#*#*#*#*#*#*#*#*#*#*#*#*#*#*#*#*

How many will you grab?

So you want to grab 1

*#*#*#*#*#*#*#*#*#*#*#*#*#*#*#*#*

You grabbed the last one
                so I win!!
```

And here is the listing of that program:

```
10 REM Nimgrab
20 CLS
30 PRINT "Press 'S' to start the game..."
40 N = 0
50 N = N + 1: IF INKEY$ = "" THEN 50
60 RANDOMIZE N
70 CLS
80 M = 0:E = 0:Z = INT(RND*8) + 16
90 IF 2*INT(Z/2) = Z THEN Z = Z + 1
100 H = 3 + INT(RND*2)
110 PRINT "The maximum you can grab is"H
120 GOSUB 320
130 IF E > 0 THEN PRINT "You took"E", and
I took"Q
140 FOR K = 1 TO Z
150 PRINT K;: IF RND >.8 THEN PRINT
160 NEXT K
170 GOSUB 320
180 PRINT "How many will you grab?"
190 E = VAL(INKEY$)
200 IF E<1 OR E>H OR E>Z THEN 190
210 PRINT:PRINT "So you want to grab"E
220 Z = Z - E
230 GOSUB 320
240 IF Z<1 THEN PRINT "You grabbed the las
t one":PRINT ,"so I win!!":END
250 Q = Z - 1 - INT((Z-1)/(H+1))*(H+1) - I
NT(RND*2) + INT(RND*2)
260 IF Q<1 OR Q>H THEN 250
270 GOSUB 320
280 Z = Z - Q
290 IF Z<1 THEN PRINT "I grabbed the last
one":PRINT ,"so you win!!":END
300 GOSUB 320
310 GOTO 110
320 PRINT
330 PRINT "*#*#*#*#*#*#*#*#*#*#*#*#*#*#*#*
#*"
340 PRINT
350 FOR O = 1 TO 200:NEXT O
360 RETURN
```

☐ TUTANKHAMEN'S TOMB

Tutankhamen was pharaoh of the 18th Dynasty of Egypt, around 1360 B.C. He became king at the age of 11. The reason he is so well known today is that his tomb, discovered by archaeologist Howard Carter in 1922, is the only Egyptian royal tomb to have been found in almost its original condition. Most of the other tombs had long been ransacked by thieves.

The Curse of the Royal Tomb hit those who dared disturb its sanctuary after such a long time, and the Curse continues its evil work in our program. The game outlines the rules, and the background:

```
YOU HAVE A LIMITED TIME IN WHICH
TO FIND AN EXPLORER LOST WITHIN
EGYPT'S GREATEST PYRAMID

{}{}{}{}{}{}{}{}{}{}{}{}{}{}{}{}{}{}


HE IS TRAPPED WITHIN THE PHARAOH'S
TOMB...AND HAS ONLY A VERY SMALL AMOUNT
OF AIR...YOU CAN TELL APPROXIMATELY
WHERE HE IS BECAUSE HE IS KNOCKING ON
ON THE SIDE OF THE TOMB AND YOU ARE
MAKING YOUR WAY TOWARDS THE SOUND...
YOU CAN HEAR KNOCKING....

{}{}{}{}{}{}{}{}{}{}{}{}{}{}{}{}{}{}


HOWEVER THE SOUND IS MUFFLED, AND
YOU CANNOT ALWAYS TELL EXACTLY WHERE
IT IS COMING FROM....

{}{}{}{}{}{}{}{}{}{}{}{}{}{}{}{}{}{}
```

You play by entering one of the following letters, which indicate the direction in which you wish to move as you continue your exploration:

U—up

D—down

R—right

L—left

F—forward

B—back

Here's the game in action:

```
THE KNOCKING APPEARS TO BE COMING FROM
TO THE RIGHT AND AHEAD OF YOU

YOU HAVE 20 MINUTES LEFT

YOU ARE IN A SERIES OF TUNNELS
WITHIN THE PYRAMID...WHICH WAY DO YOU
WANT TO TURN (U,D,R,L,F,B)? R


{}{}{}{}{}{}{}{}{}{}{}{}{}{}{}{}{}{}


THE KNOCKING APPEARS TO BE COMING FROM
TO THE RIGHT AND AHEAD OF YOU

YOU HAVE 19 MINUTES LEFT

YOU ARE IN A SERIES OF TUNNELS
WITHIN THE PYRAMID...WHICH WAY DO YOU
WANT TO TURN (U,D,R,L,F,B)? F

{}{}{}{}{}{}{}{}{}{}{}{}{}{}{}{}{}{}
```

You'll discover you soon become quite skillful at interpreting the feedback from the computer although it is—as you can see—somewhat erratic due to the imperfect sound transmission qualities of the stone. Here's the result of a successful run:

```
TO THE RIGHT
YOU HAVE 4 MINUTES LEFT

YOU ARE IN A SERIES OF TUNNELS
WITHIN THE PYRAMID...WHICH WAY DO YOU
WANT TO TURN (U,D,R,L,F,B)? R


{}{}{}{}{}{}{}{}{}{}{}{}{}{}{}{}{}{}{}


THE KNOCKING APPEARS TO BE COMING FROM

YOU HAVE 3 MINUTES LEFT

YOU ARE IN A SERIES OF TUNNELS
WITHIN THE PYRAMID...WHICH WAY DO YOU
WANT TO TURN (U,D,R,L,F,B)? R

WELL DONE....

YOU FOUND YOUR FRIEND WITH
ONLY 3 MINUTES OF AIR REMAINING...
```

And here's what you see if you fail:

```
THAT'S THE END OF THE ROAD...
YOU ARE TOO LATE...YOUR FRIEND
HAS DIED WITHIN THE PYRAMID

THE PHARAOH'S TOMB HAS BECOME
...HIS TOMB...
```

When you feel brave enough to tackle the tomb (and risk being touched by its curse), enter the following listing, and then type **RUN**:

```
10 REM TUTANKHAMEN'S TOMB
20 RANDOMIZE VAL(RIGHT$(TIME$,2))
30 A=INT(RND(1)*7)+4:B=INT(RND(1)*7)+4:C
=INT(RND(1)*7)+4
40 X=1:Y=1:Z=1
50 CLS
60 CC=21
```

```
70 PRINT "YOU HAVE A LIMITED TIME IN WHI
CH"
80 PRINT "TO FIND AN EXPLORER LOST WITHI
N"
90 PRINT "EGYPT'S GREATEST PYRAMID"
100 PRINT:PRINT "{}{}{}{}{}{}{}{}{}{}{}{}{
}{}{}{}{}{}{}":PRINT
110 FOR Q=1 TO 1000:NEXT Q
120 PRINT:PRINT "HE IS TRAPPED WITHIN TH
E PHARAOH'S"
130 PRINT "TOMB...AND HAS ONLY A VERY SM
ALL AMOUNT"
140 PRINT "OF AIR...YOU CAN TELL APPROXI
MATELY"
150 PRINT "WHERE HE IS BECAUSE HE IS KNO
CKING ON"
160 PRINT "ON THE SIDE OF THE TOMB AND Y
OU ARE"
170 PRINT "MAKING YOUR WAY TOWARDS THE S
OUND..."
180 PRINT "YOU CAN HEAR KNOCKING...."
190 PRINT:PRINT "{}{}{}{}{}{}{}{}{}{}{}{}{
}{}{}{}{}{}{}":PRINT
200 FOR Q=1 TO 1000:NEXT Q
210 PRINT:PRINT "HOWEVER THE SOUND IS MU
FFLED, AND"
220 PRINT "YOU CANNOT ALWAYS TELL EXACTL
Y WHERE"
230 PRINT "IT IS COMING FROM...."
240 FOR Q=1 TO 1000:NEXT Q
250 PRINT:PRINT "{}{}{}{}{}{}{}{}{}{}{}{}{
}{}{}{}{}{}{}":PRINT
260 PRINT:PRINT "THE KNOCKING APPEARS TO
 BE COMING FROM"
270 IF RND(1)>.7 THEN 300
280 IF X>B THEN PRINT "BELOW YOU ";
290 IF X<B THEN PRINT "ABOVE YOU ";
300 IF RND(1)>.7 THEN 340
310 IF Z>C THEN PRINT "TO THE LEFT ";
320 IF Z<C THEN PRINT "TO THE RIGHT ";
330 IF (X<>B OR Z<>C) AND Y<>A  THEN PRI
NT "AND ";
340 IF Y<A THEN PRINT "AHEAD OF YOU"
350 IF Y>A THEN PRINT "BEHIND YOU"
```

```
360 CC=CC-1
370 PRINT:PRINT "YOU HAVE";CC;"MINUTES L
EFT"
380 PRINT:PRINT "YOU ARE IN A SERIES OF
TUNNELS"
390 PRINT "WITHIN THE PYRAMID...WHICH WA
Y DO YOU"
400 INPUT "WANT TO TURN (U,D,R,L,F,B)";A
$
410 IF A$="U" THEN X=X+1:IF X>10 THEN X=
10
420 IF A$="D" THEN X=X-1:IF X<1 THEN X=1

430 IF A$="R" THEN Z=Z+1:IF Z>10 THEN Z=
10
440 IF A$="L" THEN Z=Z-1:IF Z<1 THEN Z=1

450 IF A$="F" THEN Y=Y+1:IF Y>10 THEN Y=
10
460 IF A$="B" THEN Y=Y-1:IF Y<1 THEN Y=1

470 IF X=B AND C=Z AND A=Y THEN 540
480 IF CC>1 THEN 240
490 PRINT:PRINT "THAT'S THE END OF THE R
OAD..."
500 PRINT "YOU ARE TOO LATE...YOUR FRIEN
D"
510 PRINT "HAS DIED WITHIN THE PYRAMID"
520 PRINT:PRINT "THE PHARAOH'S TOMB HAS
BECOME"
530 PRINT "...HIS TOMB...":END
540 PRINT:PRINT "WELL DONE...."
550 PRINT:PRINT "YOU FOUND YOUR FRIEND W
ITH"
560 PRINT "ONLY";CC;"MINUTES OF AIR REMA
INING..."
```

☐ ROULETTE

ROULETTE is the king of gambling games. This computer version, which faithfully follows the rules of roulette, will allow you to painlessly test your favorite "system."

This game plays with an American wheel, which has the numbers 0 to 36, plus double zero. The program speaks faultless French, as do all good croupiers, inviting you to place your bet with the words MESSIEURS, FAITES VOS JEUX (Gentlemen, place your bets). Note that the difference between the European and American wheels is discussed at the end of this introduction.

Some of the numbers on a roulette wheel are red and the balance are black. Among other bets, you can bet on the ball stopping on any red number, or any black one.

After the computer has told you how many chips you have, and asked you to place your bets, you'll be expected to enter a letter between A and Q. Q tells the computer you wish to quit (withdraw from the game), and the other letters determine which kind of bet you wish to place, according to this key:

A—a single number

B—two adjoining numbers

C—three numbers in adjoining columns

D—six numbers in adjoining columns

E—four numbers in a square

F—numbers 1 through 12 ("The First Twelve")

G—numbers 13 through 24 ("The Second Twelve")

H—numbers 25 through 36 ("The Third Twelve")

I—numbers 1 through 18 ("Low")

J—numbers 19 through 36 ("High")

K—12 numbers in a horizontal row

L—two adjacent horizontal columns

M—any red number

N—any black number

O—any even number

P—any odd number

Q—to quit the game

The red numbers are:

1, 3, 5, 7, 9, 12, 14, 16, 18, 19, 21, 23, 25, 27, 30, 32, 34, 36,

The black numbers are:

2, 4, 6, 8, 10, 11, 13, 15, 17, 20, 22, 24, 26, 28, 29, 31, 33, 35

Here's what a roulette table looks like:

```
     NOIR        PAIR        PASSE
34r  31b  28r  25r  22b  19r  16r  13b  10b  7r  4b  1r  0
35b  32r  29b  26b  23r  20b  17b  14r  11b  8b  5r  2b
36r  33b  30r  27r  24b  21r  18r  15b  12r  9r  6b  3r  00
     ROUGE       IMPAIR      MANQUE
```

As you can see, the table has three words above, and three below, the numbers. These are noir (black), pair (even), passe (numbers 19 through 36), rouge (red), impair (odd) and manque (numbers 1 through 18).

I deliberately did not include a printout of the roulette table within the program. A black and white display like the table given demands a screen width of 48 characters, which is greater than the screen width of many popular computers. As well, you are certain to be able to create a very good display using either colored graphics (which would get rid of the "r" and "b" after the numbers) or inverse numbers for the black ones and standard numbers for the white on a monochrome display.

In fact, you do not need a roulette table display within the program to run it. You may as well use this book. The most important thing about the program is its method of accepting and processing bets, after spinning the wheel, so I've concentrated on this. However, if you want to dress the program up a little, you can do so easily by incorporating a printout of the table. You may well wish to include a spinning wheel as well.

A European roulette table has the numbers 1 through 36, plus zero, while the American table has a double zero as well. It comes as quite a shock to innocent folk like me to discover that while the house take on all bets on the European wheel is 2.70% on all bets (except the even money chances, where it drops to 1.4%), the house take on the US wheel is almost doubled to 5.26%. Our wheel, as you know, follows the US system.

Here's the program in action:

```
YOU HAVE 1400 CHIPS

*#$ *#$ *#$ *#$ $#* $#* $#* $#*

MESSIEURS, FAITES VOS JEUX
? A

HOW MANY CHIPS? 365
WHICH NUMBER? 12

*#$ *#$ *#$ *#$ $#* $#* $#* $#*

THE WHEEL IS SPINNING...

*#$ *#$ *#$ *#$ $#* $#* $#* $#*
            1
                 12
                      27
                 15
           32
    3
        28
       29
         27
   25
                20
              20




THE BALL STOPPED ON 31
SORRY, BUT YOU LOST ON THAT ROUND...

*#$ *#$ *#$ *#$ $#* $#* $#* $#*

YOU HAVE 1035 CHIPS

*#$ *#$ *#$ *#$ $#* $#* $#* $#*
```

```
MESSIEURS, FAITES VOS JEUX
? N

HOW MANY CHIPS? 1035

*#$ *#$ *#$ *#$ $#* $#* $#* $#*

THE WHEEL IS SPINNING...

*#$ *#$ *#$ *#$ $#* $#* $#* $#*
    11
        31
          33
                7
                    20
    8
          29


THE BALL STOPPED ON 29

CONGRATULATIONS, YOU HAVE WON 1035 CHIPS
PLUS YOUR BET OF 1035 CHIPS

*#$ *#$ *#$ *#$ $#* $#* $#* $#*
$ YOU HAVE BROKEN THE BANK!
  $ YOU HAVE BROKEN THE BANK!
    $ YOU HAVE BROKEN THE BANK!
```

And here's the listing, so you can **FAIT** your own **JEUX**:

```
10 REM ROULETTE
20 RANDOMIZE VAL(RIGHT$(TIME$,2))
30 DIM B(24):CH=1000
40 CLS:PRINT:PRINT "YOU HAVE";CH;"CHIPS"

50 GOSUB 850
60 PRINT:PRINT "MESSIEURS, FAITES VOS JE
UX"
70 INPUT A$:IF A$="" THEN 70
80 A=ASC(A$)-64:IF A<1 OR A>17 THEN 70
90 IF A=17 THEN 700
```

```
100 FOR Q=1 TO 24:B(Q)=-99:NEXT Q
110 PRINT:INPUT "HOW MANY CHIPS";N
120 IF N<1 THEN PRINT "I CANNOT ACCEPT T
HAT BET!":GOSUB 850:GOTO 110
130 IF N>CH THEN PRINT "YOU DON'T HAVE T
HAT MANY!":GOTO 110
140 CH=CH-N
150 ON A GOSUB 430,440,450,470,490,510,5
20,530,540,550,560,580,630,650,680,690
160 GOSUB 850
170 REM *******************
180 REM **THE WHEEL SPINS**
190 PRINT:PRINT "THE WHEEL IS SPINNING..
."
200 GOSUB 850
210 FOR B=1 TO 50
220 C=INT(RND(1)*39)-1
230 PRINT TAB(RND(1)*17);
240 IF C=-1 THEN PRINT " 00" ELSE PRINT
C
250 FOR T=1 TO 3*B:NEXT T
260 NEXT B:GOSUB 850
270 CLS: IF C=-1 THEN PRINT "THE BALL ST
OPPED ON DOUBLE ZERO" ELSE PRINT "THE BA
LL STOPPED ON";C
280 Y=0:E=1
290 IF B(E)=C THEN Y=1:GOTO 310
300 IF E<24 THEN E=E+1:GOTO 290
310 IF Y=0 THEN 360
320 WI=INT(OD*N+.5):CH=CH+WI+N
330 PRINT:PRINT "CONGRATULATIONS, YOU HA
VE WON";WI;"CHIPS"
340 PRINT "PLUS YOUR BET OF";N;"CHIPS"
350 GOTO 370
360 PRINT "SORRY, BUT YOU LOST ON THAT R
OUND..."
370 GOSUB 850
380 IF CH<1 THEN 730:REM BROKE
390 IF CH>2000 THEN 800:REM BREAK THE BA
NK
400 GOTO 40
410 REM *******************
420 REM **PLACING THE BETS**
430 INPUT "WHICH NUMBER";B(1):OD=35:RETU
```

```
RN
440 INPUT "WHICH TWO NUMBERS";B(1),B(2):
OD=17:RETURN
450 INPUT "WHICH NUMBER IN LEFT COLUMN";
D
460 FOR E=0 TO 2:B(E+1)=D+E:NEXT E:OD=11
:RETURN
470 INPUT "FIRST NUMBER OF SIX";D:FOR E=
0 TO 5:B(E+1)=D+E:NEXT E
480 OD=5:RETURN
490 INPUT "FIRST NUMBER IN SQUARE";D:FOR
 E=0 TO 3:B(E+1)=D+E:IF E=2 THEN D=D+1
500 NEXT E:OD=8:RETURN
510 FOR E=1 TO 12:B(E)=E:NEXT E:OD=2:RET
URN
520 FOR E=1 TO 12:B(E)=E+12:NEXT E:OD=2:
RETURN
530 FOR E=1 TO 12:B(E)=E+24:NEXT E:OD=2:
RETURN
540 FOR E=1 TO 18:B(E)=E:NEXT E:OD=1:RET
URN
550 FOR E=1 TO 18:B(E)=E+18:NEXT E:OD=1:
RETURN
560 INPUT "LOW NUMBER AT END OF LINE";D
570 FOR E=0 TO 11:B(E+1)=3*E+D:NEXT E:OD
=2:RETURN
580 INPUT "LOW NUMBER FIRST COLUMN";D1
590 INPUT "LOW NUMBER SECOND COLUMN";D2
600 IF ABS(D1-D2)>1 THEN 580
610 FOR E=0 TO 11:B(E+1)=3*E+D1:B(E+13)=
3*E+D2:NEXT E
620 OD=.5:RETURN
630 RESTORE
640 FOR E=1 TO 18:READ B(E):NEXT E:OD=1:
RETURN
650 RESTORE
660 FOR E=1 TO 18:READ Z:NEXT E
670 FOR E=1 TO 18:READ B(E):NEXT E:OD=1:
RETURN
680 FOR E=2 TO 36 STEP 2:B(E/2)=E:NEXT E
:OD=1:RETURN
690 FOR E=1 TO 35 STEP 2:B((E+1)/2)=E:NE
XT E:OD=1:RETURN
700 PRINT:PRINT "YOU ARE WITHDRAWING FRO
```

```
M THE GAME"
710 PRINT "WITH";CH;"CHIPS"
720 END
730 FOR J=1 TO 15
740 PRINT TAB(J);"YOU HAVE LOST!"
750 FOR T=1 TO 30*J:NEXT T
760 NEXT J
770 GOSUB 850
780 PRINT:PRINT "YOU HAVE RUN OUT OF CHI
PS!"
790 END
800 FOR J=1 TO 9
810 PRINT TAB(J);"$ YOU HAVE BROKEN THE
BANK!"
820 FOR T=1 TO 50*J:NEXT T
830 NEXT J
840 END
850 PRINT:PRINT "*#$ *#$ *#$ *#$ $#* $#*
 $#* $#*"
860 FOR K=1 TO 1000:NEXT K
870 RETURN
880 DATA 1,3,5,7,9,12,14,16,18,19,21,23,
25,27,30,32,34,36
890 DATA 2,4,6,8,10,11,13,15,17,20,22,24
,26,28,29,31,33,35
```

☐ FOLLOW THE LEADER

Although the listing is not very long, so the program will only take you a few minutes to enter, you'll find FOLLOW THE LEADER a pretty hard act to follow.

The program generates a sequence of numbers which you must copy. First, it will put one number on the screen (such as 2) which will vanish after a short time. You must then enter the number. After a pause, the first number will reappear, followed by a second single digit (say, 27). You enter this, and if you've got it correct, the computer will add a third digit to the sequence (such as 273). The process continues until the computer thinks you've had enough . . . or until you make a mistake.

YOU DID IT CHAMP!! appears on the screen. Just as you're breathing a sigh of relief at having survived the ordeal, the words STAND BY FOR A MORE DIFFICULT ONE . . . come up on your screen. The game begins again, but this time the length of time the computer's number is on the screen is shortened. The computer will put you to the test five times, cutting the time to see each number as the games continue. Finally, if you survive the final mind-boggling round, you'll be told YOU ARE THE ULTIMATE CHAMP!!! and the program will stop to give you a well-earned rest.

You'll see (line 240) that, if you make a mistake, the computer generates the encouraging message:

YOU BLEW IT TURKEY!
YOUR SCORE WAS 6734

You should adjust the value of T (line 30) to produce the most suitable delay when the program cycles through the first round of the game. The number by which it is reduced (line 300) and the total which determines you are the "ultimate champ" (line 280) should also be worked out to ensure that the game is not too easy, and not absolutely impossible.

```
10  REM FOLLOW THE LEADER
20  REM **************************
30  T = 1000
40  RANDOMIZE VAL(RIGHT$(TIME$,2))
50  A=1000*INT(RND(1)*9999)+INT(RND(1)*99
99)
60  A$=STR$(A)
70  A$="2" + RIGHT$(A$,7)
80  Z=1
90  IF MID$(A$,Z,1)=" " THEN 50
100 IF Z<8 THEN Z=Z+1:GOTO 90
110 Q=1
120 REM **************************
130 CLS
140 PRINT:PRINT
150 IF Q=8 THEN 270
160 FOR Z=1 TO Q
170 PRINT MID$(A$,Z,1);
180 NEXT Z
190 FOR L = 1 TO T:NEXT L
200 CLS
210 IF INKEY$<>"" THEN 210
220 PRINT:PRINT:INPUT B$
230 IF B$="" THEN 220
240 IF B$<>LEFT$(A$,Q) THEN PRINT "YOU B
LEW IT, TURKEY!":PRINT "YOUR SCORE WAS";
37*(1100-T+10*Q):END
250 IF Q<8 THEN Q=Q+1:GOTO 130
260 REM **************************
270 PRINT:PRINT "YOU DID IT CHAMP!!"
280 IF T=500 THEN PRINT:PRINT:PRINT "YOU
 ARE THE ULTIMATE CHAMP!!!":END
290 PRINT:PRINT "STAND BY FOR A MORE DIF
FICULT ONE..."
300 T=T - 100
310 FOR Z=1 TO 3000:NEXT Z
320 GOTO 50
```

MADAME ZARA READS THE CARDS

How convenient. Not only do you save on "cross my palm with silver" coins, but the output of this program is just about as believable as the predictions laid on you by wandering fortune tellers.

Madama Zara has a totally unique deck of fortune-telling cards, The Hartnell Arcana, which contains 36 cards. The suits are Stars, Stones, Shadows, Gems, Dust, and Echoes, and the individual cards are Anchor, Tower, Elvling, Knave, Cleric, and Sovereign. The four cards which are selected, and their relationship to each other, determines the fate Madama Zara reads for you. (Actually, it doesn't happen like that at all, as it all depends on your wayward random number generator, but you don't need to tell your friends this.)

The program begins with a flashy display, then asks for your name and birthdate, and tells you the astrological sign under which you were born:

```
MADAME ZARA READS THE STARS....
* * * * * * * * * * * * * * * * *
MADAME ZARA READS THE STARS....
* FOR YOU...
 * FOR YOU...


                   * FOR YOU...
                  * FOR YOU...
WHAT IS YOUR NAME, MY DEAR? TIM

WELCOME TIM, TO ZARA'S HOUSE
OF MYSTICISM...WHERE THE VEIL OVER
THE FUTURE IS MOVED BACK...
     ...JUST FOR A MOMENT

PLEASE TELL ME WHEN YOU
WERE BORN...AS NUMBERS
THE MONTH FIRST (1 - JANUARY TO
12 - DECEMBER)? 12
```

```
THANK YOU, TIM
NOW WHAT DAY OF THE MONTH WERE YOU BORN? 30

                                        *
                                          *


TIM, YOU WERE BORN UNDER
THE SIGN OF CAPRICORN
*
  *

                                    *
                                      *

NOW I SHALL GAZE INTO THE FUTURE...
*
  *

I AM TURNING UP THE CARDS FROM
THE HARTNELL ARCANA...
---------------------------------------
THIS IS THE SOVEREIGN OF STONES
---------------------------------------
---------------------------------------
THIS IS THE CLERIC OF STARS
---------------------------------------
---------------------------------------
THIS IS THE ANCHOR OF STARS
---------------------------------------
---------------------------------------
THIS IS THE KNAVE OF DUST
---------------------------------------

AND THESE CARDS TELL ME...

GOOD HEALTH WILL BE YOURS

YOU WILL BE TREATED GENTLY TODAY

STRENGTH IS ON YOUR SIDE

RICHES THROUGH PROPERTY INDICATED
---------------------------------------
THANK YOU FOR CONSULTING THE
THE WISDOM OF ZARA....
---------------------------------------
```

I WOULD LIKE TO SEE YOU
AGAIN SOME TIME, TIM

Here's the program so you can go into the fortune-telling business for yourself:

```
10 REM MADAME ZARA READS THE CARDS
20 GOSUB 770
30 PRINT:PRINT "WELCOME ";A$;", TO ZARA
'S HOUSE"
40 PRINT "OF MYSTICISM...WHERE THE VEIL
OVER"
50 PRINT "THE FUTURE IS MOVED BACK..."
60 PRINT TAB(7);"...JUST FOR A MOMENT"
70 FOR Y=1 TO 1500:NEXT Y
80 PRINT:PRINT "PLEASE TELL ME WHEN YOU"

90 PRINT "WERE BORN...AS NUMBERS"
100 PRINT "THE MONTH FIRST (1 - JANUARY
TO"
110 INPUT "12 - DECEMBER)";B1:IF B1<1 OR
 B1>12 THEN 80
120 PRINT:PRINT "THANK YOU, ";A$
130 INPUT "NOW WHAT DAY OF THE MONTH WER
E YOU BORN";B2
140 IF B2<1 OR B2>31 THEN 120
150 B=100*B1+B2
160 CLS
170 FOR Y=1 TO 32:PRINT TAB(Y);"*":NEXT
Y
180 PRINT:PRINT A$;", YOU WERE BORN UNDE
R"
190 PRINT "THE SIGN OF ";
200 IF B>=101 AND B<=120 OR B>=1223 AND
B<=1231 THEN PRINT "CAPRICORN"
210 IF B>=121 AND B<=219 THEN PRINT "AQU
ARIUS"
220 IF B>=220 AND B<=321 THEN PRINT "PIS
CES"
230 IF B>=332 AND B<=420 THEN PRINT "ARI
ES"
240 IF B>=421 AND B<=521 THEN PRINT "TAU
RUS"
```

```
250 IF B>=522 AND B<=621 THEN PRINT "GEM
INI"
260 IF B>=622 AND B<=723 THEN PRINT "CAN
CER"
270 IF B>=724 AND B<=823 THEN PRINT "LEO
"
280 IF B>=824 AND B<=923 THEN PRINT "VIR
GO"
290 IF B>=924 AND B<=1023 THEN PRINT "LI
BRA"
300 IF B>=1024 AND B<=1122 THEN PRINT "S
CORPIO"
310 IF B>=1123 AND B<=1222 THEN PRINT "S
AGITTARIUS"
320 FOR Y=1 TO 32:PRINT TAB(Y);"*":FOR T
=1 TO 90:NEXT T:NEXT Y
330 PRINT "NOW I SHALL GAZE INTO THE FUT
URE..."
340 FOR Y=1 TO 32:PRINT TAB(Y);"*":FOR T
=1 TO 90:NEXT T:NEXT Y
350 PRINT "I AM TURNING UP THE CARDS FRO
M"
360 PRINT "THE HARTNELL ARCANA..."
370 FOR T=1 TO 1000:NEXT T
380 FOR Y=1 TO 4
390 A=INT(RND(1)*6)
400 PRINT "------------------------------
-----"
410 PRINT "THIS IS ";
420 IF A=0 THEN PRINT "THE ANCHOR ";
430 IF A=1 THEN PRINT "THE TOWER ";
440 IF A=2 THEN PRINT "THE ELVLING ";
450 IF A=3 THEN PRINT "THE KNAVE ";
460 IF A=4 THEN PRINT "THE CLERIC ";
470 IF A=5 THEN PRINT "THE SOVEREIGN ";
480 A=INT(RND(1)*6)
490 IF A=0 THEN PRINT "OF STARS"
500 IF A=1 THEN PRINT "OF STONES"
510 IF A=2 THEN PRINT "OF SHADOWS"
520 IF A=3 THEN PRINT "OF GEMS"
530 IF A=4 THEN PRINT "OF DUST"
540 IF A=5 THEN PRINT "OF ECHOES"
550 PRINT "------------------------------
-----"
```

```
560 FOR T=1 TO 3000:NEXT T
570 NEXT Y
580 FOR T=1 TO 4000:NEXT T
590 PRINT:PRINT "AND THESE CARDS TELL ME
...."
600 FOR T=1 TO 2000:NEXT T
610 PRINT:PRINT A$((INT(RND(1)*10)+1))
620 FOR T=1 TO 2000:NEXT T
630 PRINT:PRINT B$((INT(RND(1)*10)+1))
640 FOR T=1 TO 2000:NEXT T
650 PRINT:PRINT C$((INT(RND(1)*10)+1))
660 FOR T=1 TO 2000:NEXT T
670 PRINT:PRINT D$((INT(RND(1)*10)+1))
680 FOR T=1 TO 2000:NEXT T
690 PRINT "------------------------------
-----"
700 PRINT:PRINT "THANK YOU FOR CONSULTIN
G THE"
710 PRINT "THE WISDOM OF ZARA...."
720 FOR T=1 TO 3000:NEXT T
730 PRINT "------------------------------
-----"
740 PRINT:PRINT "I WOULD LIKE TO SEE YOU
"
750 PRINT "AGAIN SOME TIME, ";A$
760 END
770 DIM A$(10),B$(10),C$(10),D$(10)
780 RANDOMIZE VAL(RIGHT$(TIME$,2))
790 CLS
800 FOR T= 1 TO 10
810 PRINT "* * * * * * * * * * * * * *
* * *"
820 PRINT "MADAME ZARA READS THE STARS..
.."
830 NEXT T
840 FOR T = 1 TO 20
850 PRINT TAB(T);"* FOR YOU..."
860 NEXT T
870 FOR T= 1 TO 2000:NEXT T
880 INPUT "WHAT IS YOUR NAME, MY DEAR";A
$
890 CLS
900 FOR T=1 TO 10:READ A$(T):READ B$(T)
910 READ C$(T):READ D$(T):NEXT T
```

```
920 RETURN
930 DATA "A SUDDEN SHOCK","GREAT JOY IS
NEAR","A PARK, AND A SPECIAL FRIENDSHIP"
,"DISAPPOINTMENT IS ON ITS WAY","YOU ARE
 CLOSELY PROTECTED FROM HARM"
940 DATA "THERE IS A CHANCE TO STOP ILL-
FEELING","GOOD FRIENDS ARE NEAR","DISTRU
ST THOSE WHO WOULD ADVISE YOU","THE MOON
 IS IN A GOOD ASPECT FOR YOU"
950 DATA "SUCCESS IN SPECULATION IS LIKE
LY","CONFIDE IN THOSE NEAR YOU","SUCCESS
 IN ALL VENTURES IS INDICATED"
960 DATA "A MYSTERY WILL SOON BE SOLVED"
,"A LETTER WILL BRING YOU STRANGE NEWS",
"GOOD LUCK WILL BE YOURS TODAY"
970 DATA "HIGH HONOR IS ON ITS WAY","DOM
ESTIC HAPPINESS IS THREATENED","THE CLOU
DS ARE GATHERING","STRENGTH IS ON YOUR S
IDE"
980 DATA "SOMEONE IS WATCHING YOU WITH L
ONGING","FAMILY QUARRELS LIKELY","THE SU
N IS RISING ON YOUR HOPES"
990 DATA "EVIL CONSEQUENCES MAY BE AVERT
ED","THERE IS A CHANCE TO MAKE UP A QUAR
REL","YOUR STRUGGLES ARE TO BE REWARDED"

1000 DATA "YOU WILL BE TREATED GENTLY TO
DAY","A LONG-AWAITED WISH IS ABOUT TO CO
ME TRUE","SUSPICION IS FOCUSED ON YOU"
1010 DATA "GOOD HEALTH WILL BE YOURS","F
ULFILLMENT OF A DREAM IS JUST AROUND THE
 CORNER"
1020 DATA "BEAUTY COMES A-CALLING","GOOD
 TIDINGS ARE ON THEIR WAY","THE CURRENT
BAD SITUATION WILL NOT LAST LONG"
1030 DATA "LOSS OF PROPERTY IS PROBABLE"
,"YOU GET THE CHANCE TO WARD OFF EVIL"
1040 DATA "RICHES THROUGH PROPERTY INDIC
ATED","A MINOR FAILURE WILL TURN TO SUCC
ESS","I SEE A SAFE BULGING WITH MONEY FO
R YOU"
1050 DATA "GOOD NEWS IS ON ITS WAY","BEW
ARE OF FLATTERY"
```

☐ CADDY

Now it's time for you and your versatile computer to tackle the Microchip Golfcourse, with our next program, CADDY.

You have nine holes to negotiate, and as you'll see as you play the game, the computer obligingly keeps the score card for you. After each hole it will tell you how you are doing to date, and will work out your average score per hole. All you have to do is hit the ball! If you overshoot, the computer will automatically make sure the next shot is back toward the hole.

You'll find it pretty tricky going, especially on holes with a high difficulty factor.

Here's CADDY in action:

```
Score up to this hole is 7
<<< Hole number 2 >>>

DIFFICULTY FACTOR IS FOUR
                                    o
#############################\ /#########
############################# #########
^^^^^^^^^^^^^^^^^^^^^^^^^^^^^^^^^^^^^^^^^^


Enter stroke strength? 2


You did it!!
#############################\ /#########
############################ o #########
^^^^^^^^^^^^^^^^^^^^^^^^^^^^^^^^^^^^^^^^^^


After that stroke your score is 5
The game so far:
Hole 1 took 7 strokes
Hole 2 took 5 strokes

The average so far is 6


Score up to this hole is 12
<<< Hole number 3 >>>
```

DIFFICULTY FACTOR IS FOUR
                o
###########################\ /#########
########################### #########
^^

Enter stroke strength? 14
                          o
###########################\ /#########
############################# #########
^^

After that stroke your score is 2

You did it!!
###########################\ /#########
######################### o #########
^^

After that stroke your score is 9
The game so far:
Hole 1 took 7 strokes
Hole 2 took 5 strokes
Hole 3 took 9 strokes

The average so far is 7

The score for 3 holes is 21

Enter stroke strength? 5

You did it!!
###########################\ /#########
######################### o #########
^^

After that stroke your score is 3
The game so far:
Hole 1 took 7 strokes
Hole 2 took 5 strokes
Hole 3 took 9 strokes
Hole 4 took 9 strokes

```
Hole 5 took 6 strokes
Hole 6 took 4 strokes
Hole 7 took 7 strokes
Hole 8 took 6 strokes
Hole 9 took 3 strokes
```

```
The score for 9 holes is 56
```

```
End of that round, golfer!

You scored 56
and your average per hole was 6


Enter 'Y' for another round, or 'N' to quit

OK, thanks for playing, champ
```

Here's the listing, golf pro:

```
10 REM Caddy
20 DIM X(9):CO = 0
30 RANDOMIZE VAL(RIGHT$(TIME$,2))
40 FOR Z = 1 TO 9
50 SC = 0
60 J = INT(RND*12)
70 Q = INT(RND*3) + 3
80 IF Q = 5 THEN Q$ = "FIVE"
90 IF Q = 4 THEN Q$ = "FOUR"
100 IF Q = 3 THEN Q$ = "THREE"
110 CLS:PRINT:PRINT
120 IF Z = 2 THEN PRINT "Score up to this
hole is"X(1)
130 IF Z > 2 THEN PRINT "Score up to this
hole is"K
140 PRINT "<<< Hole number"Z">>>"
```

```
150 PRINT:PRINT "DIFFICULTY FACTOR IS "Q$
160 GOSUB 430
170 PRINT:INPUT "Enter stroke strength";A
180 IF J > 26 THEN A = -A
190 J = J + INT(A/(RND*Q+1))
200 IF J = 26 THEN GOSUB 490
210 IF J <> 26 THEN GOSUB 430
220 SC = SC + 1
230 PRINT:PRINT "After that stroke your sc
ore is"SC
240 FOR P = 1 TO 500:NEXT P
250 IF J <> 26 THEN 110
260 C = C + SC
270 X(Z) = SC
280 IF Z = 1 THEN 390
290 K = 0
300 PRINT "The game so far:"
310 FOR J = 1 TO Z
320 K = K + X(J)
330 PRINT "Hole"J"took"X(J)"strokes"
340 FOR M = 1 TO 300:NEXT M
350 NEXT J
360 IF Z < 9 THEN PRINT:PRINT "The average
 so far is"INT((K + .5)/Z)
370 FOR P = 1 TO 1000:NEXT P
380 IF Z > 1 THEN PRINT:PRINT "The score f
or"Z"holes is"C
390 IF Z = 1 THEN PRINT:PRINT "The score f
or the first hole is"C
400 FOR M = 1 TO 1000:NEXT M
410 NEXT Z
420 GOTO 560
430 IF J > 30 THEN J = 30
440 PRINT TAB(J + 2);"o"
450 PRINT "#########################\ /##
#######"
460 PRINT "######################### ###
#######"
470 PRINT "^^^^^^^^^^^^^^^^^^^^^^^^^^^^^^^^^
^^^^^^^^"
480 RETURN
490 PRINT:PRINT:PRINT "You did it!!"
500 FOR P = 1 TO 100:NEXT P
510 PRINT "#########################\ /##
```

```
######"
520 PRINT "######################### o ##
######"
530 PRINT "^^^^^^^^^^^^^^^^^^^^^^^^^^^^^^^^^
^^^^^^^^"
540 FOR P = 1 TO 2000:NEXT P
550 RETURN
560 PRINT:PRINT "End of that round, golfer
!"
570 PRINT:PRINT "You scored"C
580 PRINT "and your average per hole was"I
NT((C + .5)/9)
590 PRINT:PRINT
600 PRINT "Enter 'Y' for another round, or
 'N' to quit"
610 A$ = INKEY$
620 IF A$ <> "Y" AND A$ <> "y" AND A$ <> "
N" AND A$ <> "n" THEN 610
630 IF A$ = "Y" OR A$ = "y" THEN RUN
640 PRINT:PRINT "OK, thanks for playing, c
hamp"
```

☐ CAVALCADE OF PUZZLES

There is no need to explain CAVALCADE OF PUZZLES. The rules are all within the program, which presents a series of fun activities and games in a sequence. As you'll discover when you play it, you have to complete one game before you can move on to the next.

The listing is pretty long, but you can convince yourself it is worthwhile by thinking of the peaceful time you'll have once it is in. Whenever a well-meaning friend tells you how wonderful it is that you have a personal computer, and then adds "but what can you do with it?" all you need to do is load this program up, and then go and read a book for an hour or so in peace, while the computer does the job of entertaining.

Here is CAVALCADE OF PUZZLES underway:

```
Think of a number between
one and sixty-three



I will show you five
screenfulls of numbers.
If your number is on the screen,
just press 'Y' (for 'yes').
if it's not on the screen,
then simply press the 'N'



I'll tell you the number you
thought of at the end of the
                game

1  3  5  7  9  11  13  15  17
19 21 23 25 27 29 31
33 35 37 39 41 43 45
47 49 51 53 55 57 59
61 63
```

Press 'Y' if your number
is here, 'N' if it is not
Y

```
 2  3  6  7 10 11 14 15
18 19 22 23 26 27 30
31 34 35 38 39 42 43
46 47 50 51 54 55 58
59 62 63
```

Press 'Y' if your number
is here, 'N' if it is not
N

```
 4  5  6  7 12 13 14 15
20 21 22 23 28 29 30
31 36 37 38 39 44 45
46 47 52 53 54 55 60
61 62 63
```

Press 'Y' if your number
is here, 'N' if it is not
N

```
 8  9 10 11 12 13 14 15
24 25 26 27 28 29 30
31 40 41 42 43 44 45
46 47 56 57 58 59 60
61 62 63
```

Press 'Y' if your number
is here, 'N' if it is not
N

```
32 33 34 35 36 37 38
39 40 41 42 43 44 45
46 47 48 49 50 51 52
53 54 55 56 57 58 59
60 61 62 63
```

Press 'Y' if your number
is here, 'N' if it is not
N


```
16 17 18 19 20 21 22
23 24 25 26 27 28 29
30 31 48 49 50 51 52
53 54 55 56 57 58 59
60 61 62 63
```

Press 'Y' if your number
is here, 'N' if it is not

Y

Your number was...

                17 !

I'm going to think of a number
between one and 40 and you
have just six guesses to get
it right...if you do, you
get to play the next game

If you don't get it right,
you'll be given an easier
puzzle to work out...and

so on, until even someone
as stupid as a mere human
could solve it...

Please stand by...

OK, I'm thinking of my
number between one and 40

            Enter guess 1
            ? 20
            Too low!

            Enter guess 2
            ? 30
            Too high!

            Enter guess 3
            ? 25
            Too low!

            Enter guess 4
            ? 26

            Wowee!!! Zap!!!

            You did it baby...

Now, it's time to
be amazed...

Follow these instructions,
and press RETURN after
you've carried them out...

Start by multiplying your
age by two...
?

Now add five to that...
?

Now multiply that by 50...
?

Now subtract 365 from that...
?

Now add the amount of loose
change in your pocket...
?

Now give me the number
you've ended up with...
? 1402

You have 17 change...

and are 15 years old...

Now to get your mind
back into gear...

In this game, we start
with two sets of four
objects in a line, with
a space between them,
like this:

$$$$ ****

You have to get them so
they look like this:
**** $$$$
in the shortest possible
time...

You can only slide into
empty space, or jump over
one piece into an empty
square....as I'll now
demonstrate...

$$$*$* **

and so on....

Press RETURN when you're
ready to play...
?

That was move 9

$ $ * * $ $ * *
1 2 3 4 5 6 7 8 9

You have 3 correct
Which number piece to move?

That brings us to the end
of our cavalcade of puzzles

Enter 'Y' to play them again
or 'N' to quit...

    Thanks for spending so
    much time playing with
    me...it sure was fun!

    See you again some time...

And here's that long listing I promised you:

```
10  REM Cavalcade of Puzzles
20  GOSUB 2530
30  X = .5:N = 0
40  PRINT "Think of a number between"
50  PRINT "one and sixty-three"
60  GOSUB 2550
70  PRINT "I will show you five"
80  PRINT "screenfulls of numbers."
90  GOSUB 2550
100 PRINT "If your number is on the screen,"
110 PRINT "just press 'Y' (for 'yes')."
120 PRINT "if it's not on the screen,"
130 PRINT "then simply press the 'N'"
140 GOSUB 2550
150 PRINT "I'll tell you the number you"
160 PRINT "thought of at the end of the"
170 PRINT ,"game"
180 GOSUB 2560:GOSUB 2560
190 GOSUB 2530
200 PRINT "1 3 5 7 9 11 13 15 17"
210 PRINT "19 21 23 25 27 29 31"
220 PRINT "33 35 37 39 41 43 45"
230 PRINT "47 49 51 53 55 57 59"
240 PRINT "61 63"
250 GOSUB 630
260 PRINT " 2 3 6 7 10 11 14 15"
270 PRINT "18 19 22 23 26 27 30"
280 PRINT "31 34 35 38 39 42 43"
290 PRINT "46 47 50 51 54 55 58"
300 PRINT "59 62 63"
310 GOSUB 630
320 PRINT " 4 5 6 7 12 13 14 15"
330 PRINT "20 21 22 23 28 29 30"
340 PRINT "31 36 37 38 39 44 45"
350 PRINT "46 47 52 53 54 55 60"
360 PRINT "61 62 63"
370 GOSUB 630
380 PRINT "8 9 10 11 12 13 14 15"
390 PRINT "24 25 26 27 28 29 30"
400 PRINT "31 40 41 42 43 44 45"
```

```
410 PRINT "46 47 56 57 58 59 60"
420 PRINT "61 62 63"
430 GOSUB 630
440 PRINT "16 17 18 19 20 21 22"
450 PRINT "23 24 25 26 27 28 29"
460 PRINT "30 31 48 49 50 51 52"
470 PRINT "53 54 55 56 57 58 59"
480 PRINT "60 61 62 63"
490 GOSUB 630
500 PRINT "32 33 34 35 36 37 38"
510 PRINT "39 40 41 42 43 44 45"
520 PRINT "46 47 48 49 50 51 52"
530 PRINT "53 54 55 56 57 58 59"
540 PRINT "60 61 62 63"
550 GOSUB 630
560 GOSUB 2550:GOSUB 2550
570 GOSUB 2530
580 PRINT "Your number was..."
590 GOSUB 2550
600 PRINT ,N"!"
610 GOSUB 2550
620 GOTO 730
630 X = X + X
640 GOSUB 2550
650 PRINT "Press 'Y' if your number"
660 PRINT "is here, 'N' if it is not"
670 A$ = INKEY$
680 IF A$ <> "n" AND A$ <> "N" AND A$ <> "Y"
    AND A$ <> "y" THEN 670
690 IF A$ = "y" OR A$ = "Y" THEN N = N + X
700 GOSUB 2530
710 RETURN
720 REM *****************************
730 GOSUB 2530
740 PRINT "Now it's time for something"
750 PRINT "almost completely different!"
760 GOSUB 2550
770 W = 40
780 PRINT "I'm going to think of a number"
790 PRINT "between one and"W"and you"
800 PRINT "have just six guesses to get"
810 PRINT "it right...if you do, you"
820 PRINT "get to play the next game"
830 GOSUB 2550
```

```
840 PRINT "If you don't get it right,"
850 PRINT "you'll be given an easier"
860 PRINT "puzzle to work out...and"
870 PRINT "so on, until even someone"
880 PRINT "as stupid as a mere human"
890 PRINT "could solve it..."
900 PRINT:PRINT
910 PRINT "Please stand by..."
920 GOSUB 2550
930 GOSUB 2530
940 PRINT "OK, I'm thinking of my"
950 PRINT "number between one and"W
960 N = INT(RND*W) + 1
970 J = 0
980 J = J + 1
990 PRINT:PRINT "Enter guess"J
1000 INPUT Q
1010 IF Q = N THEN 1140
1020 IF Q<1 OR Q>W THEN 1000
1030 IF Q<N THEN PRINT "Too low!"
1040 IF Q>N THEN PRINT "Too high!"
1050 IF J<6 THEN 980
1060 PRINT:PRINT "Pretty hopeless..."
1070 PRINT "I was thinking of"N
1080 IF W = 5 THEN PRINT "You're hopeless...
let's try":PRINT "something else":GOSUB 2550
:GOTO 1190
1090 PRINT
1100 PRINT "Well, I guess I'll have"
1110 PRINT "to give you another go..."
1120 W = W/2
1130 GOTO 940
1140 GOSUB 2550
1150 PRINT "Wowee!!! Zap!!!"
1160 GOSUB 2550
1170 PRINT "You did it baby..."
1180 GOSUB 2550
1190 GOSUB 2530
1200 REM ********************
1210 PRINT "Now, it's time to"
1220 PRINT "be amazed..."
1230 GOSUB 2550
1240 PRINT "Follow these instructions,"
1250 PRINT "and press RETURN after"
```

```
1260 PRINT "you've carried them out..."
1270 GOSUB 2550
1280 GOSUB 2530
1290 PRINT "Start by multiplying your"
1300 PRINT "age by two..."
1310 INPUT A$
1320 GOSUB 2530
1330 PRINT "Now add five to that..."
1340 INPUT A$
1350 GOSUB 2530
1360 PRINT "Now multiply that by 50..."
1370 INPUT A$
1380 GOSUB 2530
1390 PRINT "Now subtract 365 from that..."
1400 INPUT A$
1410 GOSUB 2530
1420 PRINT "Now add the amount of loose"
1430 PRINT "change in your pocket..."
1440 INPUT A$
1450 GOSUB 2530
1460 PRINT "Now give me the number"
1470 PRINT "you've ended up with..."
1480 INPUT A
1490 A = A + 115
1500 B = INT(A/100)
1510 A = A - 100*B
1520 GOSUB 2530
1530 PRINT "You have"A"change..."
1540 GOSUB 2550
1550 PRINT "and are"B"years old..."
1560 GOSUB 2550
1570 REM ******************
1580 GOSUB 2530
1590 PRINT "Now to get your mind"
1600 PRINT "back into gear..."
1610 GOSUB 2550
1620 PRINT "In this game, we start"
1630 PRINT "with two sets of four"
1640 PRINT "objects in a line, with"
1650 PRINT "a space between them,"
1660 PRINT "like this:"
1670 PRINT
1680 PRINT "$$$$ ****"
1690 GOSUB 2550
```

```
1700 PRINT "You have to get them so"
1710 PRINT "they look like this:"
1720 PRINT "**** $$$$"
1730 PRINT "in the shortest possible"
1740 PRINT "time..."
1750 GOSUB 2550
1760 PRINT "You can only slide into"
1770 PRINT "empty space, or jump over"
1780 PRINT "one piece into an empty"
1790 PRINT "square....as I'll now"
1800 PRINT "demonstrate..."
1810 GOSUB 2550:GOSUB 2550
1820 FOR J = 1 TO 3
1830 CLS
1840 PRINT "$$$$ ****"
1850 FOR Z = 1 TO 500:NEXT Z:CLS
1860 PRINT "$$$ $****"
1870 FOR Z = 1 TO 500:NEXT Z:CLS
1880 PRINT "$$$*$ ***"
1890 FOR Z = 1 TO 500:NEXT Z:CLS
1900 PRINT "$$$*$* **"
1910 NEXT J
1920 PRINT:PRINT "and so on...."
1930 GOSUB 2550
1940 PRINT "Press RETURN when you're"
1950 PRINT "ready to play..."
1960 INPUT A$
1970 X = -1:M = 9
1980 DIM A(M)
1990 FOR Q = 1 TO M
2000 IF Q < 5 THEN A(Q) = ASC("$")
2010 IF Q > 5 THEN A(Q) = ASC("*")
2020 NEXT Q
2030 GOSUB 2530
2040 C = 0
2050 X = X + 1
2060 IF X = 0 THEN 2080
2070 PRINT "That was move"X
2080 PRINT
2090 FOR Q = 1 TO M
2100 PRINT CHR$(A(Q));" ";
2110 IF Q < 5 AND A(Q) = ASC("*") THEN C = C
     + 1
2120 IF A(Q) = 0 THEN H = Q
```

270

```
2130 IF Q > 5 AND A(Q) = ASC("$") THEN C = C
     + 1
2140 NEXT Q
2150 PRINT:PRINT "1 2 3 4 5 6 7 8 9"
2160 PRINT
2170 PRINT:PRINT "You have"C"correct"
2180 GOSUB 2220
2190 IF C = 8 THEN 2260
2200 PRINT:PRINT
2210 GOTO 2030
2220 INPUT "Which number piece to move";T
2230 K = A(T)
2240 A(T) = 0:A(H) = K
2250 RETURN
2260 PRINT:PRINT "Well done.....You"
2270 PRINT "solved it in just"X"moves!"
2280 GOSUB 2550
2290 GOSUB 2530
2300 REM *********************
2310 PRINT "That brings us to the end"
2320 PRINT "of our cavalcade of puzzles"
2330 GOSUB 2550
2340 PRINT "Enter 'Y' to play them again"
2350 PRINT "or 'N' to quit..."
2360 A$ = INKEY$
2370 IF A$ <> "n" AND A$ <> "N" AND A$ <> "y
     " AND A$ <> "Y" THEN 2360
2380 IF A$ = "Y" OR A$ = "y" THEN 2460
2390 GOSUB 2530
2400 PRINT "Thanks for spending so"
2410 PRINT "much time playing with"
2420 PRINT "me...it sure was fun!"
2430 GOSUB 2550
2440 PRINT "See you again some time..."
2450 END
2460 GOSUB 2550
2470 PRINT "OK, here we go again..."
2480 GOSUB 2550
2490 CLEAR
2500 GOTO 10
2510 END
2520 REM *********************
2530 REM Delay, cls, print
2540 CLS
```

```
2550 PRINT:PRINT:PRINT
2560 FOR Z = 1 TO 1000:NEXT Z
2570 RETURN
```

☐ ROBOT MINEFIELD

Time now to face the terrors, the dangers, and the horrors of the **ROBOT MINEFIELD**. There you are, peacefully tripping along one day in the sun, when suddenly you find yourself trapped in a walled area, with a number of manic robots, all bent on your destruction.

The robots are shown on the display as dollar signs, the H is you, and the asterisks (*) are mines which are deadly to both you and robots. Robots, pretty pretty clumsily programmed, can detect you, but they cannot detect mines. Therefore, your salvation lies in getting a mine or two in between you and the robots, so that when they come toward you they'll smash into mines and be wiped out.

The robots have one trick up their sleeves. They can merge into one another, so you may think only one robot is approaching you, when at the last minute it splits into two or more, one going each way around a mine. This is not a game for those who seek the quiet life.

You can move north, south, east, or west (with north at the top of the screen), and you enter the move you want to make by entering the initial of the desired direction (so you enter "N" to go north, "S" to go south and so on).

Just to show you that the odds are definitely not in your favor, here's one game:

```
X X X X X X X X X X X X X X
X *  .  .  .  .  .  .  .  .  .  .  *  .  X
X .  .  .  .  .  .  .  .  .  .  .  .  .  X
X .  .  .  .  .  .  .  .  .  .  .  $  .  X
X .  .  .  .  *  .  .  .  .  .  .  .  .  X
X H  .  $  .  *  *  .  .  .  .  .  .  X
X .  .  .  .  .  .  .  .  .  .  .  .  X
X .  .  .  .  .  .  $  .  *  .  .  .  X
X .  *  .  .  .  *  .  *  .  .  .  X
X .  .  .  .  *  .  .  .  .  .  .  X
X .  .  .  .  .  *  .  .  .  .  .  X
X .  .  .  .  *  *  .  $  *  *  .  .  X     Dead robot tally: 1
X .  .  .  .  .  .  *  *  .  .  .  X
X .  .  .  .  .  .  .  .  .  .  .  X X X X X X X X X X X X X X X
X X X X X X X X X X X X X X  X *  .  .  .  .  .  .  .  .  .  *  .  X
                             X .  .  .  .  .  .  .  .  .  .  .  .  X
                             X .  .  .  .  .  .  .  .  .  .  .  .  X
                             X H  .  .  .  *  .  .  .  .  $  .  .  X
                             X .  $  .  .  *  *  .  .  .  .  .  .  X
                             X .  .  .  .  .  .  .  .  .  .  .  .  X
                             X .  .  .  .  .  $  .  .  *  .  .  .  X
              A robot has got you!!  X .  *  .  .  *  .  .  .  *  .  .  .  X
                             X .  .  .  *  .  .  .  .  .  .  .  X
X X X X X X X X X X X X X X X  X .  .  .  .  .  *  .  .  .  .  X
X *  .  .  .  .  .  .  .  .  *  .  X  X .  .  .  *  *  .  *  *  .  .  X
X .  .  .  .  .  .  .  .  .  .  .  X  X .  .  .  .  *  *  .  .  .  X
X .  .  .  .  .  .  .  .  .  .  .  X  X .  .  .  .  .  .  .  .  .  X
X $  .  .  .  *  .  .  .  .  $  .  .  X X X X X X X X X X X X X X
X .  .  .  .  *  *  .  .  .  .  .  X
X .  .  .  .  $  .  .  .  .  .  X
X .  .  .  .  .  .  *  .  .  .  X
X .  *  .  .  *  .  .  .  .  .  X
X .  .  .  *  .  .  .  .  .  .  X
X .  .  .  .  .  *  .  .  .  .  X
X .  .  .  .  *  *  .  *  *  .  .  X
X .  .  .  .  .  *  *  .  .  .  X
X .  .  .  .  .  .  .  .  .  X
X X X X X X X X X X X X X X
```

And here's a game in which the human race (represented by me at the computer console) fared a little better:

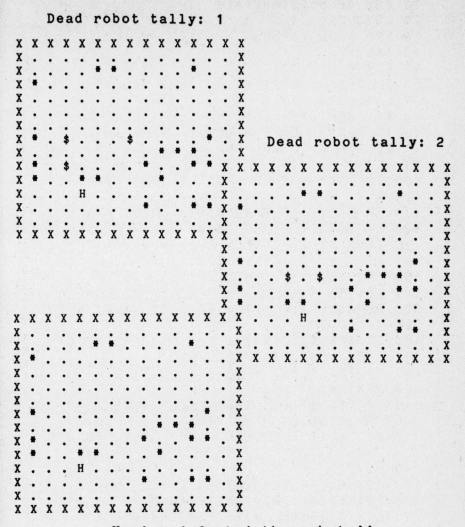

You've defeated the robots!!

This is the listing of **ROBOT MINEFIELD**.

```
10 REM Robot Minefield
20 GOTO 250
30 REM move robots
40 TALLY = 0
50 FOR E = 1 TO 4
60 IF A(B(E),C(E)) = 42 THEN TALLY = TAL
LY + 1:GOTO 200
70 X = B(E):Y = C(E)
80 IF B(E) < D THEN B(E) = B(E) + 1
90 IF B(E) > D AND RND>.3 THEN B(E) = B(
E) - 1
100 IF C(E) < F AND RND>.3 THEN C(E) = C
(E) + 1
110 IF C(E) > F THEN C(E) = C(E) - 1
120 IF B(E) < 2 THEN B(E) = 2
130 IF B(E) > 14 THEN B(E) = 14
140 IF C(E) < 2 THEN C(E) = 2
150 IF C(E) > 14 THEN C(E) = 14
160 A(X,Y) = 46
170 IF A(B(E),C(E)) = 42 THEN TALLY = TA
LLY + 1:GOTO 200
180 IF A(B(E),C(E)) = 72 THEN A(B(E),C(E
)) = 36: GOSUB 300:GOTO 910
190 A(B(E),C(E)) = 36
200 NEXT E
210 IF TALLY < CH THEN TALLY = CH
220 CH = TALLY
230 IF TALLY = 4 THEN GOSUB 300:GOTO 970

240 RETURN
250 GOSUB 530:REM INITIALISE
260 GOSUB 300:PRINT MINEFIELD
270 GOSUB 30:REM ROBOTS MOVE
280 GOSUB 420:REM HUMAN MOVE
290 GOTO 260
300 REM print minefield
310 CLS
320 IF TALLY > 0 THEN PRINT "Dead robot
tally:"TALLY:PRINT
330 IF TALLY = 0 THEN PRINT:PRINT
340 PRINT:PRINT:PRINT
```

```
350 FOR B = 1 TO 15
360 FOR C = 1 TO 15
370 PRINT CHR$(A(B,C));" ";
380 NEXT C
390 PRINT
400 NEXT B
410 RETURN
420 REM player move
430 A(D,F) = 46
440 A$ = INKEY$
450 IF A$ = "" THEN 440
460 IF A$ = "N" AND D>2 THEN D = D - 1
470 IF A$ = "S" AND D<14 THEN D = D + 1
480 IF A$ = "E" AND F<14 THEN F = F + 1
490 IF A$ = "W" AND F>2 THEN F = F - 1
500 IF A(D,F) = 42 THEN GOSUB 300:GOTO 9
90
510 A(D,F) = 72
520 RETURN
530 REM initialise
540 DEFINT A - Z
550 DIM A(15,15),B(4),C(4)
560 CLS
570 PRINT:PRINT "Please stand by for a m
oment..."
580 CH = 0
590 N = (VAL(RIGHT$(TIME$,2)))
600 RANDOMIZE N
610 REM place walls
620 FOR B = 1 TO 15
630 FOR C = 1 TO 15
640 A(B,C) = 46
650 IF B = 1 OR B = 15 OR C = 1 OR C = 1
5 THEN A(B,C) = 88
660 NEXT C:NEXT B
670 REM place mines
680 FOR B = 1 TO 20
690 C = INT(RND*13) + 1
700 D = INT(RND*13) + 1
710 IF A(C,D) = 88 THEN 690
720 A(C,D) = 42
730 NEXT B
740 DATA 4,4,13,8,8,3,12,7
750 REM place robots
```

```
760 FOR E = 1 TO 4
770 D = INT(RND*13) + 2
780 F = INT(RND*13) + 2
790 IF A(D,F) <> 46 THEN 770
800 B(E) = D:C(E) = F
810 A(B(E),C(E)) = 36
820 NEXT E
830 REM place human
840 D = INT(RND*13) + 2
850 F = INT(RND*13) + 2
860 IF A(D,F) <> 46 THEN 830
870 A(D,F) = 72
880 RETURN
890 REM human at d,f
900 REM robots at b(e),c(e)
910 REM end of game
920 CLS:PRINT "A robot has got you!!"
930 CH = 0:TALLY = 0:GOSUB 340
940 A$ = ""
950 IF INKEY$ <> "" THEN 950
960 GOSUB 570:GOTO 260
970 CLS:PRINT "You've defeated the robot
s!!"
980 GOTO 930
990 CLS:PRINT "You've run into a mine!!"

1000 GOTO 930
```

☐ NOUGHTS AND CROSSES

I'm sure that NOUGHTS AND CROSSES (Tic-Tac-Toe) needs no introduction. Here is a program which plays fairly well, but not in a totally predictable manner, so you stand a fair chance of winning a few games.

This may not sound like a big deal. However, many NOUGHTS AND CROSSES programs have been written so that a draw is the best you can do, if you are not actually beaten by the machine.

This program decides who will go first in each game, and responds swiftly to your moves. You move just by entering the number of the square into which you want to move.

Let's see NOUGHTS AND CROSSES in action:

```
Enter your move...          Enter your move...


1 2 3    -  -  -
4 5 6    -  X  -            1 2 3    0  X  0
7 8 9    -  -  -            4 5 6    -  X  -
                           7 8 9    -  -  X

1 2 3    -  -  0
4 5 6    -  X  -
7 8 9    -  -  -            1 2 3    0  X  0
                           4 5 6    -  X  -
                           7 8 9    -  0  X

Enter your move...

                           1 2 3    0  X  0
1 2 3    -  -  0           4 5 6    X  X  -
4 5 6    -  X  -           7 8 9    -  0  X
7 8 9    -  -  X


1 2 3    0  -  0           1 2 3    0  X  0
4 5 6    -  X  -           4 5 6    X  X  0
7 8 9    -  -  X           7 8 9    -  0  X
```

Enter your move...

```
1 2 3      0  X  0
4 5 6      X  X  0
7 8 9      X  0  X
```

It's a draw!

I'll have the first move

```
1 2 3      -  -  -
4 5 6      -  -  -
7 8 9      -  -  -
```

```
1 2 3      -  -  -
4 5 6      -  0  -
7 8 9      -  -  -
```

Enter your move...

```
1 2 3      -  -  -
4 5 6      -  0  -
7 8 9      -  X  -
```

```
1 2 3      -  -  0
4 5 6      -  0  -
7 8 9      -  X  -
```

Enter your move...

```
1 2 3      -  -  0
4 5 6      -  0  -
7 8 9      X  X  -
```

```
1 2 3      -  -  0
4 5 6      -  0  -
7 8 9      X  X  0
```

Enter your move...

```
1 2 3      -  -  0
4 5 6      -  0  X
7 8 9      X  X  0
```

```
1 2 3      0  -  0
4 5 6      -  0  X
7 8 9      X  X  0
```

I'm the winner!

Here's the program listing:

```
10  REM Noughts and CRosses
20  DEFINT A - Z
30  CLS
40  N = 0
50  PRINT "Press any key when"
60  PRINT "you're ready to play"
70  N = N + 1: IF INKEY$ = "" THEN 70
80  CLS
90  DIM A(9)
100 RANDOMIZE N
110 CLS:FOR N = 1 TO 9:A(N) = 0:NEXT N
120 IF RND >.5 THEN PRINT "I'll have the
 first move":FOR J = 1 TO 1000:NEXT:CLS:
GOTO 160
130 GOSUB 750
140 GOSUB 480
150 GOSUB 670
160 GOSUB 750
170 GOSUB 480
180 IF A(5) = 0 THEN A(5) = 1:GOTO 130
190 REM To complete row/block
200 D = 1
210 B = 1
220 IF B = 1 THEN X = 1:Y = 2:Z = 3
230 IF B = 2 THEN X = 1:Y = 4:Z = 7
240 IF B = 3 THEN X = 1:Y = 5:Z = 9
250 IF B = 4 THEN X = 3:Z = 7
260 C = 1
270 IF A(X) = D AND A(Y) = D AND A(Z) =
0 THEN A(Z) = 1:GOTO 130
280 IF A(X) = D AND A(Y) = 0 AND A(Z) =
D THEN A(Y) = 1:GOTO 130
290 IF A(X) = 0 AND A(Y) = D AND A(Z) =
D THEN A(X) = 1:GOTO 130
300 IF B = 1 THEN X = X + 3:Y = Y + 3:Z
= Z + 3
310 IF B = 2 THEN X = X + 1:Y = Y + 1:Z
= Z + 1
320 IF C < 3 THEN C = C + 1:GOTO 270
330 IF B < 4 THEN B = B + 1:GOTO 230
340 IF D < 2 THEN D = D + 1:GOTO 210
350 REM Move at random
```

```
360 B = 1
370 D = INT(RND*9) + 1
380 IF A(C) = 0 THEN A(C) = 1:GOTO 130
390 B = B + 1
400 IF B<21 THEN 370
410 B = 0
420 B = B + 1
430 IF A(B) = 0 THEN A(B) = 1: GOTO 130
440 IF B < 9 THEN 420
450 GOSUB 750
460 PRINT:PRINT "It's a draw!"
470 GOTO 650
480 REM Win check
490 FOR B = 1 TO 4
500 IF B = 1 THEN X = 1:Y = 2:Z = 3
510 IF B = 2 THEN X = 1:Y = 4:Z = 7
520 IF B = 3 THEN X = 1:Y = 5:Z = 9
530 IF B = 4 THEN X = 3:Z = 7
540 FOR C = 1 TO 3
550 IF A(X) = A(Y) THEN IF A(Y) = A(Z) T
HEN IF A(X) <> 0 THEN 610
560 IF B = 1 THEN X = X + 3:Y = Y + 3:Z
= Z + 3
570 IF B = 2 THEN X = X + 1:Y = Y + 1: Z
= Z + 1
580 NEXT C
590 NEXT B
600 RETURN
610 REM The Winner!
620 PRINT
630 IF A(X) = 1 THEN PRINT "I'm the winn
er!"
640 IF A(X) = 2 THEN PRINT "You're the w
inner!"
650 FOR O = 1 TO 1000:NEXT O
660 GOTO 110
670 REM Player move
680 PRINT:PRINT "Enter your move..."
690 A$ = INKEY$
700 IF A$ < "1" OR A$ > "9" THEN 690
710  B = VAL (A$)
720 IF A(B) <> 0 THEN 690
730 A(B) = 2
740 RETURN
```

```
750 REM Printout
760 CLS
770 PRINT:PRINT:PRINT:PRINT
780 PRINT "1 2 3     ";
790 FLAG = 0
800 FOR B = 1 TO 9
810 IF A(B) = 0 THEN FLAG = 1
820 IF A(B) = 0 THEN PRINT " - ";
830 IF A(B) = 1 THEN PRINT " O ";
840 IF A(B) = 2 THEN PRINT " X ";
850 IF B = 3 THEN PRINT:PRINT:PRINT "4 5
    6   ";
860 IF B = 6 THEN PRINT:PRINT:PRINT "7 8
    9   ";
870 NEXT B
880 PRINT:PRINT
890 IF FLAG = 0 THEN 460
900 RETURN
```

☐ LAS VEGAS HIGH

Finally, in this section of the book, we have a slot machine game, LAS VEGAS HIGH. You need only decide how much you'll bet before pulling the handle on the machine (which you do by pressing the spacebar) and the reels will whirl away.

Your winnings—as you'd expect—are related to the relative difficulty of the various combinations coming up. The computer keeps up the chatter as the game, and your wealth (or poverty) unfold.

Here's the making of a million (or so):

```
Hi there, gambler!

You have $ 250

How much do you want to bet? 140


OK, sir, $ 140 it is!


Press the spacebar to play


/^^^^^^^^^^^^^^^^^^^^^^^^^^^^^^^^^^^^^^^^^^^^^^^^^\
      * {{PLUM}} * << Lemon >> * {{PLUM}} *

>> A PAIR <<


And you've won $ 98 !


So you now have $ 348


You're doing well tonight!

You have $ 348

How much do you want to bet? 172
```

OK, sir, $ 172 it is!

Press the spacebar to play

/^^^\
    * # Cherry # * << Lemon >> * * Bell * *
A BELL at the end is a bonus!

And you've won $ 103 !

So you now have $ 451

   _____

Lady Luck has certainly smiled on you!
You have $ 758
How much do you want to bet? 500

OK, sir, $ 500 it is!

Press the spacebar to play

/^^^\
    * << Lemon >> * $ Apple $ * # Cherry # *

And you've lost $ 500

So you now have $ 258

Hi there, gambler!

You have $ 8

How much do you want to bet? 1000000
You ain't got that much!

How much do you want to bet? 8

OK, sir, $ 8 it is!

Press the spacebar to play

/^^^\
        * $ Apple $ * << Lemon >> * {{PLUM}} *

And you've lost $ 8

That's the end of the line,
oh once mighty gambler...

You're stone, flat broke!!

Press 'Y' if you'd like to
have another go at breaking
!!!!! LAS VEGAS HIGH !!!!!
(or press 'N' if you wish to leave)

And this is the way to do it:

```
10  REM Las Vegas High
20  GOSUB 1110:REM Initialise
30  GOSUB 870:REM Player input
40  GOSUB 520:REM Operate slot machine
50  IF CASH < 1 THEN 90
60  IF CASH > 2500 THEN 290
70  GOTO 30
80  REM *****
90  REM  Broke
100 REM *****
110 GOSUB 410
120 PRINT "That's the end of the line,"
130 PRINT "oh once mighty gambler..."
140 GOSUB 410
150 PRINT "You're stone, flat broke!!"
160 GOSUB 410
170 PRINT "Press 'Y' if you'd like to"
180 PRINT "have another go at breaking"
190 PRINT "!!!!! LAS VEGAS HIGH !!!!!"
200 PRINT "(or press 'N' if you wish to lea
ve)"
210 A$ = INKEY$
220 IF A$ <> "Y" AND A$ <> "y" AND A$ <> "N
" AND A$ <> "n" THEN 210
230 IF A$ = "Y" OR A$ = "y" THEN RUN
240 PRINT:PRINT "OK, punter..."
250 GOSUB 410
260 PRINT "Thanks for the game!"
270 END
280 REM **************
290 REM Broke the bank
300 REM **************
310 GOSUB 410
320 PRINT "Well done, gambler!!"
330 GOSUB 410
340 PRINT "You've reached our house limit"
350 PRINT "so we'll have to throw you out"
360 GOSUB 410
370 PRINT "People with luck like yours give
"
380 PRINT "our casino a bad name..........
"
```

```
390 GOTO 160
400 REM *****
410 REM Delay
420 REM *****
430 FOR P = 1 TO 1000:NEXT P
440 PRINT:PRINT
450 RETURN
460 REM **********
470 REM Delay two
480 REM **********
490 FOR P = 1 TO 1000:NEXT P
500 RETURN
510 REM ********************
520 REM Operate slot machine
530 REM ********************
540 CLS
550 GOSUB 410
560 PRINT "/^^^^^^^^^^^^^^^^^^^^^^^^^^^^^^^^^^^
^^^^^^^^^^^^^^^^^^^^^\"
570 PRINT TAB(5);" * ";
580 FOR M = 1 TO 3
590 GOSUB 460
600 A = INT(43*RND)
610 IF A < 2 THEN PRINT A$(4);:C(M) = 1
620 IF A > 1 AND A < 6 THEN PRINT A$(3);:C(
M) = 2
630 IF A > 5 AND A < 12 THEN PRINT A$(1);:C
(M) = 3
640 IF A > 11 AND A < 20 THEN PRINT A$(2);:
C(M) = 4
650 IF A > 19 AND A < 31 THEN PRINT A$(5);:
C(M) = 5
660 IF A > 30 THEN PRINT A$(6);:C(M) = 6
670 PRINT " * ";
680 NEXT M
690 GOSUB 410
700 WIN = 0
710 IF C(1) + C(2) + C(3) = 3 THEN PRINT "T
hree BARs!!!":GOSUB 410:"That's jackpot sty
le!!":WIN = WIN + 9:GOTO 750
720 IF C(1) = C(2) AND C(3) = C(2) AND C(1)
 = 2 THEN PRINT "Three Bells!!!":WIN = WIN
+ 3.9:GOTO 750
730 IF C(1) = C(2) AND C(3) = C(2) AND C(1)
```

```
    <> 1 AND C(2) <> 3 THEN PRINT "Three of a
kind":WIN = WIN + 3.5:GOTO 750
740 IF C(1) = C(2) OR C(1) = C(3) OR C(2) =
    C(3) THEN PRINT ">> A PAIR <<":WIN = WIN +
    .7
750 IF C(3) = 2 THEN PRINT "A BELL at the e
nd is a bonus!":WIN = WIN + .6
760 IF C(1) = 3 AND C(3) = 3 THEN PRINT "An
 Apple at each side is good":WIN = WIN + .5

770 IF C(1) = 4 AND C(2) = 3 AND C(3) = 4 T
HEN PRINT "THAT OLD 'cherry,bell,cherry'":P
RINT "COMBINATION IS ONE OF MY FAVORITES!":
WIN = WIN + .4
780 GOSUB 410
790 WIN = INT(BET*WIN)
800 IF WIN > 0 THEN PRINT "And you've won $
"WIN"!":CASH = CASH + WIN
810 IF WIN = 0 THEN PRINT "And you've lost
$"BET:CASH = CASH - BET
820 GOSUB 410
830 IF CASH > 0 THEN PRINT "So you now have
  $"CASH
840 GOSUB 460
850 RETURN
860 REM ************
870 REM Player input
880 REM ************
890 CLS
900 GOSUB 410
910 IF CASH < 300 THEN PRINT "Hi there, gam
bler!"
920 IF CASH > 299 AND CASH < 600  THEN PRIN
T "You're doing well tonight!"
930 IF CASH > 599 AND CASH < 900  THEN PRIN
T "Lady Luck has certainly smiled on you!"
940 IF CASH > 899 AND CASH < 1200  THEN PRI
NT "The Fates are being extremely kind"
950 IF CASH > 1199 THEN PRINT "It is so goo
d to see an expert at work"
960 GOSUB 470
970 PRINT:PRINT "You have $"CASH
980 PRINT:INPUT "How much do you want to be
t";BET
```

```basic
990 IF BET > CASH THEN PRINT "You ain't got
   that much!":GOTO 980
1000 GOSUB 410
1010 PRINT "OK, sir, $"BET"it is!"
1020 GOSUB 410
1030 PRINT "Press the spacebar to play"
1040 IF INKEY$ <> " " THEN 1040
1050 FOR T = 1 TO 40
1060 PRINT TAB(T/2);"******* Stand by *****
**"
1070 PRINT
1080 NEXT T
1090 RETURN
1100 REM **********
1110 REM Initialise
1120 REM **********
1130 CLS
1140 DIM A$(6),C(6)
1150 RANDOMIZE VAL(RIGHT$(TIME$,2))
1160 CASH = 250
1170 FOR B = 1 TO 6
1180 READ A$(B)
1190 NEXT B
1200 RETURN
1210 DATA "$ Apple $","# Cherry #","* Bell
*","!! BAR !!","<< Lemon >>","{{PLUM}}"
```

Fun with your Printer

☐ CELESTIA

The first of the two programs in this section is CELESTIA, which you can run either on your TV screen, or on the screen and to the printer at the same time. It produces an infinite series of evolving patterns.

The patterns develop according to the rules of the famous computer game of LIFE, developed by John Conway while at Gonville and Caius College at Cambridge in the UK. Martin Gardiner spread the game throughout the world when he wrote about in *Scientific American* in October, 1970.

In LIFE, cells are born, grow and die according to rules which Conway invented. Each cell on a grid (the colony of cells is imagined to be evolving on a grid) is surrounded by eight others, and the state of those eight other cells dictates what happens to the cell in question in the following generation.

The rules which govern the evolution of the cells are as follows:

- If a cell has two or three surrounding it, it survives to the next generation

- If there are three, and just three, full cells next to an empty one, a cell will be "born" in that empty space in the next generation

- Any cell with four of its neighboring cells occupied dies in the next generation

Don't worry, you don't have to know the rules, as the computer interprets them quite happily by itself. The rules produce patterns which are far more attractive (and far less predictable) than you could possibly imagine by reading the rules. There is just one extra twist in this program, which makes it even more effective. CELESTIA actually prints out four colonies each time a colony evolves. The original colony is in one quadrant of the screen, and the other three quarters of the screen contain reflections of the original one.

CELESTIA is incredibly effective, as you can see:

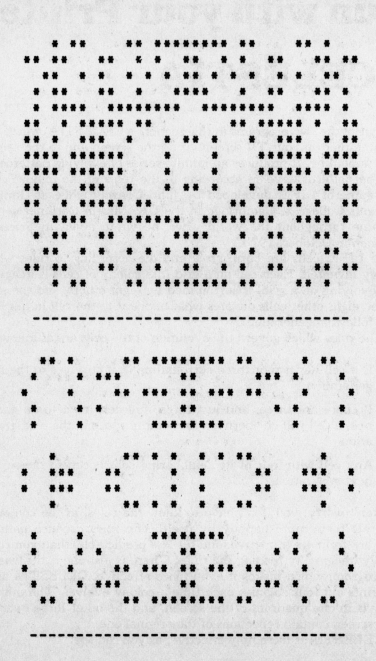

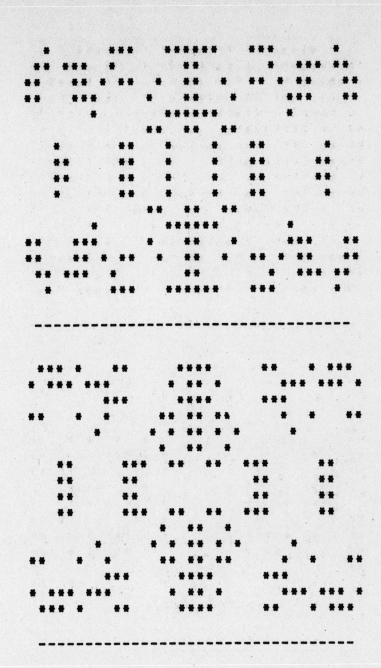

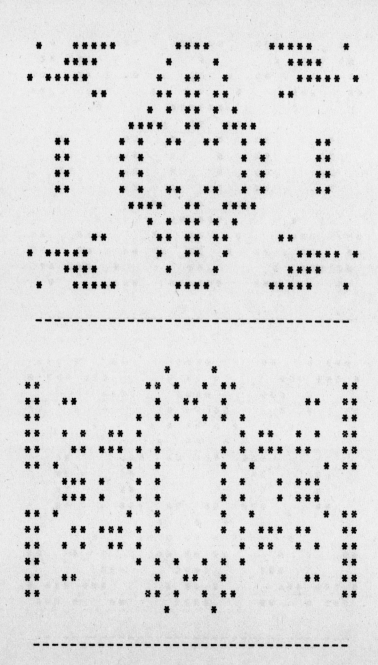

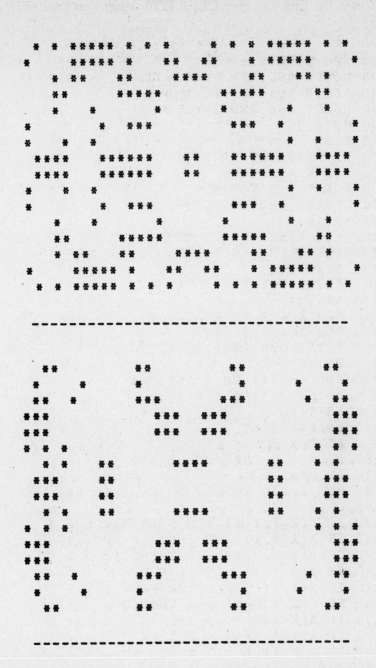

This is the listing to give CELESTIA designs on your microcomputer:

```
10 REM Celestia
20 GOSUB 450:REM Initialise
30 GOSUB 60:REM Print out
40 GOSUB 280:REM Evolve
50 GOTO 30
60 CLS
70 PRINT:PRINT:PRINT,
80 FOR X = 2 TO 9
90 FOR Y = 2 TO 19
100 PRINT CHR$(A(X,Y));
110 NEXT Y
120 FOR Y = 19 TO 2 STEP -1
130 PRINT CHR$(A(X,Y));
140 NEXT Y
150 PRINT:PRINT ,
160 NEXT X
170 FOR X = 9 TO 2 STEP - 1
180 FOR Y = 2 TO 19
190 PRINT CHR$(A(X,Y));
200 NEXT Y
210 FOR Y = 19 TO 2 STEP -1
220 PRINT CHR$(A(X,Y));
230 NEXT Y
240 PRINT:PRINT ,
250 NEXT X
260 IF N = 0 THEN GOSUB 640
270 RETURN
280 FOR X = 2 TO 9:FOR Y = 2 TO 19
290 C = 0
300 IF A(X-1,Y-1) = B THEN C = C + 1
310 IF A(X-1,Y) = B THEN C = C + 1
320 IF A(X-1,Y+1) = B THEN C = C + 1
330 IF A(X,Y-1) = B THEN C = C + 1
340 IF A(X,Y+1) = B THEN C = C + 1
350 IF A(X+1,Y-1) = B THEN C = C + 1
360 IF A(X+1,Y) = B THEN C = C + 1
370 IF A(X+1,Y+1) = B THEN C = C + 1
380 IF A(X,Y)=B AND C<>3 AND C<>2 THEN B
(X,Y)=E
390 IF A(X,Y)=E AND C=3 THEN B(X,Y)=B
```

```
400 NEXT Y:NEXT X
410 FOR X  = 2 TO 9:FOR Y = 2 TO 19
420 A(X,Y) = B(X,Y)
430 NEXT Y:NEXT X
440 RETURN
450 REM initialise
460 CLS
470 PRINT "Press the space bar":PRINT"wh
en you're ready to begin"
480 N = 1
490 IF INKEY$ = "" THEN N = N + 1:GOTO 4
90
500 RANDOMIZE N:CLS
510 PRINT "Do you want a copy on"
520 PRINT "your printer (Y or N)"
530 A$ = INKEY$: IF A$ <>"n" AND A$ <> "
N" AND A$ <> "y" AND A$ <>"Y" THEN 530
540 IF A$ = "y" OR A$ = "Y" THEN N = 0
550 CLS
560 B = ASC("*"): E = ASC(" ")
570 DIM A(10,20),B(10,20)
580 FOR X = 2 TO 9:FOR Y = 2 TO 19
590 A(X,Y) = E
600 IF RND > .45 THEN A(X,Y) = B
610 B(X,Y) = A(X,Y)
620 NEXT Y:NEXT X
630 RETURN
640 LPRINT "      ------------------------
-------------":REM 6 spaces, 34 -'s
650 LPRINT:LPRINT:LPRINT "      ";
660 FOR X = 2 TO 9
670 FOR Y = 2 TO 19
680 LPRINT CHR$(A(X,Y));
690 NEXT Y
700 FOR Y = 19 TO 2 STEP - 1
710 LPRINT CHR$(A(X,Y));
720 NEXT Y
730 LPRINT:LPRINT "      ";
740 NEXT X
750 FOR X = 9 TO 2 STEP -1
760 FOR Y = 2 TO 19
770 LPRINT CHR$(A(X,Y));
780 NEXT Y
```

```
790 FOR Y = 19 TO 2 STEP - 1
800 LPRINT CHR$(A(X,Y));
810 NEXT Y
820 LPRINT:LPRINT "        ";
830 NEXT X
840 LPRINT
850 RETURN
```

☐ **BILLBOARD**

BILLBOARD, as you can see from the following sample run, takes a message of any length (up to the maximum string length permitted by your system) and turns it into a printed message down the side of your printer paper. The printed letters can then be used to decorate your walls, cut up to form posters, or used however your imagination dictates.

You don't need any further instructions to get great results like these:

```
T  H  E
Q  U  I  C  K
B  R  O  W  N
F  O  X
J  U  M  P  E  D
O  V  E  E  R
```

```
    TTTTTTT  HHHHHH  EEEEEE
       T     H    H  E
       T     HHHHHH  EEEEE
       T     H    H  E
       T     H    H  EEEEEE

LLLLLL   AAAAA   ZZZZZZ   YY   YY
L        A   A       ZZ    Y   Y
L        AAAAA     ZZ       YYY
L        A   A   ZZ          Y
LLLLLL   A   A   ZZZZZZ      Y

DDDDDD   OOOOO   GGGGG   @@@@
D    D   O   O   G       @@@@
D    D   O   O   G  GG
D    D   O   O   GG  G
DDDDDD   OOOOO   GGGGG   @@
                        @@
```

This is the listing for **BILLBOARD**:

```
10  REM Billboard
20  REM All input must be in upper case
30  CLS
40  INPUT "Enter your message      ",A$
50  B = LEN (A$)
60  FOR C = 1 TO B
70  D = ASC(MID$(A$,C)) - 64
80  IF D = -18 THEN GOSUB 410:GOTO 130:REM
Period (.)
90  IF D = -31 THEN GOSUB 420:GOTO 130:REM
Exclamation mark (!)
100 IF D = -32 THEN GOSUB 430:GOTO 130:REM
 Space
110 IF D < 1 OR D > 26 THEN GOSUB 430:GOTO
 130:REM UNKNOWN CHARACTER
120 ON D GOSUB 150,160,170,180,190,200,210
,220,230,240,250,260,270,280,290,300,310,3
20,330,340,350,360,370,380,390,400
130 LPRINT:NEXT C
140 END
150 LPRINT "AAAAA":LPRINT "    A A":LPRINT
"    A A":LPRINT "    A A":LPRINT "AAAAA":R
ETURN
160 LPRINT "BBBBBBB":LPRINT "B  B  B":LPRI
NT "B  B  B":LPRINT "B  B  B":LPRINT " BB
BB":RETURN
```

```
170 LPRINT " CCCCC ":LPRINT "C        C":LPRI
NT "C        C":LPRINT "C        C":LPRINT " C
  C":RETURN
180 LPRINT "DDDDDDD":LPRINT "D        D":LPRI
NT "D        D":LPRINT "D        D":LPRINT " DDD
DD":RETURN
190 LPRINT "EEEEEEE":LPRINT "E  E  E":LPRI
NT "E  E  E":LPRINT "E        E":LPRINT "E":R
ETURN
200 LPRINT "FFFFFFF":LPRINT "  F  F":LPRI
NT "  F  F":LPRINT "  F  F":LPRINT "
  F":RETURN
210 LPRINT " GGGGG":LPRINT "G        G":LPRIN
T "G        G":LPRINT "G G     G":LPRINT " GG
G":RETURN
220 LPRINT "HHHHHHH":LPRINT "    H":LPRINT
"    H":LPRINT "    H":LPRINT "HHHHHHH":RETU
RN
230 LPRINT:LPRINT "I        I":LPRINT "IIIIII
I":LPRINT "I        I":LPRINT:RETURN
240 LPRINT :LPRINT "JJJ":LPRINT "J        J":
LPRINT "J        J":LPRINT " JJJJJ":RETURN
250 LPRINT "KKKKKKK":LPRINT "    K":LPRINT
"  K K":LPRINT " K    K":LPRINT "K        K":R
ETURN
260 LPRINT "LLLLLLL":FOR Z = 1 TO 4:LPRINT
 "L":NEXT Z:RETURN
270 LPRINT "MMMMMMM":LPRINT "      M":LPRIN
T "    MM":LPRINT "      M":LPRINT "MMMMMMM"
:RETURN
280 LPRINT "NNNNNNN":LPRINT "      NN":LPRI
NT "    NN":LPRINT " NN":LPRINT "NNNNNNN":R
ETURN
290 LPRINT " OOOOO":LPRINT "O        O":LPRIN
T "O        O":LPRINT "O        O":LPRINT " OOOO
O":RETURN
300 LPRINT "PPPPPP":LPRINT "  P  P":LPRIN
T "  P  P":LPRINT "  P  P":LPRINT "      P
P":RETURN
310 LPRINT " QQQQQ":LPRINT "Q        Q":LPRIN
T "Q Q    Q":LPRINT "QQ     Q":LPRINT " QQQQ
Q":RETURN
320 LPRINT "RRRRRR":LPRINT "    R  R":LPRIN
T " RR  R":LPRINT " R R  R":LPRINT "R    R
```

```
R":RETURN
330 LPRINT " S  SS":LPRINT "S  S  S":LPRIN
T "S  S  S":LPRINT "S  S  S":LPRINT " SS
S":RETURN
340 LPRINT "      T":LPRINT "       T":LPRI
NT "TTTTTTT":LPRINT "       T":LPRINT "
   T":RETURN
350 LPRINT " UUUUUU":LPRINT "U":LPRINT "U"
:LPRINT "U":LPRINT " UUUUUU":RETURN
360 LPRINT "    VVVV":LPRINT " VV":LPRINT "
V":LPRINT " VV":LPRINT "    VVVV":RETURN
370 LPRINT " WWWWWW":LPRINT "W":LPRINT "WW
WWW":LPRINT "W":LPRINT " WWWWWW":RETURN
380 LPRINT "X     X":LPRINT " XX XX":LPRIN
T "   X":LPRINT " XX XX":LPRINT "X     X":
RETURN
390 LPRINT "      YY":LPRINT "     Y":LPRINT
 "YYYY":LPRINT "     Y":LPRINT "      YY":RE
TURN
400 LPRINT "ZZ    Z":LPRINT "Z Z   Z":LPRI
NT "Z  Z  Z":LPRINT "Z   Z Z":LPRINT "Z
 ZZ":RETURN
410 LPRINT "@@":LPRINT "@@":LPRINT:LPRINT:
LPRINT:RETURN
420 LPRINT "@@ @@@@":LPRINT "@@ @@@@":LPRI
NT:LPRINT:LPRINT:RETURN
430 LPRINT:LPRINT:RETURN
```

Space Games

Good old space, the final frontier. No collection of computer games would be complete without a few space games. Unfortunately, most games of this type rely on use of a particular computer's graphics set, and on moving graphics. Of course, to make this a game collection which would be "universal" we couldn't assume access to a particular type of screen. Display file PEEKs and POKEs are among the least transportable aspects of any program.

Therefore, the space games in this collection rely on either just text output, or graphics output of a limited nature (such as using⟨*⟩ to represent a space ship). Even this apparently limited approach works surprisingly well, and it should not take you long, once you get the programs up and running, to adapt them to take advantage of your particular computer's facilities.

☐ MOONLANDER I AND II

There are two versions of our **MOONLANDER** program. I suggest you start off with the simpler of the two—just called **MOON-LANDER**—and when you're confident you can land on the moon successfully two times out of three, you can graduate to **REALTIME LANDER**, which uses INKEY$ to strobe the keyboard, and demands quick thinking to save your craft from disaster.

The scenario of these programs is pretty familiar. You are landing on the moon, with limited fuel, and for some reason your onboard computer is incapable of doing anything except reporting the state of the flight to you. The information you get is, of necessity, limited but adequate.

You are told, at all times, your height above the moon's surface, how much fuel you have left, and the speed with which you are descending. You have to enter the correct amount of thrust to ensure you land gently on the surface. The fuel you have is limited, so you must ration it to ensure you have enough left in the last few seconds of flight to cushion your impact. A "high-score" feature (lines 370 and 380) ensures you and your friends return to this program time and time again in an effort to get a better "galactic rating" and to create a less deep crater.

Here is MOONLANDER in action:

```
Height: 674    Velocity: -24
       Fuel: 259




          <*>




Thrust? 17
```

Your ship crashed at 106.5 kph
creating a 4792 meter deep crater

Your galactic rating is 6.5

Best rating so far is 6.5

Please stand by for your next mission

___

This is the listing for the simpler version of the game:

```
10 REM Moonlander
20 HS = - 10000
30 RANDOMIZE VAL(RIGHT$(TIME$,2))
40 A = - 20 - INT(RND*60):REM Initial ve
locity
50 B = 1200 + INT(RND*380):REM Height
60 C = 320 + INT(RND*90): REM Fuel
70 CLS
80 PRINT:PRINT:PRINT
90 B = INT(B):A = INT(A):C = INT(C)
100 PRINT "Height:"B,"Velocity: "A
110 PRINT "    Fuel:"C
120 FOR Q = 1 TO 16 - B/100
130 PRINT
140 NEXT Q
150 PRINT TAB(5 + RND*3 - RND*3);"<*>"
160 FOR Q = 16 - B/100 TO 16
170 PRINT
180 NEXT Q
190 FOR P = 1 TO 500:NEXT P
200 INPUT "Thrust";T
210 FOR P = 1 TO 500:NEXT P
220 IF T > C THEN T = 0
230 C = C - T
240 B = B + A + (T - 5)/2
```

```
250 A = A + (T - 5)/2
260 IF C < 1 AND B > 100 THEN 300
270 IF ABS(B) < 20 AND ABS(A) < 15 THEN
PRINT "You have landed safely":PRINT:PRI
NT "Well done, intrepid captain":SCORE =
 C*234:GOTO 340
280 IF B > 19 THEN 70
290 IF C > 1 THEN 310
300 PRINT "You have run out of fuel"
310 PRINT "Your ship crashed at"ABS(A)"k
ph"
320 PRINT "creating a"INT(ABS(A)*45)"met
er deep crater"
330 SCORE = 100 - ABS(A)
340 FOR P = 1 TO 1000:NEXT P
350 PRINT:PRINT
360 PRINT "Your galactic rating is"SCORE

370 IF SCORE > HS THEN HS = SCORE
380 PRINT:PRINT "Best rating so far is"H
S
390 PRINT:PRINT "Please stand by for you
r next mission"
400 FOR P = 1 TO 1500:NEXT P
410 GOTO 40
```

This version is for experienced space jockeys only:

```
10 REM Realtime Lander
20 HS = - 10000
30 RANDOMIZE VAL(RIGHT$(TIME$,2))
40 A = 0
50 B = 1200 + INT(RND*380):B1 = B:REM He
ight
60 C = 720 + INT(RND*90): REM Fuel
70 CLS
80 PRINT:PRINT:PRINT
90 B = INT(B):A = INT(A):C = INT(C)
100 IF B > B1 THEN B = B1
110 PRINT "Height:"B,"Velocity: "A
120 PRINT "    Fuel:"C
130 FOR Q = 1 TO 16 - B/100
140 PRINT
```

```
150 NEXT Q
160 PRINT TAB(5 + RND*3 - RND*3);"<*>"
170 FOR Q = 16 - B/100 TO 16
180 PRINT
190 NEXT Q
200 T = 0
210 T$ = INKEY$:T = VAL(T$)*1.7
220 IF T > C THEN T = 0
230 C = C - T
240 B = B + A + (T - 5)/2
250 A = A + (T - 5)/2
260 IF C < 1 AND B > 100 THEN 300
270 IF ABS(B) < 40 AND ABS(A) < 25 THEN
PRINT "You have landed safely":PRINT:PRI
NT "Well done, intrepid captain":SCORE =
 C*234:GOTO 340
280 IF B > 39 THEN 70
290 IF C > 1 THEN 310
300 PRINT "You have run out of fuel"
310 PRINT "Your ship crashed at"ABS(A)"k
ph"
320 PRINT "creating a"INT(ABS(A)*45)"met
er deep crater"
330 SCORE = 100 - ABS(A)
340 FOR P = 1 TO 1000:NEXT P
350 PRINT:PRINT
360 PRINT "Your galactic rating is"SCORE

370 IF SCORE > HS THEN HS = SCORE
380 PRINT:PRINT "Best rating so far is"H
S
390 PRINT:PRINT "Please stand by for you
r next mission"
400 FOR P = 1 TO 1500:NEXT P
410 IF INKEY$ <> "" THEN 410
420 GOTO 40
```

☐ HYPERWAR

HYPERWAR is a major space simulation, which puts you in charge of patrolling a cube-shaped sector of space, which is ten parsecs along each side. The enemy is the race known as the Dosznti. There is only one Dosznti ship in this sector, and it is moving slowly through the cube as you play. Although you cannot destroy the ship, you can kill a number of individual Dosznti. In fact, the aim of the game is to get your "alien kill total" to the highest point possible before your energy banks are exhausted. Although there are many, many more Dosznti in this sector than there are humans, the aliens are notoriously bad shots, so your chance of wiping out a lot before your mission is terminated is rather high.

You can only fire at the Dosznti when you are within three units of their position. Attempting to fire when they are out of range leads only to the crew response "The Dosznti ship is not within range, sir."

You have a limited amount of energy, and each successful hit by an alien craft diminishes your energy supply.

I will not explain the game in any more detail, because to do so would diminish the enjoyment you'll get from playing it. The "behavior of space" does not change from game to game, so you should find you begin to learn the tricks of space warfare after the first game, leading to higher and higher scores as you continue to play it. The game tends to explain the rules to you as you play, and the screen display has been organized to make it as clear as possible what is going on.

Here's a snapshot of HYPERWAR in action:

```
**********************************************
Status report from master control:

Energy in main and auxiliary banks: 53.75
             Stardate timer reads 49
**********************************************
>>>Ships galactic co-ordinates are 10   4   2

>>>>>Dosznti mothership located at 10   2   5

The Dosznti is to the west behind us,
   captain
**********************************************
```

```
What is your order, captain?
    N, S, E, W
    A(dvance), R(etreat)
    H(yperspace)
    L(aser
? L


Lasers armed and ready, sir


You damaged the Dosznti ship, captain
                           Well done!!!
Well done!!!
 Well done!!!
 Well done!!!
                   Well done!!!
                   Well done!!!
                   Well done!!!
     Well done!!!
   Well done!!!
 Well done!!!


Energy in main and auxiliary banks: 4
               Stardate timer reads 1
!!!!!Warning - Mission time running out!!!!!
********************************************

Dosznti destruction tally is 234563
>>>Ships galactic co-ordinates are 4  1  6

>>>>>Dosznti mothership located at 9  10  1

The Dosznti is to the south east in front of
  us, sir

********************************************


What is your order, captain?
    N, S, E, W
    A(dvance), R(etreat)
    H(yperspace)
    L(aser
? S
```

```
*****************************
*Deep space scanners read:*
*     N/S - 3               *
*     E/W --1               *
*     A/R - 3               *
*****************************
```

You have stayed in space too long

You defeated 234563 Dosznti

Life support systems fading...

   fading...

      fading...

This program will enable you to turn your computer console into one within your space ship, as you set out to rid the 10 parsec cube of the menace of the Dosznti mothership:

```
10 REM Hyperwar
20 HS = 0
30 GOSUB 1410
40 GOSUB 1150
50 IF L < 0 THEN 670
60 GOSUB 1660
70 L = L - .25
80 TI = TI - 1
90 PRINT "What is your order, captain?"
100 PRINT "   N, S, E, W"
110 PRINT "    A(dvance), R(etreat)"
120 PRINT "    H(yperspace)"
130 PRINT "    L(aser"
140 INPUT Z$
150 IF Z$ = "N" OR Z$ = "n" THEN X = X - 1
160 IF Z$ = "S" OR Z$ = "s" THEN X = X + 1
```

```
170 IF Z$ = "E" OR Z$ = "e" THEN Y = Y + 1
180 IF Z$ = "W" OR Z$ = "w" THEN Y = Y - 1
190 IF Z$ = "A" OR Z$ = "a" THEN Z = Z - 1
200 IF Z$ = "R" OR Z$ = "r" THEN Z = Z + 1
210 IF Z$ = "L" OR Z$ = "l" THEN GOSUB 490
220 IF Z$ = "H" OR Z$ = "h" THEN GOSUB 1520
230 IF X < 1 THEN X = 1
240 IF Y < 1 THEN Y = 1
250 IF Z < 1 THEN Z = 1
260 IF X > 10 THEN X = 10
270 IF Y > 10 THEN Y = 10
280 IF Z > 10 THEN Z = 10
290 GOSUB 890
300 IF RND < .7 THEN 40
310 PRINT "******************************"
320 PRINT "*Deep space scanners read:*"
330 PRINT "*   N/S -"A - X"              *"
340 PRINT "*   E/W -"B - Y"              *"
350 PRINT "*   A/R -"C - Z"              *"
360 PRINT "******************************"
370 A = A + INT(RND*2 - RND*2)
380 B = B + INT(RND*2 - RND*2)
390 C = C + INT(RND*2 - RND*2)
400 IF A < 1 THEN A = 1
410 IF A > 10 THEN A = 10
420 IF B < 1 THEN B = 1
430 IF B > 10 THEN B = 10
440 IF C < 1 THEN C = 1
450 IF C > 10 THEN C = 10
460 GOSUB 1650
470 GOTO 40
480 REM ******************************
490 REM Laser option
500 L = L - .75
510 GOSUB 1620
520 IF ABS(A - X)>3 OR ABS(B - Y)>3 OR ABS(C
  - Z)>3 THEN PRINT "The Dosznti ship is not
within range, sir"
530 IF ABS(A - X)>3 OR ABS(B - Y)>3 OR ABS(C
  - Z)>3 THEN GOSUB 1650:RETURN
540 PRINT "Lasers armed and ready, sir"
550 GOSUB 1650
560 IF RND > .5 THEN 590
570 PRINT "Laser fire was unsuccessful, capt
```

```
ain"
580 GOTO 650
590 PRINT "You damaged the Dosznti ship, cap
tain"
600 FOR J = 1 TO 30
610 FOR H = 1 TO 30 - J/3:PRINT " ";:NEXT H
620 PRINT "Well done!!!";
630 NEXT J
640 T = T + INT(RND*1000) + 784
650 GOSUB 1620
660 RETURN
670 REM Out of energy
680 GOSUB 1620
690 PRINT "This is ship's master control"
700 GOSUB 1650
710 IF L <= 0 THEN PRINT "Energy reserves de
pleted"
720 IF TI = 0 THEN PRINT "You have stayed in
 space too long"
730 PRINT:PRINT "You defeated"T"Dosznti":GOS
UB 1650
740 PRINT "Life support systems fading..."
750 GOSUB 1650
760 PRINT "   fading..."
770 GOSUB 1650
780 PRINT "        fading..."
790 GOSUB 1650
800 PRINT "Tally was "T:IF T > HS THEN HS =
T
810 PRINT:PRINT "Best so far is"HS:GOSUB 165
0
820 PRINT:PRINT "Stand by for your next miss
ion"
830 GOSUB 1650:GOSUB 1650:GOTO 30
840 REM *******************************
850 GOSUB 1650
860 PRINT "You have collided with the Dosznt
i ship!!"
870 GOSUB 1650
880 GOTO 690
890 REM Dosznti report
900 IF ABS(A - X)>5 OR ABS(B - Y)>5 OR ABS(C
 - Z)>5 OR RND < .7 THEN RETURN
910 GOSUB 1620
```

```
920 PRINT "Condition red!  Condition red!"
930 GOSUB 1650:IF RND < .25 THEN GOSUB 1620:
PRINT "Condition amber!":GOSUB 1650:RETURN
940 PRINT "Dosznti are firing at us, sir"
950 GOSUB 1650
960 PRINT "Condition red!  Condition red!"
970 GOSUB 1650
980 IF RND > .7 THEN 1110
990 PRINT "Dosznti fire has hit our ship, ca
ptain"
1000 DA = INT(RND*9) + 2
1010 GOSUB 1650
1020 PRINT "Master control reports damage ra
ting of"DA
1030 PRINT "to the ";
1040 IF DA = 2 THEN PRINT "foreward section,
 sir"
1050 IF DA > 2 AND DA < 4 THEN PRINT "crew s
ection, captain"
1060 IF DA > 3 AND DA < 7 THEN PRINT "main d
rive, sir"
1070 IF DA > 6 THEN PRINT "power reserve cha
mber, captain"
1080 L = L - DA
1090 GOSUB 1620
1100 RETURN
1110 GOSUB 1650
1120 PRINT "The Dosznti fire missed our ship
, captain"
1130 GOSUB 1650
1140 RETURN
1150 REM Status report
1160 CLS
1170 PRINT "*****************************************
************"
1180 PRINT:PRINT "Status report from master
control:"
1190 GOSUB 1650
1200 PRINT "Energy in main and auxiliary ban
ks:"L
1210 IF L<3 THEN PRINT:PRINT "Warning...ener
gy level is":PRINT "dangerously low!"
1220 PRINT ,"Stardate timer reads"TI
1230 IF TI < 8 THEN PRINT "!!!!!Warning - Mi
```

```
ssion time running out!!!!!"
1240 IF TI < 1 THEN 680
1250 PRINT "*********************************
***********"
1260 IF T > 0 THEN PRINT:PRINT "Dosznti dest
ruction tally is"T
1270 PRINT ">>>Ships galactic co-ordinates a
re"X;Y;Z
1280 PRINT:PRINT ">>>>>Dosznti mothership lo
cated at"A;B;C
1290 PRINT:PRINT "The Dosznti is ";
1300 IF A<>X OR B<>Y THEN PRINT "to the";
1310 IF A < X THEN PRINT " north";
1320 IF A > X THEN PRINT " south";
1330 IF B > Y THEN PRINT " east";
1340 IF B < Y THEN PRINT " west";
1350 IF C = Z THEN PRINT " of your ship, sir
"
1360 IF C > Z THEN PRINT " behind us, captai
n"
1370 IF C < Z THEN PRINT " in front of us, s
ir"
1380 PRINT "*********************************
***********"
1390 RETURN
1400 REM ******************************
1410 REM Initialise
1420 CLS
1430 RANDOMIZE VAL(RIGHT$(TIME$,2))
1440 L = 35 + INT(RND*30):T = 0:TI = 50
1450 A = INT(RND*10) + 1
1460 B = INT(RND*10) + 1
1470 C = INT(RND*10) + 1
1480 X = INT(RND*10) + 1
1490 Y = INT(RND*10) + 1
1500 Z = INT(RND*10) + 1
1510 RETURN
1520 REM Hyperspace option
1530 X = INT(RND*10) + 1
1540 Y = INT(RND*10) + 1
1550 X = INT(RND*10) + 1
1560 FOR J = 1 TO 40
1570 PRINT TAB(J);"*":PRINT
1580 FOR H = 1 TO J:NEXT H
```

```
1590 NEXT J
1600 CLS
1610 RETURN
1620 FOR P = 1 TO 1000:NEXT P
1630 CLS
1640 GOTO 1660
1650 FOR P = 1 TO 1000:NEXT P
1660 PRINT:PRINT
1670 RETURN
```

Brain Games

I guess 90% of all games could, without stretching the definition too much, be called "brain games." After all, they demand a certain amount of brain-power and application from you to play.

However, the programs in this section under the heading of "brain games" are here because they demand a little more intellectual effort than several of the other games in the book.

Here you'll find FASTERMIND, where you'll have to deduce a four-digit code invented by your computer, tax your mathematical ability as you solve magic stars and squares (IDAHO STARS and IDAHO SQUARES), and save your precious neck by deducing a word the computer has chosen in EXECUTIONER.

As well, you'll try to unlock a twisted cube in CUBIC, will settle down to a game or two of MUMBLE MARBLE (also known as "solitaire" and named as it is here because the game in "real life" uses marbles on a board), and will have to work under the pressure of a relentless clock to locate some atoms within a CYCLOTRON.

If your brain still has any power left after all that, you can attempt a task which may appear impossible in FLIPPER and work out an algorithm to solve the SWITCHEROO problem in the fewest number of moves.

Finally, when your brain has been brought into shape by the exercise of solving all the other problems in this section, you can attempt to deduce the map of a cave system in SEARCHING FOR DARYL. Don't expect this one to be easy. Concentration and patience are vital to solving it.

☐ FASTERMIND

We'll start with something fairly simple—FASTERMIND. You are probably already familiar with this kind of game, in which you have to try and crack a code developed by another player.

In this program, the computer thinks of a four-digit code (using the numbers 1 to 9, and making sure that no digit is repeated within the code) and you have to try and work out what it is within eight goes.

Each guess will get feedback in terms of "blacks" and "whites," where a black is your reward for getting a correct digit in the correct position, and a white is awarded if you have a digit right, but it is not in the right position within the code.

And here's the listing so you can get your brain working with a sixpack or two of FASTERMIND:

```
10  REM Fastermind
20  CLS
30  N = 1
40  PRINT "Press a key"
50  N = N + 1
60  IF INKEY$ = "" THEN 50
70  RANDOMIZE N
80  CLS
90  PRINT "Fastermind"
100 PRINT
110 PRINT "When you are told to do"
120 PRINT "so, enter a 4-digit number"
130 PRINT "and then press RETURN."
140 PRINT
150 PRINT "Digits can be repeated."
160 PRINT
170 PRINT "You have 8 goes to break"
180 PRINT "the difficult code."
190 FOR Z=1 TO 3000:NEXT Z
200 CLS
210 DIM B(4)
220 DIM D(4)
230 LET H=0
240 FOR A=1 TO 4
```

```
250 LET B(A)= INT (RND*9)+1:REM
    Or RND(1)*9 + 1
260 NEXT A
270 FOR C=1 TO 8
280 PRINT
290 PRINT "Enter guess number";C;
300 INPUT X
310 IF X>9999 THEN GOTO 290
320 IF X<1000 THEN GOTO 290
330 LET P=INT (X/1000)
340 LET Q=INT ((X-1000*P)/100)
350 LET R=INT ((X-1000*P - 100*Q)/10)
360 LET S=INT (X-1000*P - 100*Q - 10*R)
370 LET D(1)=P
380 LET D(2)=Q
390 LET D(3)=R
400 LET D(4)=S
410 FOR E=1 TO 4
420 IF D(E)<>B(E) THEN GOTO 470
430 PRINT " Black";
440 LET B(E)=B(E) + 10
450 LET D(E)=D(E) + 20
460 LET H=H + 1
470 NEXT E
480 IF H=4 THEN GOTO 680
490 FOR F=1 TO 4
500 LET D=D(F)
510 FOR G=1 TO 4
520 IF D<>B(G) THEN GOTO 560
530 PRINT "  White";
540 LET B(G)=B(G) + 10
550 GOTO 570
560 NEXT G
570 NEXT F
580 FOR G=1 TO 4
590 IF B(G)<10 THEN GOTO 610
600 LET B(G)=B(G) - 10
610 NEXT G
620 LET H =0
630 PRINT
640 NEXT C
650 PRINT:PRINT "You didn't get it..."
660 PRINT "The answer is:   ";B(1);B(2);B
(3);B(4)
```

```
670 END
680 PRINT:PRINT:PRINT "Well done, Master
   brain!"
690 PRINT
700 PRINT:PRINT "You got the answer in"
710 PRINT TAB(5);"just";C;"goes"
```

◻ IDAHO STARS

IDAHO STARS are stars with a special property—numbers placed on the crossover points of the lines forming them will, when added together, produce the same total, no matter which line of numbers is chosen.

Here, for example, is one such star:

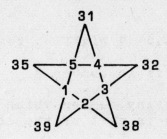

As you can see, each line on the star sums to the same total. In this program, the computer generates an IDAHO STAR, leaving two or three of the numbers as zeroes for you to work out as quickly as you can:

Here's the program in action:

```
                    0


        10      0      10      5

                2           5

                    6

        20                  18


        This is go number 1

        Enter any number which you
        think is part of the star? 11
```

```
                    0

        10      11      10      5

            2       5

                    6

        20              18


You have 9 right so far

This is go number 2

Enter any number which you
think is part of the star? 3



                    3

        10      11      10      5

            2       5

                    6

        20              18



Yes, you've solved it!

And it only took 2 goes...
Press 'Y' if you'd like to
try another Star of Idaho,
press 'N' to stop........
```

```
                    0

        10      16      13      9

                7       9

                    8

        22              0
```

This is go number 1

Enter any number which you
think is part of the star? 7


```
                    0

        10      16      13      9

                7       9

                    8

        22              0
```

You have 8 right so far

This is go number 3

Enter any number which you
think is part of the star? 15

```
            3

    10    16    13    9

        7         9

            8

    22              23


    Yes, you've solved it!

    And it only took 5 goes...
    Press 'Y' if you'd like to
    try another Star of Idaho,
    press 'N' to stop........

    OK, thanks for playing
```

This is the listing to produce your own IDAHO STARS (and note you can change the 3 in line 630 to a higher number if you want to produce stars which are more difficult to solve):

```
10 REM Idaho Stars
20 GOSUB 480:REM Set up star
30 GOSUB 340:REM Print Star
40 GOSUB 70:REM Ask for guess
50 GOTO 30
60 REM ******************
70 REM Ask for Guess
80 IF SCORE > 0 AND SCORE < 10 THEN PRINT
 "You have"SCORE"right so far":PRINT
90 GO = GO + 1
100 PRINT "This is go number"GO:PRINT
110 PRINT "Enter any number which you"
120 INPUT "think is part of the star";G
130 SCORE = 0
140 FOR J = 1 TO 10
150 IF G = A(J) THEN B(J) = A(J)
```

```
160 IF B(J) <> 0 THEN SCORE = SCORE + 1
170 NEXT J
180 FOR P = 1 TO 1000:NEXT P
190 IF SCORE < 10 THEN RETURN
200 REM ******************
210 GOSUB 340
220 PRINT:PRINT "Yes, you've solved it!"
230 PRINT:PRINT "And it only took"GO"goes
..."
240 FOR P = 1 TO 1000:NEXT P
250 PRINT "Press 'Y' if you'd like to"
260 PRINT "try another Star of Idaho,"
270 PRINT "press 'N' to stop........."
280 A$ = INKEY$
290 IF A$ <> "n" AND A$ <> "N" AND A$ <>
"Y" AND A$ <> "y" THEN 280
300 IF A$ = "Y" OR A$ = "y" THEN RUN
310 PRINT:PRINT "OK, thanks for playing"
320 END
330 REM *************
340 REM Print star
350 CLS:PRINT:PRINT
360 PRINT TAB(11);B(1)
370 PRINT:PRINT
380 PRINT TAB(2);" ";B(2);"   ";B(3);" ";B
(4);" ";B(5)
390 PRINT
400 PRINT TAB(7);B(6);"     ";B(7)
410 PRINT
420 PRINT TAB(10);B(8)
430 PRINT
440 PRINT TAB(4);B(9);"         ";B(10)
450 PRINT:PRINT
460 RETURN
470 REM *************
480 REM Set up star
490 CLS
500 RANDOMIZE VAL(RIGHT$(TIME$,2))
510 DIM A(10),B(10)
520 DEFINT A - Z
530 GO = 0:SCORE = 0
540 A = INT(RND*9) + 1
550 B = INT(RND*9) + 1
560 C = INT(RND*9) + 1
```

```
570 D = INT(RND*9) + 1
580 E = INT(RND*9) + 1
590 IF A = B OR A = C OR A = D OR A = E T
HEN 550
600 IF B = C OR B = D OR B = E THEN 550
610 IF C = D OR C = E THEN 550
620 IF D = E THEN 550
630 X = INT(RND*3) + 1
640 A(1) = X
650 A(2) = X - B + C + D
660 A(3) = A + E
670 A(4) = A + D
680 A(5) = X - B - C + E
690 A(6) = A
700 A(7) = A + C
710 A(8) = A + B
720 A(9) = X - 2*B + 2*D + E
730 A(10) = X - 2*B - C + D + 2*E
740 FOR J = 1 TO 10
750 B(J) = A(J)
760 IF A(J) = 0 THEN RUN
770 NEXT J
780 B(INT(RND*10) + 1) = 0
790 B(INT(RND*10) + 1) = 0
800 B(INT(RND*10) + 1) = 0
810 RETURN
```

☐ IDAHO SQUARES

As expected, IDAHO SQUARES are like IDAHO STARS, except that the digits which add up to a common total lie along the horizontal, vertical and diagonal lines of a nine by nine grid, rather than along the lines forming a star.

Here's an IDAHO SQUARE being solved:

```
13    2    0

 0    0   10

 6   16    0
```

```
THIS IS GUESS NUMBER 1

YOU HAVE 5 RIGHT

ENTER YOUR GUESS? 4        13    2    0

                            0    0   10

                            6   16    5
```

```
13    2    0          THIS IS GUESS NUMBER 3

 0    0   10          YOU HAVE 6 RIGHT

 6   16    0          ENTER YOUR GUESS? 12
```

```
THIS IS GUESS NUMBER 2

YOU HAVE 5 RIGHT

ENTER YOUR GUESS? 5
```

331

```
13   2   12

 0   0   10

 6  16   5
```

THIS IS GUESS NUMBER 4

YOU HAVE 7 RIGHT

ENTER YOUR GUESS? 8

```
13   2   12

 8   0   10

 6  16   5
```

THIS IS GUESS NUMBER 5

YOU HAVE 8 RIGHT

ENTER YOUR GUESS? 9

```
13   2   12

 8   9   10

 6  16   5
```

YOU'VE SOLVED IT
IN JUST 5 GUESSES!

As you can see, you simply enter any number which you think may make up part of the grid, and the computer checks to see if your number is one, or more, of the missing numbers. If your guess is correct, the relevant zero (or zeroes) in the grid changes magically into the number you've entered. A tally is kept of the number of guesses it has taken you to solve it.

Here's the listing to produce your very own IDAHO SQUARES. You can change the nines in lines 250 to 280 to a lower digit for squares which are easier to solve, and to a higher one for squares which are more difficult.

```
10 REM IDAHO SQUARES
20 GOSUB 230:REM INITIALISE
30 J=J+1
40 CLS
50 PRINT:PRINT:PRINT TAB(3);
60 M=0
70 FOR Z=1 TO 9
80 PRINT B(Z);" ";
90 IF 3*INT(Z/3)=Z THEN PRINT:PRINT:PRIN
T TAB(3);
100 IF B(Z)=A(Z) THEN M=M+1
110 NEXT Z
120 PRINT
130 IF M=9 THEN PRINT "YOU'VE SOLVED IT"
:PRINT "IN JUST";J-1;"GUESSES!":END
140 PRINT:PRINT "THIS IS GUESS NUMBER";J

150 PRINT:PRINT "YOU HAVE";M;"RIGHT":PRI
NT
160 INPUT "ENTER YOUR GUESS";X
170 FOR Z=1 TO 9
180 IF B(Z)=0 AND A(Z)=X THEN B(Z)=X
190 NEXT Z
200 GOTO 30
210 END
220 REM ********************
230 DIM A(9),B(9)
240 RANDOMIZE VAL(RIGHT$(TIME$,2))
250 A=INT(RND(1)*9)+1
260 B=INT(RND(1)*9)+1
270 C=INT(RND(1)*9)+1
280 D=INT(RND(1)*9)+1
290 IF A=B OR B=C OR A=C OR A=D OR B=D O
R C=D THEN 260
300 A(1)=A+B
310 A(2)=A-(B+C)
320 A(3)=A+C
330 A(4)=A-B+C
340 A(5)=A
```

```
350 A(6)=A+B-C
360 A(7)=A-C
370 A(8)=A+B+C
380 A(9)=A-B
390 FOR Q=1 TO 9
400 B(Q)=A(Q)
410 NEXT Q
420 B(A)=0
430 B(B)=0
440 B(C)=0
450 B(D)=0
460 J=0
470 RETURN
```

☐ EXECUTIONER

As you can tell, this game is a computer variation of the old pencil-and-paper game, "hangman." In this game, the computer chooses a word from its store (held in the DATA statements from 500 to 540) and then challenges you to guess it.

The number of guesses you'll get is related to the length of the word (see lines 120 and 170).

Let's see some hapless human (me) try to work out which word the computer has chosen:

```
. . . . .

You have 0 correct letters


  8 chances left...

Enter your next guess? E



.E...

You have 1 correct letters


  8 chances left...

Enter your next guess? T



.E..T

You have 2 correct letters


  8 chances left...

Enter your next guess? Y
```

```
.E..T
You have 2 correct letters

 7 chances left...
Enter your next guess? A


ME..T
You have 3 correct letters

 2 chances left...
Enter your next guess?


ME.IT
You have 4 correct letters

 2 chances left...
Enter your next guess?
                    MERIT


Whew! You've staved off
execution for another day
You got it in 11 guesses

The Executioner's word was MERIT
```

This listing will enable you to risk your neck in the noble cause of increasing your vocabulary:

```
10 REM Executioner
20 CLS
30 N = 0:Y = 0
40 PRINT "Press 'E' when you're ready"
50 PRINT "to face the Executioner..."
60 N = N + 1:IF INKEY$ <> "e" AND INKEY$
 <> "E" THEN 60
70 RANDOMIZE N
80 FOR G = 1 TO RND*22 + 1
90 READ A$
100 NEXT G
110 GOSUB 480
120 N = LEN(A$):DIM B(N),D(N)
130 FOR G = 1 TO N
140 B(G) = ASC(MID$(A$,G,1))
150 D(G) = B(G)
160 NEXT G
170 Q = INT(N + N/2 + .5)
180 CLS:PRINT:PRINT "You have to guess t
he executioner's"
190 PRINT "word in just"Q"guesses
200 GOSUB 480
210 FOR J = 1 TO Q:Y = Y + 1
220 GOSUB 400
230 IF H = N THEN 340
240 PRINT:PRINT:PRINT Q + 1 - J "chances
 left..."
250 PRINT:INPUT "Enter your next guess";
C$
260 F = ASC(C$)
270 FOR G = 1 TO N
280 IF D(G) = F THEN D(G) = 0: J = J - 1

290 NEXT G:NEXT J
300 GOSUB 480
310 GOSUB 400
320 PRINT:PRINT:PRINT "So sorry, but you
 gotta go now!"
330 GOTO 370
340 PRINT:PRINT "Whew! You've staved off
"
```

```
350 PRINT "execution for another day"
360 PRINT "You got it in"Y - 1"guesses"
370 PRINT:PRINT "The Executioner's word
was ";A$
380 END
400 H = 0:CLS:PRINT:PRINT:PRINT
410 FOR E = 1 TO N
420 IF B(E) = D(E) THEN PRINT ".";
430 IF B(E) <> D(E) THEN PRINT CHR$(B(E)
);:H = H + 1
440 NEXT E
450 PRINT:PRINT:IF H <> N THEN PRINT "Yo
u have"H"correct letters"
460 PRINT
470 RETURN
480 FOR O = 1 TO 500:NEXT O
490 RETURN
500 DATA "MERIDIAN","MERIT","MERMAID","M
ERRIMENT"
510 DATA "OVERSEER","OXIDANT","OXYGEN","
PALPABLE","UNORTHODOX"
520 DATA "PANDEMONIUM","PANEGYRIC","PARA
DOXICAL","PHEASANT"
530 DATA "RUMPUS","RUMMAGE","SACRAMENT",
"SABRE","SCHEMATIC"
540 DATA "SEDIMENT","SEXAGENARIAN","TEMP
ERATE","TELESCOPE"
```

☐ CUBIST

This is a two-dimensional version of the colored cube puzzle which swept the world from Hungary.

The "cube" starts off looking like this:

```
1 1 2 2
1 1 2 2
3 3 4 4
3 3 4 4
```

After some manipulation by the computer, it will look something like this:

```
1 2 1 2
3 3 3 2
3 1 4 1
4 2 4 4
```

Your job is to get it back into its original state in as few moves as possible. The numbers on the cube rotate in groups of four, spinning in a clockwise direction. This means that

```
1 2
3 4
```

when rotated will look like this:

```
3 1
4 2
```

You enter a number in order to rotate the elements of the cube. The key to move is as follows:

```
 2  3  4
 6  7  8
10 11 12
```

Let's look at the effect of a couple of twists on the cube shown on the previous page:

```
Enter your choice (2 - 12) but
not 5 or 9? 6


    1   2   1   2
    3   3   3   2
    1   3   4   1
    4   2   4   4
```

Your cubist twist number 1


```
Enter your choice (2 - 12) but
not 5 or 9? 6


    1   2   1   2
    1   3   3   2
    3   3   4   1
    4   2   4   4
```


Your cubist twist number 2

This is the listing for CUBIST:

```
10  REM Cubist
20  DIM A(4),B(16)
30  RANDOMIZE VAL(RIGHT$(TIME$,2))
40  CLS
50  B = 1:F = 0
60  FOR D = 1 TO 4
70  C = 0
80  IF B = 1 THEN C = 1
90  IF B = 3 THEN C = 2
100 IF B = 9 THEN C = 3
110 IF B = 11 THEN C = 4
120 B(B) = C
130 B(B + 1) = C
140 B(B + 4) = C
150 B(B + 5) = C
```

```
160 C = 0
170 IF B = 1 THEN C = 2
180 IF B = 3 THEN C = 6
190 IF B = 9 THEN C = 2
200 B = B + C
210 NEXT D
220 GOSUB 410
230 PRINT:PRINT
240 IF F < 11 THEN PRINT "Twisting..."
250 F = F + 1
260 FOR P = 1 TO 900:NEXT P
270 IF F < 11 THEN X = INT(RND*12) + 1
280 IF F > 10 THEN PRINT "Enter your choic
e (2 - 12) but":INPUT "not 5 or 9";X
290 IF X < 2 OR X = 5 OR X = 9 OR X > 12 T
HEN 270
300 A(1) = B(X)
310 A(2) = B(X + 4)
320 A(3) = B(X + 3)
330 A(4) = B(X - 1)
340 B(X) = A(4)
350 B(X + 4) = A(1)
360 B(X + 3) = A(2)
370 B(X - 1) = A(3)
380 GOSUB 410
390 F = F + 1
400 GOTO 270
410 CLS
420 PRINT:PRINT:PRINT
430 FOR B = 1 TO 16
440 PRINT B(B);
450 IF B/4 = INT(B/4) THEN PRINT
460 NEXT B
470 PRINT:PRINT
480 IF F < 10 THEN PRINT:PRINT "Twist numb
er"F
490 IF F > 10 THEN PRINT:PRINT "Your cubis
t twist number"F  - 10:PRINT
500 IF F < 11 THEN RETURN
510 P = 0
520 IF B(1) = 1 AND B(2) = 1 AND B(3) = 2
AND B(4) = 2 AND B(5) = 1 AND B(6) = 1 AND
 B(7) = 2 AND B(8) = 2 THEN P = P + 1
530 IF B(9) = 3 AND B(10) = 3 AND B(11) =
```

```
    4 AND B(12) = 4 AND B(13) = 3 AND B(14) =
    3 AND B(15) = 4 AND B(16) = 4 THEN P = P +
     1
540 IF P <> 2 THEN RETURN
550 PRINT:PRINT "You solved it in just"F -
    10" twists"
560 PRINT:PRINT "Well done, cubist!"
```

□ MUMBLE MARBLE

Our next brain game is a computer version of the game you may know as "solitaire," in which you have to move marbles around a board. At the start of the game only the center hole is empty. You can jump over marbles into empty holes, and you remove the marble so jumped over. The idea of the game is to end up with just one marble in the center hole.

Many stories have been told about the origin of this game. The most interesting of these tales is the one that says the idea of the game was worked out by a prisoner in solitary confinement in the Bastille, who devised it as a way to relieve the monotony of his imprisonment. Whether that story is true or not, there is no doubt that the game can become quite addictive, as you try to devise a foolproof way to solve it.

Here's what the MUMBLE MARBLE display looks like at the start of the game:

```
Enter side co-ordinate first
   Enter 99 to concede

   1 2 3 4 5 6 7
         0 0 0        1
         0 0 0        2
   0 0 0 0 0 0 0      3
   0 0 0 * 0 0 0      4
   0 0 0 0 0 0 0      5
         0 0 0        6
         0 0 0        7


Moves so far: 0
```

A few moves later it could look like this:

```
1 2 3 4 5 6 7
    0 0 0       1
    0 * 0       2
0 * 0 0 0 0 0   3
0 0 * 0 0 0 0   4
0 0 0 0 0 0 0   5
    * 0 0       6
    * 0 0       7
```

Moves so far: 4

There are 28 marbles on the board
Which marble do you want to move? 41
  41 to where? 43

Here's the listing, so you can set out to solve the problem yourself:

```
10 REM Mumble Marble
20 GOSUB 400
30 GOSUB 250
40 REM ACCEPT MOVE
50 PRINT "Which marble do you want to mov
e";
60 INPUT A
70 IF A = 99 THEN GOTO 240
80 IF A<11 OR A>77 THEN GOTO 50
90 IF A(A) <> 79 THEN GOTO 50
100 PRINT A"to where";
110 INPUT B
120 IF B<11 OR B>77 THEN GOTO 110
130 IF A(B) <> E THEN GOTO 110
140 LET A((A + B)/2) = E: LET A(A) = E:LE
T A(B) = 79
150 LET MOVE = MOVE + 1
160 LET COUNT = 0
170 FOR F=11 TO 75
180 IF A(F) = 79 THEN LET COUNT = COUNT +
  1
190 NEXT F
200 GOSUB 250
```

```
210 PRINT "There are";COUNT;"marbles on t
he board"
220 IF COUNT <> 1 THEN GOTO 40
230 IF A(44) = 79 THEN PRINT "You did it,
 in just";MOVE;"moves!":END
240 PRINT "The game is over, and you've f
ailed!":END
250 REM print out
260 CLS: REM Put HOME here if your
        computer supports it
270 PRINT "Enter side co-ordinate first"
280 PRINT TAB(5);"Enter 99 to concede"
290 PRINT "    1 2 3 4 5 6 7"
300 PRINT TAB(5);
310 FOR D = 11 TO 75
320 T = 10*(INT(D/10))
330 IF D - T = 8 THEN LET D = D + 2: PRIN
T T/10:PRINT TAB(5);:GOTO 350
340 PRINT CHR$(A(D));" ";
350 NEXT D:PRINT "      7"
360 PRINT:PRINT:PRINT
370 PRINT "Moves so far:";MOVE
380 PRINT: PRINT
390 RETURN
400 REM INITIALISE
410 CLS
420 DIM A(87)
430 LET E = 42
440 FOR D = 11 TO 75
450 LET T = 10*(INT(D/10))
460 IF D - T = 8 THEN LET D = D + 3
470 READ A(D)
480 NEXT D
490 LET MOVE = 0
500 RETURN
510 REM 42 is ASC ("*")
520 REM 79 is ASC("O")
530 DATA 32,32,79,79,79,32,32
540 DATA 32,32,79,79,79,32,32
550 DATA 79,79,79,79,79,79,79
560 DATA 79,79,79,42,79,79,79
570 DATA 79,79,79,79,79,79,79
580 DATA 32,32,79,79,79,32,32
590 DATA 32,32,79,79,79
```

☐ CYCLOTRON

In CYCLOTRON, you fire atoms into the machine from the top, by specifying a number, and you have to try and locate particles of antimatter hidden within the machine from the behavior of the atom.

If the atom hits a particle of antimatter it will either be absorbed, or deflected to the right or left. An atom may be affected by more than one particle of antimatter, which makes the resolution of the problem even more difficult.

There are always three particles of antimatter in the machine, although they could well all be in the same number cyclotron. You have an extremely limited number of goes in order to locate the antimatter. At each go, you can either enter the number where you want to enter an atom, or be reckless and enter 8, which gives you a chance to guess the location of the antimatter particles.

This is what it looks like when it is up and running:

```
You have 6 seconds
Enter cyclotron number,
or 8 if you think you know
where the antimatter lies
? 3
```

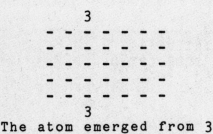

```
           3
   - - - - - -
     - - - - - -
   - - - - - -
   - - - - - -
   - - - - - -
           3
The atom emerged from 3
```

```
You have 5 seconds
Enter cyclotron number,
or 8 if you think you know
where the antimatter lies
? 5
```

```
- - - - - - -
- - - - - - -
- - - - - - -
- - - - - - -
- - - - - - -
```

The atom has been absorbed

You have 2 seconds
Enter cyclotron number,
or 8 if you think you know
where the antimatter lies
? 8
Where do you think
the antimatter lies?
? 3,5,4
Well done. You located the
antimatter with 2 seconds
                  to spare

Your best time so far is 4

And here's the listing for your very own cyclotron:

```
10 REM Cyclotron
20 CLS
30 N = 0:HS = 9:DIM B(7),Q(3),W(3)
40 PRINT "Press a key when you're"
50 PRINT "ready to play"
60 N = N + 1:IF INKEY$ = "" THEN 60
70 RANDOMIZE N
80 REM Place antimatter
90 FOR A = 1 TO 3
100 B(A) = INT(RND*7) + 1
110 NEXT A
120 FOR H = 6 TO 1 STEP - 1
130 CLS
140 PRINT:PRINT:PRINT "You have"H"seconds"

150 PRINT "Enter cyclotron number,"
160 PRINT "or 8 if you think you know"
```

```basic
170 PRINT "where the antimatter lies"
180 INPUT C
190 IF C = 8 THEN GOTO 520
200 GOSUB 450
210 D = 1
220 IF B(D) = C THEN 350
230 IF D<3 THEN D = D + 1:GOTO 220
240 GOSUB 500
250 PRINT "The atom emerged from"C
260 FOR Z = 1 TO 2000:NEXT Z
270 NEXT H
280 PRINT:PRINT:PRINT
290 PRINT "Sorry, time is up"
300 PRINT:PRINT "The antimatter was in"
310 FOR A = 1 TO 3
320 PRINT B(A);
330 NEXT A
340 END
350 REM Antimatter acts
360 IF RND > .9 THEN 420
370 IF C = 1 THEN C = 2:GOTO 210
380 IF C = 7 THEN C = 6:GOTO 210
390 F = INT(RND*2) - 1
400 C = C + F
410 GOTO 210
420 REM Antimatter absorbs atom
430 PRINT "The atom has been absorbed"
440 GOTO 260
450 PRINT:PRINT:PRINT  TAB(3 + 2*C);C
460 FOR Z = 1 TO 5
470 PRINT TAB(6);"- - - - - -"
480 NEXT Z
490 RETURN
500 PRINT TAB(3 + 2*C);C
510 RETURN
520 REM Location attempt
530 PRINT "Where do you think"
540 PRINT "the antimatter lies?"
550 INPUT Q(1),Q(2),Q(3)
560 FOR T = 1 TO 3:W(T) = B(T):NEXT T
570 SR = 0
580 FOR X = 1 TO 3:FOR Y = 1 TO 3
590 IF Q(X) = B(Y) THEN SR = SR  + 1:B(Y)
 = 0:Q(X) = 0
```

```
600 NEXT Y:NEXT X
610 GOTO 650
620 FOR P = 1 TO 3
630 B(P) = W(P)
640 NEXT P
650 IF SR > 2 THEN 700
660 IF SR > 0 THEN PRINT "You located"SR"c
orrectly"
670 IF SR = 0 THEN PRINT "You are complete
ly wrong!"
680 FOR T = 1 TO 3:B(T) = W(T):NEXT T
690 GOTO 260
700 PRINT "Well done. You located the"
710 PRINT "antimatter with"H"seconds"
720 PRINT ,"to spare"
730 IF 6 - H < HS THEN HS = 6 - H
740 PRINT:PRINT "Your best time so far is"
HS
750 FOR Z = 1 TO 2000:NEXT Z
760 GOTO 90
```

☐ SWITCHEROO

In SWITCHEROO, you are presented with the digits 1 to 9 arranged in a random order, and you have to get them into 123456789 order, in as few moves as possible.

You enter your moves as numbers, and the computer performs a "switcheroo" using the number you've entered. It works like this:

```
Please stand by...
7
                    Move number 1
79

798
                    798654321
7986
                    Which number to switcheroo?
79865

798654              Move number 3

7986543

79865432            123456897

                    Which number to switcheroo?


                    Move number 4


                    123456879

                    Which number to switcheroo?
```

Move number 6

123456798

Which number to switcheroo?

123456789

You did it, champ!

And it took just 7 moves...

This is the listing for the game:

```
10 REM Switcheroo
20 CLS
30 PRINT:PRINT "Please stand by..."
40 GOSUB 100
50 GOSUB 230
60 IF A$ = "123456789" THEN 400
70 M = M + 1
80 GOTO 50
90 END
100 RANDOMIZE VAL(RIGHT$(TIME$,2))
110 M = 1:X = 0
120 A$ = ""
130 FOR T = 1 TO 9
140 L = INT(RND#9) + 49
150 Q = 1
160 IF MID$(A$,Q,1) = CHR$(L) THEN 140
170 IF Q<T THEN Q = Q + 1:GOTO 160
180 A$ = A$ + CHR$(L)
190 PRINT A$
200 PRINT
210 NEXT T
220 RETURN
230 REM Print out
```

```
240 CLS
250 PRINT:PRINT:PRINT
260 PRINT "Move number"M
270 PRINT:PRINT:PRINT
280 PRINT A$
290 PRINT:PRINT "Which number to switcheroo
?"
300 IF INKEY$ <> "" THEN 300
310 C$ = INKEY$
320 R = VAL(C$)
330 IF R<1 OR R>8 THEN 310
340 B$ = ""
350 FOR T = 9 TO R STEP - 1
360 B$ = B$ + MID$(A$,T,1)
370 NEXT T
380 A$ = LEFT$(A$,R-1) + B$
390 RETURN
400 PRINT:PRINT:PRINT
410 PRINT A$
420 PRINT:PRINT:PRINT
430 PRINT "You did it, champ!"
440 PRINT:PRINT "And it took just"M"moves..
."
450 END
```

☐ FLIPPER

This intriguing game can provide you with a considerable degree of mental stretching. When you run the game, you'll see a mix of X's and *'s on a three by three grid. You have to end up with an X in the middle, and eight *'s surrounding it.

You enter the number of the place you want to hit with your flipper. Flipping a corner piece causes those adjoining it to change into their opposites (that is an X becomes an *, and an * becomes an X). Hitting the middle piece on a side with your flipper causes the two on either side of it to change, and hitting the middle piece changes the middle pieces on each of the sides.

The piece you hit always changes in each case.

Here's what it looks like in action:

```
You flipped 5

1  2  3        X X X

4  5  6        * X *

7  8  9        * X *

That was move 1

Number of X is 5

You only need one - in the middle square

Which one do you want to flip?


You flipped 9

1  2  3        X X X

4  5  6        * * X

7  8  9        * * X
```

That was move 2

Number of X is 5

You only need one - in the middle square

Which one do you want to flip?

You flipped 4

```
1  2  3      * X X
4  5  6      X * X
7  8  9      X * X
```

That was move 3

Number of X is 6

You only need one - in the middle square

Which one do you want to flip?

You flipped 1

```
1  2  3      X * X
4  5  6      * X X
7  8  9      X * X
```

That was move 4

Number of X is 6

You only need one - in the middle square

Which one do you want to flip?

This is what you're aiming for:

```
You flipped 5

 1   2   3        * * *

 4   5   6        * X *

 7   8   9        * * *


You solved it in just 22 moves
```

Here's the listing so you can do it yourself:

```
10 REM FLIPPER
20 DIM A(10),F(4)
30 M = -1:Q = 42:X = 88:P = 0
40 RANDOMIZE VAL(RIGHT$(TIME$,2))
50 FOR C = 1 TO 9
60 A(C) = Q
70 IF INT(RND + .5) = 0 THEN A(C) = X
80 NEXT C
90 GOSUB 270
100 M = M + 1
110 N = 0
120 FOR C = 1 TO 9
130 IF A(C) = X THEN N = N + 1
140 NEXT C
150 IF N = 1 AND A(5) = X THEN 350
160 IF M > 0 THEN PRINT:PRINT "That was mo
ve"M
170 PRINT:PRINT "Number of X is"N
180 PRINT:PRINT "You only need one - in th
e middle square"
190 PRINT:PRINT "Which one do you want to
flip?"
200 IF INKEY$ <> "" THEN 200
210 A$ = INKEY$
220 N = VAL(A$):IF N<1 OR N>9 THEN 210
230 P = N
240 GOSUB 380
```

```
250 GOTO 90
260 END
270 CLS:PRINT:PRINT
280 IF P <> 0 THEN PRINT "You flipped"P
290 PRINT:PRINT:PRINT "1   2   3",CHR$(A(1))
;" ";CHR$(A(2));" ";CHR$(A(3))
300 PRINT
310 PRINT "4   5   6",CHR$(A(4));" ";CHR$(A(
5));" ";CHR$(A(6))
320 PRINT
330 PRINT "7   8   9",CHR$(A(7));" ";CHR$(A(
8));" ";CHR$(A(9))
340 RETURN
350 PRINT:PRINT
360 PRINT "You solved it in just"M"moves"
370 END
380 IF A(N) = X THEN RETURN
390 IF N = 1 THEN F(1)=2:F(2)=4:F(3)=5:F(4
)=10
400 IF N = 2 THEN F(1)=1:F(2)=3:F(3)=10:F(
4)=10
410 IF N = 3 THEN F(1)=2:F(2)=5:F(3)=6:F(4
)=10
420 IF N = 4 THEN F(1)=1:F(2)=7:F(3)=10:F(
4)=10
430 IF N = 5 THEN F(1)=2:F(2)=4:F(3)=8:F(4
)=6
440 IF N = 6 THEN F(1)=3:F(2)=9:F(3)=10:F(
4)=10
450 IF N = 7 THEN F(1)=4:F(2)=5:F(3)=8:F(4
)=10
460 IF N = 8 THEN F(1)=7:F(2)=9:F(3)=10:F(
4)=10
470 IF N = 9 THEN F(1)=8:F(2)=5:F(3)=6:F(4
)=10
480 FOR G = 1 TO 4
490 F = 0
500 IF A(F(G)) = X THEN F = 1
510 IF F = 1 THEN A(F(G)) = Q
520 IF F = 0 AND A(F(G)) = Q THEN A(F(G))
= X
530 NEXT G
540 A(N) = X
550 RETURN
```

□ SEARCHING FOR DARYL

Finally, we have the most troubling program of all. Daryl is lost in an underground cave system of the most perplexing complexity.

You have to enter the system, and work your way to Daryl, who is in cave 29, and then get out again.

The caves are connected by a stable, coherent set of tunnels, and you should try and solve this puzzle by making a map as you work out how the caves link up. Be warned that some tunnels travel underneath other ones. The caves are not laid out in neat numerical order. Rather, the cave numbers are provided just so you can refer to them easily.

You may find the problem difficult, but it is by no means impossible. The references within the program to directions (such as N for north and so on) should be examined with care. In fact, north is *not* up in the case, nor is south *down*. Rather, they refer to directions as if the entire cave system was being viewed from above, and the direction at the top of the system was the north, the east was the right hand side and so on. Anyway, the direction clues are more likely than not to confuse you when you first try this program.

Don't give up easily. It can be done. The number of possible routes is extraordinarily high, so once you've solved it one way, you may like to work out another way of getting through the system. Veterans of the program like to get to Daryl by a new route each time they run it, and then return to the entrance (carrying Daryl) by a completely different route.

To prove the problem can be solved, here is one route to Daryl, with another one getting out of the system:

```
You are on your way to find
Daryl, trapped in this cave system

You are in cave 1

Tunnels lead from this cave to:
  2  7  10

Daryl is to the north of you
```

Your Daryl-proximeter meter reads 30

Which cave do you wish to enter? 2

You are on your way to find
Daryl, trapped in this cave system

You are in cave 2

Tunnels lead from this cave to:
 25 11 1 8

Daryl is to the northeast of you

Your Daryl-proximeter meter reads 12

Which cave do you wish to enter? 8

You are on your way to find
Daryl, trapped in this cave system

You are in cave 8

Tunnels lead from this cave to:
 26 2

Daryl is to the northeast of you

Your Daryl-proximeter meter reads 33

Which cave do you wish to enter? 26

You are on your way to find
Daryl, trapped in this cave system

You are in cave 26

Tunnels lead from this cave to:
  8   3   23   12

Daryl is to the northeast of you

Your Daryl-proximeter meter reads 54

Which cave do you wish to enter? 23

You are on your way to find
Daryl, trapped in this cave system

You are in cave 23

Tunnels lead from this cave to:
  18   26

Daryl is to the northeast of you

Your Daryl-proximeter meter reads 86

Which cave do you wish to enter? 18

You are on your way to find
Daryl, trapped in this cave system

You are in cave 18

Tunnels lead from this cave to:
  13   15   22   23

Daryl is to the northwest of you

Your Daryl-proximeter meter reads 54

Which cave do you wish to enter? 22

You are in cave 22

Tunnels lead from this cave to:
 18 29

Daryl is to the northwest of you

Your Daryl-proximeter meter reads 74

Which cave do you wish to enter? 29

Well done, you've found Daryl
apparently safe and well....

You have found Daryl, and are
returning to the entrance

You are in cave 29

Tunnels lead from this cave to:
 22

The exit is to the northwest of you

Your Exit-proximeter meter reads 55

Which cave do you wish to enter? 22

You have found Daryl, and are
returning to the entrance

You are in cave 22

Tunnels lead from this cave to:
 18 29

The exit is to the northwest of you

Your Exit-proximeter meter reads 44

Which cave do you wish to enter? 18

You have found Daryl, and are
returning to the entrance

You are in cave 18

Tunnels lead from this cave to:
 13 15 22 23

The exit is to the northwest of you

Your Exit-proximeter meter reads 24

Which cave do you wish to enter? 15

You have found Daryl, and are
returning to the entrance

You are in cave 15

Tunnels lead from this cave to:
 18 6

The exit is to the southwest of you

Your Exit-proximeter meter reads 15

Which cave do you wish to enter? 6

You have found Daryl, and are
returning to the entrance

You are in cave 6

Tunnels lead from this cave to:
 15 19

The exit is to the east of you

Your Exit-proximeter meter reads 5

Which cave do you wish to enter? 19

You have found Daryl, and are
returning to the entrance

You are in cave 19

Tunnels lead from this cave to:
 20 6

The exit is to the southeast of you

Your Exit-proximeter meter reads 46

Which cave do you wish to enter? 20

You have found Daryl, and are
returning to the entrance

You are in cave 20

Tunnels lead from this cave to:
 19 14 21

The exit is to the southeast of you

Your Exit-proximeter meter reads 25

Which cave do you wish to enter? 21

You have found Daryl, and are
returning to the entrance

You are in cave 21

Tunnels lead from this cave to:
 11 25 20

The exit is to the southeast of you

Your Exit-proximeter meter reads 63

Which cave do you wish to enter? 25

You have found Daryl, and are
returning to the entrance

You are in cave 25

Tunnels lead from this cave to:
 21 2

The exit is to the southeast of you

Your Exit-proximeter meter reads 43

Which cave do you wish to enter? 2

You have found Daryl, and are
returning to the entrance

You are in cave 2

Tunnels lead from this cave to:
  25 11 1 8

The exit is to the southeast of you

Your Exit-proximeter meter reads 22

Which cave do you wish to enter? 1

You are a hero!!!

You've made it back with
Daryl safe and well....

Go straight to Washington
to be decorated by the
President.....
See you later, hero!

And this is the listing for our final **BRAIN GAME**:

```
10 REM Searching for Daryl
20 GOSUB 770:REM Initialise
30 GOSUB 480:REM Location description
40 GOSUB 360:REM Move
50 IF DA = 0 AND CAVE = 29 THEN GOSUB 90:RE
M Daryl found
60 IF DA = 1 AND CAVE = 1 THEN 210:REM Back
 home safely
70 GOTO 30
80 REM ***********
90 REM   Daryl found
100 REM ***********
110 PRINT:PRINT "Well done, you've found Da
ryl"
120 PRINT "apparently safe and well...."
130 FOR P = 1 TO 1000:NEXT P
140 PRINT:PRINT "Now it's time to try"
150 PRINT "return to the exit, with"
160 PRINT "Daryl...."
170 FOR P = 1 TO 1000:NEXT P
180 DA = 1
190 RETURN
200 REM ****************
210 REM Back home safely
220 REM ****************
230 PRINT:PRINT
240 PRINT "You are a hero!!!"
250 FOR P = 1 TO 1000:NEXT P
260 PRINT:PRINT "You've made it back with"
270 PRINT "Daryl safe and well...."
280 PRINT:PRINT
290 PRINT "Go straight to Washington"
300 PRINT "to be decorated by the"
310 PRINT "President....."
320 FOR P = 1 TO 1000:NEXT P
330 PRINT "See you later, hero!"
340 END
350 REM *********
360 REM Make move
370 REM *********
380 PRINT:PRINT
390 INPUT "Which cave do you wish to enter"
```

```
;J
400 FLAG = 0
410 FOR K = 1 TO 4
420 IF Z(CAVE,K) = J THEN FLAG = 1
430 NEXT K
440 IF FLAG = 0 THEN PRINT "There is no tun
nel to cave"J:FOR P = 1 TO 1000:NEXT P:GOTO
 390
450 CAVE = J
460 RETURN
470 REM *********************
480 REM Location description
490 REM *********************
500 CLS:PRINT:PRINT
510 IF DA = 0 THEN PRINT "You are on your w
ay to find":PRINT "Daryl, trapped in this c
ave system"
520 IF DA = 1 THEN PRINT "You have found Da
ryl, and are":PRINT "returning to the entra
nce"
530 PRINT:PRINT "You are in cave"CAVE
540 PRINT:PRINT "Tunnels lead from this cav
e to:"
550 FOR Q = 1 TO 4
560 IF Z(CAVE,Q) > 0 THEN PRINT Z(CAVE,Q);
570 NEXT Q
580 PRINT:PRINT
590 IF DA = 1 THEN 660
600 PRINT "Daryl is to the ";
610 IF Z(CAVE,5) > 4 THEN PRINT "north";
620 IF Z(CAVE,5) < 4 THEN PRINT "south";
630 IF Z(CAVE,6) < 7 THEN PRINT "east";
640 IF Z(CAVE,6) > 7 THEN PRINT "west";
650 GOTO 710
660 PRINT "The exit is to the ";
670 IF Z(CAVE,5) > 7 THEN PRINT "north";
680 IF Z(CAVE,5) < 7 THEN PRINT "south";
690 IF Z(CAVE,6) < 7 THEN PRINT "east";
700 IF Z(CAVE,6) > 7 THEN PRINT "west";
710 PRINT " of you"
720 PRINT:PRINT
730 IF DA = 0 THEN PRINT "Your Daryl-proxim
eter meter reads"10*(ABS(Z(CAVE,5) - 4)) +
ABS(Z(CAVE,6) - 7)
```

```
740 IF DA = 1 THEN PRINT "Your Exit-proxime
ter meter reads"10*(ABS(Z(CAVE,5) - 7)) + A
BS(Z(CAVE,6) - 7)
750 RETURN
760 REM **********
770 REM Initialise
780 REM **********
790 CLS
800 DIM Z(29,6)
810 FOR H = 1 TO 29
820 READ B:READ C:READ D
830 READ E:READ F:READ G
840 Z(H,1) = B:Z(H,2) = C:Z(H,3) = D
850 Z(H,4) = E:Z(H,5) = F:Z(H,6) = G
860 NEXT H
870 DA = 0:REM You have not yet found Daryl

880 CAVE = 1:REM Starting position
890 RETURN
900 DATA 2,7,10,0,7,7,25,11,1,8,5,5
910 DATA 26,0,0,0,10,1,24,9,7,0,2,10
920 DATA 27,28,0,0,10,8,15,19,0,0,7,2
930 DATA 4,1,0,0,5,8,26,2,0,0,7,4
940 DATA 4,24,10,0,4,11,1,9,0,0,7,9
950 DATA 21,2,0,0,2,7,26,28,0,0,11,4
960 DATA 18,16,0,0,8,10,20,0,0,0,2,2
970 DATA 18,6,0,0,6,12,13,17,0,0,9,5
980 DATA 16,28,0,0,11,6,13,15,22,23,9,11
990 DATA 20,6,0,0,3,1,19,14,21,0,5,2
1000 DATA 11,25,20,0,1,4,18,29,0,0,11,11
1010 DATA 18,26,0,0,12,1,4,9,0,0,1,12
1020 DATA 21,2,0,0,3,4,8,3,23,12,9,3
1030 DATA 5,0,0,0,9,7,17,5,12,0,12,7
1040 DATA 22,0,0,0,12,12
```

Creating your
own Games

☐ CREATING GAMES

You may well find, after you've been programming for some time, that although you've got many of the skills you need to write games of your own, you're a little short on ideas. If that's the case, you should find this section of the book of interest to you. I'm going to outline a number of games which seem to me to be ideal for conversion to computer games.

A second book of computer games programs is now in preparation, and I'm looking for new programs to include in that volume. If you've written any games which you think would be suitable (that is, they are worthwhile, original programs, and are not machine-dependent) I'd very much like to see them, with a view to purchasing them to use in the next volume. You'll be given full credit for the program, of course. Only printed listings, dumped direct from the computer, can be considered. Write to me care of the publisher.

The reason I've mentioned that at this point is that I'm quite willing to consider programs based on ideas given in this section of the book, or programs which are based entirely on your own ideas.

Let's get back now to writing your own games. Unless you're converting a well-known game, such as checkers, when your program will be expected to coincide in every respect with the non-computer version, you do not need to ensure that your computer developments of these ideas slavishly follows the outlines here. You'll probably find that, after a certain degree of development, the game takes off on its own, and may well end up in due course bearing little resemblance to its "parent." This is all to the good.

☐ GAMES TO ADAPT

SHUFFLEBOARD: Players slide flat, circular pieces along a board toward a triangular "target" which contains painted circles with numbers on them. A piece ending up entirely within the numbered circle gives the player the score of that number. There are many possible variations of this, including darts-like target games. Once you get a shuffleboard program running, you may well find that only cosmetic changes are needed to convert it into a ten-pin bowling game.

HORSESHOE: Starting with a board like this, with one player's pieces at the positions marked A, and one at those marked B, the players take it in turns to move along a line to a vacant spot:

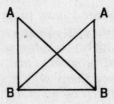

The game ends when a player discovers he or she (or it) cannot move. Despite its simplicity, this is an interesting game, as you'll discover when you play it.

DAMOCLES: This game is like **HORSESHOE**, but uses a larger board, and three pieces per player. The aim of the game is the same as **HORSESHOE**, and uses this board:

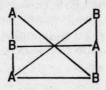

MU-TORERE: This game, which originated among the Maoris in New Zealand, is played on a board shaped like an eight-pointed star, with each point of the star joined to a circle in the middle. This circle is called the *putahi*. The players start with four pieces each, which are placed on the outside points, with all of one player's pieces occupying points next to each other. The aim of the game, as in the last two we've discussed, is to make it impossible for a player to move. You can move from one point to an adjacent empty point, or from the putahi to any vacant point. The third possible move is from a point to the putahi, but this move can only be made if at least one of the points immediately adjacent to the one from which you intend to move is occupied by an opponent's piece.

BINGO: This game is usually played with cards marked with numbers, which are crossed off as numbers are drawn at random from a pool, the winner being the player who first crosses off five in a row on his card, in any direction. It can be greatly simplified for computer use, with the computer generating two "cards" at random, using numbers from 0 to 99, and printing them on a five by five grid. The computer can then choose numbers at random from 0 to 99, and do the crossings off, and look for possible wins. The program can be made more interesting to look at by, instead of just generating a random number, including two "dials" with spinning arrows. The first dial, the "tens," is marked from zero to nine, and this is spun first. The second dial is marked the same as the first one, except that it represents the "ones."

Dice Games

As I said in the notes regarding the dice games in the dice section of this book, you should find dice games relatively easy to program on your computer, especially if the computer is not expected to exhibit too much intelligence when playing. There are a number of dice games which you may wish to try and adapt for computer play, including:

DROP DEAD: You need five dice for this. The dice are thrown by the first player, and any which show two or five are removed. The total of the rest is written down, and the dice which fell with a two or a five are thrown again. After this throw, the dice landing two and five are removed, and the total of the remaining dice is added to the total from the first throw. This process continues until there are no dice left, at which point that particular player's move ends. It is then player two's go, and the same procedure is followed. The winner is the player with the biggest total after both have had their throws. You can make the game the best of, say, three rounds, or limit the total number of throws any player can have per go, regardless of how many dice he or she has left.

MARTINETTI: You need three dice for this, and a score sheet marked with a row of boxes marked from 1 to 12, and two tokens, one each for you and the computer. You are aiming to traverse the numbers in order, before your opponent manages to do so. Each player takes it in turn to throw the dice. If the throw contains a one, the player's token can be placed in the one square. If the first throw also contained a two, the token could be moved into the two. After box one, players can either take the pip shown on an individual die for a move, or can add together the pips showing to get a desired number. A variation of this game (often called EVEREST) is to "climb down" through the numbers, after 1 through 12 has been achieved. The winner of EVEREST is the first player getting back to base camp on one.

INDIAN DICE: This game is similar to POKER DICE and is played with five dice. The aim is simply to get the best possible "poker hands." There is no provision for getting additional "cards" in one deal. You throw the five dice at once, and that is your hand. The ranking of the hands is as follows (with six highest and ones wild):

• five of a kind

• four of a kind

• full house (three of a kind plus a pair)

• two pairs

• one pair

• highest die

BIDOU: This game is also similar to POKER DICE, however, you aim to get rid of all your chips, rather than win them. The winner of the game is, paradoxically, the person who has lost the most rounds. You need three dice for this game, and a supply of chips which are distributed equally between the two players. A bet is made, and matched, before the players take it in turns to throw the three dice. The throws are ranked as follows, with "winning throws" coming first:

2 1 1; 2 2 1; 4 2 1; 6 6 6; 5 5 5; 4 4 4;
3 3 3; 2 2 2; 1 1 1; 3 3 6; 3 3 5; 3 3 4;
3 3 2; 3 3 1; 1 1 6; 1 1 5; 1 1 4; 1 1 3;
3 2 1; 4 3 2; 5 4 3; 6 5 4

If the combination thrown is not in the list, the pips are added, with the highest total winning.

BARBOOTH: Also known as BARBUDI, this game is played with two dice, and features winning and losing throws. It is suggested you

374

start with a bank of 30 chips, and give both players a starting stake of 15 chips each, charging two chips per player per round. The players take it in turns to throw the dice. Winning throws are 3 3; 5 5; 6 5; and 6 6. Losing throws are 1 1; 2 2; 2 1 and 4 4. If the players both get winning throws, the one closest to the start of the list wins (that is, 3 3 is better than 6 6). If both throw the same winning throw, the bank gets the money. If one player throws a combination which is not a winning one or a losing one, and the other throws a losing throw, the loser's chips go into the bank, and the other player retains his or her chips.

If one player throws a winning throw, and the other a non-ranking combination, the winner gets his own chips back, as well as those bet by the loser. If, however, one player throws a winning combination, and the other a losing combination, the bank contributes the same number of chips as have been bet in total. The game continues until either player, or the bank, runs out of chips. The player holding the maximum number of chips at this point wins. Note that this way of distributing the wins and losses is not the same as BARBOOTH when played as a 'professional' gambling game, but is a pay-off scheme which is relatively easy to computerize, and makes for an interesting game.

FIVE THOUSAND: There are no prizes for guessing that the first player to score over 5000 points in this game is the winner. Played with as many players as you like, all you'll need in the way of game equipment is five six-sided dice. Each player takes it in turn to throw the five dice, and scoring is carried out in the following way:

- A 5 is worth 100.

- A 2 is worth 50.

- Three 5's thrown in one go are worth 1000.

- Three 2's thrown in a go score 500.

- Three of a kind (apart from 2's and 5's) are worth 100 times their value (that is, three 1's are worth 100 points, and three 6's are worth 600).

- If the sequence 1, 2, 3, 4, and 5 is thrown in a single go, this scores 1500.

- 2, 3, 4, 5, and 6 in one throw are worth 2000 points.

Note that 4's and 6's do not score in this game, except as part of a sequence. Once you've thrown, you can—if you like—throw the non-scoring dice again. However, if the next throw gains no score, the turn ends, and the overall score for the throw is zero. So long as a scoring throw has been made, any dice "left over" can be thrown.

The game rewards the slow and careful player with a reasonable score, but gives him or her no chance against a player who decides to take a chance and try to get a massive score in a single throw.

Card Games

Once you've worked out a routine to get the computer to hold, shuffle, and deal the cards (and such a routine is in my version of "concentration" in this book) you have the raw bones of a host of games. Any book of card games will give you more ideas than you can possibly cope with. Here are a few to start you off:

TRENTE AND QUARANTE: This game, which originated in 17th century Europe, is also known as ROUGE ET NOIR. Six decks of cards are used in the casino version, but it works well with a single deck. The cards are dealt into two rows, with the total of each row being examined after each row has had an additional card. Face cards (jack, queen, king) count as ten, with all other cards (including the ace) counting as their face value. The moment the total of a row equals or exceeds 31, no more cards are added to that row. However, the dealer keeps adding to the other row until it, too, equals or exceeds 31. The first row is called "black," regardless of the suits of the cards involved, and the second row is "red."

You can bet that, at the end, the red row or the black row total will be closer to 31. You can also bet that the color of the *first* card to be dealt will match the color name of the winning row. All bets are made against the bank, and winners receive their bet back, plus that amount again (odds of one to one). If both rows equal 31, the bank takes half the stake and returns the rest to the player.

CARD CRAPS: This game was devised to get around laws passed by some US States which outlawed craps played with dice. You use a special deck of 48 cards, made up from the aces, 2's, 3's, 4's, 5's, and 6's, from two decks of cards. The game follows the standard rules of craps (which are similar to those used in the game SEVEN/ELEVEN in this book).

In its simplified form, without the somewhat complex betting combinations, you play as follows:

- A total of 2, 3 or 12 is "craps" and the dealer loses, passing the cards to the next player to deal.

- A total of 7 or 11 is a "natural" and the dealer wins.

- Any other number (4, 5, 6, 8, 9, or 10) is the player's "point" and he or she must continue dealing in pairs until the point is dealt again, at which point the dealer wins. However if a 7 is dealt before the point is obtained, the dealer loses.

THREE CARD BRAG: This game was the forerunner of poker, and as its name suggests, it is played with hands of three, rather than five, cards. Here are the winning combinations, ranked from highest to lowest:

- "Pryle," three of a kind

- "On a bike," three in sequence from the same suit

- "Run," three cards in sequence

- "Flush," three cards from the same suit

- "Pair," two of a kind

- "High card"

A normal deck is used, and aces rank high, except for "on a bike" and "run," when 3, 2, ace beats ace, king, queen. You can vary the game by making it SEVEN CARD BRAG, in which the players split their seven cards into two three-card hands of their choice, or NINE CARD BRAG, when three hands are created.

ACE-DEUCE-JACK: This is a simple game, heavily loaded in the dealer's favor, in which players bet on the likelihood that the next card which appears will be an ace, a two (a "deuce"), or a jack.

PUT AND TAKE: This gambling game uses an eight-sided top, which is spun. The game begins with all players having 10 chips, with 30 in the pot. The players take it in turn to spin the top, and—obeying the instructions which come up on the top—put chips into the pot, or take them out. A player is out when he or she runs out of chips, and the game ends when the pot is empty. The instructions written on the sides of the top are:

- PUT ONE

- TAKE ONE

- PUT THREE

- TAKE THREE

- PUT FOUR
- TAKE FOUR
- PUT ALL
- TAKE ALL

BOULE: This is a simplified form of roulette which appeared in the 18th century. It is often found in European casinos. The wheel is divided into 18 segments, numbered from one to nine, twice. You can bet on the winning number, whether it will be a red or a black number, even or odd, high or low. Except for the fives on the wheel, which are usually yellow, the reds and blacks alternate, so that there is, for example, a red six and a black six, a red nine and a black nine, and so on. A "high" number is above five, while "low" numbers are below it. If you bet successfully on a single number, you'll be paid at seven to one, with a one to one return on the "characteristic" of a number (such as its being "high" or "odd").

Glossary

Accumulator—part of the computer's logic unit which stores the intermediate results of computations

Address—a number which refers to a location, generally in the computer's memory, where information is stored

Algorithm—the sequence of steps used to solve a problem

Alphanumeric—generally used to describe a keyboard, and signifying that the keyboard has alphabetical and numerical keys. A numeric keypad, by contrast, only has keys for the digits one to nine

APL—this stands for Automatic Programming Language, a language developed by Iverson in the early 1960s, which supports a large set of operators and data structures. It uses a non-standard set of characters

Application software—these are programs which are tailored for a specific task, such as word processing, or to handle mailing lists

ASCII—stands for American Standard Code for Information Interchange. This is an almost universal code for letters, numbers, and symbols

Assembler—this is a program which converts another program written in an assembly language (which is a computer program in which a single instruction, such as ADD, converts into a single instruction for the computer) into the language the computer uses directly

BASIC—stands for Beginner's All-purpose Symbolic Instruction Code, the most common language used on microcomputers. It is easy to learn, with many of its statements being very close to English

Batch—a group of transactions which are to be processed by a computer in one lot, without interruption by an operator

Baud—a measure of the speed of transfer of data. It generally stands for the number of bits (discrete units of information) per second

Benchmark—a test which is used to measure some aspect of the performance of a computer, which can be compared to the result of running a similar test on a different computer

Binary—a system of counting in which there are only two symbols, 0 and 1 (as opposed to the ordinary decimal system, in which there are ten symbols, 0, 1, 2, 3, 4, 5, 6, 7, 8, and 9). Your computer "thinks" in binary

Boolean Algebra—the algebra of decision-making and logic, developed by English mathematician George Boole, and at the heart of your computer's ability to make decisions

Bootstrap—a program, run into the computer when it is first turned on, which puts the computer into the state where it can accept and understand other programs

Buffer—a storage mechanism which holds input from a device such as keyboard, then releases it at a rate which the computer dictates

Bug—an error in a program

Bus—a group of electrical connections used to link a computer with an ancillary device, or another computer

Byte—the smallest group of bits which makes up a computer word. Generally a computer is described as being "8 bit" or "16 bit," meaning the word consists of a combination of eight or sixteen zeros or ones

Central Processing Unit (CPU)—the heart of the computer, where arithmetic, logic, and control functions are carried out

Character code—the number of ASCII (see ASCII) which refers to a particular symbol, such as 32 for a space and 65 for the letter "A"

COBOL—stands for Common Business Oriented Language, a standard programming language, close to English, which is used primarily for business

Compiler—a program which translates a program written in a high level (human-like) language into a machine language which the computer understands directly

Concatenate—to add (adding two strings together is known as "concatenation")

CP/M—stands for Control Program/Microcomputer, an almost universal disk operating system developed and marketed by Digital Research, Pacific Grove, California

380

Data—a general term for information processed by a computer

Database—a collection of data organized to permit rapid access by computer

Debug—to remove bugs (errors) from a program

Disk—a magnetic storage medium (further described as a "hard disk," "floppy disk," or even "floppy") used to store computer information and programs. The disks resemble, to a limited extent, 45 rpm sound records, and are generally eight, five and a quarter, or three inches in diameter. Smaller "microdisks" are also available for some systems

Documentation—the written instructions and explanations which accompany a program

DOS—stands for Disk Operating System (and generally pronounced "doss"), the versatile program which allows a computer to control a disk system

Dot-matrix printer—a printer which forms the letters and symbols by a collection of dots, usually on an eight by eight, or seven by five, grid

Double-density—adjective used to describe disks when recorded using a special technique which, as the name suggests, doubles the amount of storage the disk can provide

Dynamic memory—computer memory which requires constant recharging to retain its contents

EPROM—stands for Erasable Programmable Read Only Memory, a device which contains computer information in a semi-permanent form, demanding sustained exposure to ultra-violet light to erase its contents

Error messages—information from the computer to the user, sometimes consisting only of numbers or a few letters, but generally of a phrase (such as "Out of memory") which points out a programming or operational error which has caused the computer to halt program executions

Field—A collection of characters which form a distinct group, such as an identifying code, a name or a date; a field is generally part of a record

File—A group of related records which are processed together, such as an inventory file or a student file

Firmware—The solid components of a computer system are often called the "hardware," the programs, in machine-readable form on disk or cassette, are called the "software," and programs which are hard-wired into a circuit are called "firmware." Firmware can be altered, to a limited extent, by software in some circumstances

Flag—this is an indicator within a program, with the "state of the flag" (i.e., the value it holds) giving information regarding a particular condition

Floppy disk—see "disk"

Flowchart—a written layout of program structure and flow, using various shapes, such as a rectangle with sloping sides for a computer action, and a diamond for a computer decision. A flowchart is generally written before any lines of program are entered into the computer

FORTRAN—a high level computer language, generally used for scientific work (from FORmula TRANslation)

Gate—a computer "component" which makes decisions, allowing the circuit to flow in one direction or another, depending on the conditions to be satisfied

GIGO—acronym for "Garbage In Garbage Out," suggesting that if rubbish or wrong data is fed into a computer, the result of its processing of such data (the output) must also be rubbish

Global—a set of conditions which affects the entire program is called "global," as opposed to "local"

Hard copy—information dumped to paper by a printer

Hardware—the solid parts of the computer (see "software" and "firmware")

Hexadecimal—a counting system much beloved by machine code programmers because it is closely related to the number storage methods used by computers, based on the number 16 (as opposed to our "ordinary" number system which is based on 10)

Hex pad—a keyboard, somewhat like a calculator, which is used for direct entry of hexadecimal numbers

High-level languages—programming languages which are close to English. Low-level languages are closer to those which the computer understands. Because high-level languages have to be compiled into a form which the computer can understand before they are processed, high-level languages run more slowly than do their low-level counterparts

Input—any information which is fed into a program during execution

I/O—stands for Input/Output port, a device the computer uses to communicate with the outside world

Instruction—an element of programming code, which tells the computer to carry out a specific task. An instruction in assembler language, for example, is ADD which (as you've probably guessed) tells the computer to carry out an addition

Interpreter—converts the high-level ("human-understandable") program into a form which the computer can understand

Joystick—an analog device which feeds a signal into a computer which is related to the position which the joystick is occupying; generally used in games programs

Kilobyte—the unit of language measurement; one kilobyte (generally abbreviated as K) equals 1024 bits

Line printer—a printer which prints a complete line of characters at one time

Low-level language—a language which is close to that used within the computer (see "high-level language")

Machine language—the step below a low-level language; the language which the computer understands directly

Mainframe—the term for "giant" computers such as the IBM 370. Computers are also classed as minicomputer and microcomputer (such as the computer you own)

Memory—the device or devices used by a computer to hold information and programs being currently processed, and for the instruction set fixed within a computer which tells it how to carry out the demands of the program. There are basically two types of memory (see "RAM" and "ROM")

Microprocessor—the "chip" which lies at the heart of your computer. This does the "thinking"

Modem—stands for MOdulator/DEModulator, and is a device which allows one computer to communicate with another via the telephone

Monitor—(a) a dedicated television screen for use as a computer display unit; contains no tuning apparatus; (b) the information within a computer which enables it to understand and execute program instructions

Motherboard—a unit, generally external, which has slots to allow additional "boards" (circuits) to be plugged into the computer to provide facilities (such as high-resolution graphics, or "robot control") which are not provided with the standard machine

Mouse—a control unit, slightly smaller than a box of cigarettes, which is rolled over the desk, moving an on-screen cursor in parallel to select options and make decisions within a program. "Mouses" work either by sensing the action of their wheels, or by reading a grid pattern on the surface upon which they are moved

Network—a group of computers working in tandem

Numeric pad—a device primarily for entering numeric information into a computer, similar to a calculator

Octal—a numbering system based on eight (using the digits 0, 1, 2, 3, 4, 5, 6, and 7)

On-line—device which is under the direct control of the computer

Operating system—this is the "big boss" program or series of programs within the computer which controls the computer's operation, doing such things as calling up routines when they are needed and assigning priorities

Output—any data produced by the computer while it is processing, whether this data is displayed on the screen or dumped to the printer, or is used internally

Pascal—a high level language, developed in the late 1960s by Niklaus Wirth, which encourages disciplined, structured programming

Port—an output or input "hole" in the computer, through which data is transferred

Program—the series of instructions which the computer follows to carry out a predetermined task

PILOT—a high-level language, generally used to develop computer programs for education

RAM—stands for "Random Access Memory," and is the memory on board the computer which holds the current program. The contents of RAM can be changed, while the contents of ROM (Read Only Memory) cannot be changed under software control

Real-time—when a computer event is progressing in line with time in the "real world," the event is said to be occurring in real time. An example would be a program which showed the development of a colony of bacteria which developed at the same rate that such a real colony would develop. Many games which require reactions in real time have been developed. Most "arcade action" programs occur in real time

Refresh—The contents of dynamic memories (see "memory") must receive periodic bursts of power in order for them to maintain their contents. The signal which "reminds" the memory of its contents is called the "refresh signal"

Register—a location in computer memory which holds data

Reset—a signal which returns the computer to the point it was in when first turned on

ROM—see "RAM"

RS-232—a standard serial interface (defined by the Electronic Industries Association) which connects a modem and associated terminal equipment to a computer

S-100 bus—this is a standard interface (see "RS-232") made up of 100 parallel common communication lines which are used to connect circuit boards within microcomputers

SNOBOL—a high-level language, developed by Bell Laboratories, which uses pattern recognition and string manipulation

Software—the program which the computer follows (see "firmware")

Stack—the end point of a series of events which are accessed on a last in, first out basis

Subroutine—a block of code, or program, which is called up a number of times within another program

Syntax—as in human languages, the syntax is the structure rules which govern the use of a computer language

Systems software—sections of code which carry out administrative tasks, or assist with the writing of other programs, but which are not actually used to carry out the computer's final task

Thermal printer—a device which prints the output from the computer on heat-sensitive paper. Although thermal printers are quieter than other printers, the output is not always easy to read, nor is the used paper easy to store

Time-sharing—this term is used to refer to a large number of users, on independent terminals, making use of a single computer, which divides its time between the users in such a way that each of them appears to have the "full attention" of the computer

Turnkey system—a computer system (generally for business use) which is ready to run when delivered, needing only the "turn of a key" to get it working

Volatile memory—a memory device which loses its contents when the power supply is cut off (see "memory," "refresh," "ROM," and "RAM")

Word processor—a dedicated computer (or a computer operating a word processing program) which gives access to an "intelligent typewriter" with a large range of correction and adjustment features

BASIC Conversion Chart

The programs in this book were written in Microsoft BASIC on an IBM PC (and are fully compatible with MSX BASIC). Converting the programs to the versions of BASIC used on other microcomputers is relatively easy. Use the chart on the next page to convert the programs in the book so that they'll run on your computer. If the column under a command has been left blank, your computer uses the same command that is used in the programs in the book. In all cases, a little thought (and perhaps a quick check of your BASIC manual) should be sufficient to get the programs running on your system.

Program statements which test a number of conditions and which are too long for your computer can be split into several IF/THEN statements, one for each of the conditions tested for in the original statement. Note that some BASICs (such as Atari BASIC) won't let you specify a prompt string within an INPUT statement. Use a separate PRINT statement (before the INPUT statement) to put the prompt string on the screen. Some BASICs won't READ values directly into an array, as in READ X$(7). Use a separate READ statement before the array assignment; for example, READ A$: X$(7) = A$.

	In Text: CLS	INKEY$	IF/THEN/ELSE	Line Length	Strings
Commodore 64 and VIC 20	PRINT "CLR" (inverse heart)	GET A$	Split into 2 IF/THEN Lines	4 Lines Use abbreviations for key words; split where 2 Lines needed	
Apple (all)	HOME	GET A$	Split into 2 IF/THEN Lines		
TI 99/4a Extended BASIC	CALL CLEAR	CALL KEY		6 Lines max.	SEG$(A$,2,3) for MID$(A$(2,3))
Timex-Sinclair 2068					A$(2 TO 5) for MID$(A$(2,3))
Atari (all)	PRINT "CLR" or ? CHR$(125) or GRAPHICS 0	INPUT A$ DIM A$(1) must be in program		120 char. max. Split if needed	A$(2,5) for MID$(A$(2,3))

ABOUT THE AUTHOR

Tim Hartnell has written more than 30 books on personal computers, including many game books. He owns a computer book publishing company, called Interface Publications, based in London. He is also the author of a number of programming guides, including *PROGRAMMING YOUR IBM PC* * *If You've Never Programmed a Computer Before; PROGRAMMING YOUR APPLE IIe* * *If You've Never Programmed a Computer Before;* and *PROGRAMMING YOUR COMMODORE 64* * *If You've Never Programmed a Computer Before* (Ballantine). He lives in Australia.